KT-520-165

# HOUSING TRANSITIONS THROUGH THE LIFE COURSE

## Aspirations, needs and policy

Andrew Beer and Debbie Faulkner

*with*

Chris Paris and Terry Clower

First published in Great Britain in 2011 by

The Policy Press
University of Bristol
Fourth Floor
Beacon House
Queen's Road
Bristol BS8 1QU, UK
t: +44 (0)117 331 4054
f: +44 (0)117 331 4093
tpp-info@bristol.ac.uk
www.policypress.co.uk

North American office:
The Policy Press
c/o International Specialized Books Services (ISBS)
920 NE 58th Avenue, Suite 300
Portland, OR 97213-3786, USA
t: +1  503 287 3093
f: +1 503 280 8832
info@isbs.com

© The Policy Press 2011

British Library Cataloguing in Publication Data
A catalogue record for this book is available from the British Library.

Library of Congress Cataloging-in-Publication Data
A catalog record for this book has been requested.

ISBN 978 1 84742 428 0 (hardcover)

Cover design by The  Policy Press
*Front cover:* photograph kindly supplied by plainpicture/René Wolf
Printed and bound in Great Britain by TJ International, Padstow
The Policy Press uses environmentally responsible print partners

# Contents

# List of figures and tables

## Figures

## Tables

# Notes about the authors

**Andrew Beer** is a Professor in Geography at the University of Adelaide and was previously based at Flinders University. His interests include the relationship between housing and the life course, regional economic development policies and homelessness.

**Debbie Faulkner** is a Research Fellow in the Department of Geography and Environmental Studies at the University of Adelaide. Debbie has research interests in population issues including housing, ageing, homelessness and at risk groups in the community.

**Terry Clower** is director of the Center for Economic Development and Research at the University of North Texas (UNT) and an associate professor of applied economics. Dr Clower has served as project manager, staff researcher and statistical analyst on numerous projects reflecting experience in economic and community development, economic and fiscal impact analysis, survey research design, housing market issues, land use planning, labour market analysis, transportation, and forecasting.

**Chris Paris** was Professor of Housing Studies at the University of Ulster from 1992 to 2008. He has held visiting professorships at the RMIT and Hong Kong Universities and visiting fellowships in many other universities including Cambridge and Oxford in the UK, and the ANU, La Trobe, Flinders and QUT in Australia. His current research includes multiple home ownership in affluent societies and the housing needs of older people.

# Acknowledgements

The support, assistance and encouragement of many people made possible the writing of this book. Many of our colleagues at Flinders University – Michael Kroehn, Emma Baker, Selina Tually, Louise O'Loughlin, Kate Deller-Evans and Cecile Cutler – helped us undertake the research presented in this publication and turn it into a finished monograph. Thanks also are due to other colleagues including Michelle Gabriel, Maryann Wulff, Gabriel Gwyther, Joe Flood, John Minnery, Robin Zakharov and Lise Saugeres. Much of the research that underpins this book was made possible through the the financial assistance of the Australian Housing and Urban Research Institute (AHURI) Ltd and the Australian Research Council's Linkage Program (LP 0776660). Several staff within AHURI made important contributions to this research with thanks going to Ian Winter, Andrew Hollows, Sonia Whitely, Simone Finch and Grania Sheehan. AHURI provided the financial resources necessary to undertake the large scale survey analysed in this monograph. Acknowledgement is also due to Flinders University for facilitating the study leave that made the writing of this manuscript possible.

Finally we need to thank all the people who gave freely of their time to participate in the Housing 21 Survey.

# Preface

Housing and housing markets across the developed world have been in a state of considerable flux since 2005 when the ideas for this book first began to take shape. In many parts of the developed world it was a time of economic growth, financial stability, booming housing markets and policy reformation, but that environment has both changed and become more fragmented over the past five years. These external shocks have inevitably influenced the development of this book.

In common with much contemporary social science, *Housing Transitions* has its origins in research undertaken for the public sector, albeit a public sector attracted to, and intrigued by, the long-running academic literature on 'housing careers'. Through discussions with the Australian Housing and Urban Research Institute (AHURI), Australian government housing bodies began to ask, 'how are housing careers changing in the 21st century, and what are the implications for the forms of government assistance that will be needed now and into the future?' In particular, government bodies in Australia were concerned about three questions of policy relevance. First, over the coming decades what will be the impact of the ageing of the 'baby boom' cohort in terms of housing and the demand for housing assistance? Second, is the apparent decline in entry into homeownership amongst 25- to 34-year-olds robust, and what are the implications of this for the demand for housing assistance in the long term? Third, what forms of government housing assistance will be necessary and appropriate in the 21st century given changes in household structure, labour markets and philosophical shifts in attitudes to government intervention?

One of the public sector drivers for establishing research into 21st century housing careers was recognition that the ageing baby boomer cohort had the potential to challenge the future stability of the housing system. There was a perception that the decisions this generation took upon leaving paid work, and potentially seeking new housing in retirement, carried risks for society, governments and individuals. Older people make substantial use of public assistance, including in the housing sector, and the rapid escalation in the population aged over 60 could lead to an exponential growth in demand for housing support. Moreover, the 'leading edge' of the baby boom those – aged 55 to 60 – was seen to be a significant indicator of trends and developments likely to take place over the next two to three decades.

The second major challenge exercising the minds of public sector policy makers was the apparent decline in the number of younger Australians entering homeownership. Australia has been a nation of homeowners since 1945, recording one of the earliest increases in the owner occupation rate amongst the developed economies. The owner occupation rate has, however, been relatively static since 1966, moving in a narrow band of around two-thirds of households in homeownership. Australia's rate of homeownership has been surpassed by a number of other nations including Ireland, Spain and the United Kingdom (UK) (Badcock and Beer, 2000). More importantly, the economist Judy Yates has documented that since the mid 1990s (Yates, 1996) younger generations have become less likely to enter homeownership than either their parents' or grandparents' generation. More recent work by Flood and Baker (2010) has confirmed this trend and highlighted the ongoing difficulties younger Australians face in seeking to enter home purchase. Australian governments have been concerned about this trend because homeownership has been an important pillar of the nation's welfare state, with Castles (1998) arguing that promotion of homeownership, rather than the development of a more comprehensive welfare state, was the 'Really Big Tradeoff' implicit within Australian social democracy. High rates of homeownership amongst the aged have reduced the cost of income security to Australian governments (Yates and Bradbury, 2010) and enabled a range of other social policy innovations. It is important to acknowledge that similar systems of asset-based welfare apply in many European and Asian nations (Doling and Ronald, 2010).

Ongoing change in the philosophies of assistance connected with housing was a third major imperative for research into housing careers in the 21st century. Australia has a 60-year history of substantial direct government intervention in the housing market, most notably in the form of public sector provision for low income households (Neutze, 1978). But over recent decades housing assistance has become much more tightly targeted to the very poor within society, partly as a result of a broader shift to neoliberal philosophies of government (Beer and Paris, 2005; Larner, 2005; Dodson, 2007). Other shifts within society have also driven change in the interactions between individuals and housing assistance, namely change in household composition (with the increased presence of households who do not conform to conventional 'family' models), the ageing of the population and shifts in the labour market. In addition, high levels of migration have also called into question conventional forms of policy action. Finally, it is important to acknowledge that the 'mainstreaming' of services to particularly disadvantaged groups, such as persons with a disability and family members with care responsibilities, has created new challenges for government housing providers and policy makers. Fresh solutions are needed for these evolving dilemmas.

The origins of this work lie in research undertaken in Australia, but the themes, issues and concerns are common across the developed world, and especially for English-speaking nations. The ageing of the baby boom generation has affected many nations, as has the rise in homeownership rates and shifts in government philosophies. It is important to acknowledge that under Epsing-Anderson's (1990) schema of 'welfare capitalism' Australia is grouped with the United States (US) and New Zealand as a 'neoliberal' nation, but it has much in common with the UK and some other European nations. Importantly, the rising tide of global affluence in developed economies has had comparable impacts on housing markets across nations and has fundamentally reshaped attitudes to, and expectations of, housing. There are, therefore, strong commonalities across nations in their attitudes to the use and consumption of housing across the life course. It is, however, important to acknowledge the differences. In Australia, for instance, the small but significant

Indigenous population generates housing market dynamics and patterns unknown in Europe and even in other nations, such as New Zealand, Canada or the US, with comparable communities.

Ensuring the ideas presented in a book are relevant to both the current and future environment is a challenge for all authors. In this instance, the task was all the greater because work on the manuscript began in a period of economic prosperity. The financial market turmoil commonly referred to in Australia as the global financial crisis (GFC) unfolded as work continued. For this book there is a danger that the housing market conditions that have been documented are seen to be part of the past and not relevant to a more economically challenged present or future. There are two responses to this concern: first, we would argue that the attitudes, behaviours and market conditions discussed in this work are the product of long-term structural trends – demographic, labour market and economic – and that they represent the inevitable future for housing in developed economies. Second, we would argue there is mounting evidence that the economic tide has already turned. We can conclude that in early 2010 the global economy appears to have entered a period of post financial crisis with some nations recovering much more quickly than others. Parts of Europe (Germany and France) appear to be relatively robust, while the Australian economy is booming on the back of strong demand for resources from China (Uren, 2010). Elsewhere, New Zealand, Ireland and the UK remain mired in recession, while growth in the US is low but picking up pace. This book is not primarily concerned with the difficulties confronting the global financial system in 2007 through to 2009. It does touch, and shed light upon, the crisis because housing market conditions were the pivotal trigger. We can also be confident that economic cycles will turn and that those economies currently in a downturn will revive and their housing markets – and the aspirations of their consumers – will re-emerge.

*Andrew Beer and Debbie Faulkner*
*July 2010*

# ONE

# Housing markets and policy in the 21st century

## Housing through the life course: questions, challenges and opportunities

Housing remains one of the fundamental pillars of both life and lifestyle for us as individuals. Housing is also important within our economies and societies as it is a source of employment within the building industry, an object of public policy attention and action, and a focus of concern for debates around fairness or inclusion within society. This book considers the role housing plays in the lives of individuals and households through their life course, and along the way it confronts issues about the part housing plays within society, economy and culture. Most writing on housing takes a cross-sectional view that considers the housing market or the system of social provision at a single point in time. This may be during a census or other period of data collection, or as a generalised set of conditions lacking a temporal reference. But this is not our lived experience of housing: at a personal level we know housing through our engagement with the housing system; as a child being raised by parents or carers; as a young person searching for our first accommodation; as an adult entering a relationship and seeking a home to share; and as a household decision maker seeking a dwelling that is convenient to employment, recreation and, potentially, schooling for children.

There is a substantial body of work on housing through the life course that spans more than four decades. Research in this vein has discussed housing histories (Farmer and Barrell 1981), housing careers (Kendig, 1990a), housing pathways (Clapham, 2002; 2004; 2005a), housing biographies (Clark et al, 2003) and more recently, housing transitions (Beer and Faulkner, 2009), but in all instances the objective focus of analysis and discussion has been on the series of housing circumstances occupied by an individual or household over their life course. Much of this work has focused on critical points of transition – such as moves into homeownership or the impact of the death of a partner – as well as the differing trajectories of groups from a range of socioeconomic backgrounds. There is, for example, a considerable North American literature on pathways into homeownership for minority groups such as African and Hispanic Americans. However, as Clark et al (2003, p 144) have observed, much of this broad body of work has paid far greater attention to 'only one move or one change in the housing career' whereas the housing careers they observed were commonly comprised of five to nine moves over a lifetime. Moreover, Clark et al (2003) noted that mobility and other studies within this research tradition have tended to place a greater emphasis on the processes of change, while largely ignoring the periods of stability between housing shifts. For Clark et al (2003) it is important to think of housing over the life course as a sequence, with periods of stability interspersed by often significant change.

Understanding how the sequence of housing plays out in the life course of individuals and households presents significant technical and conceptual challenges. Technically, it is difficult to find aggregate measures or indicators of significant housing careers. Kendig (1979) presented an idealised housing career for young households in Australia, while Farmer and Barrell (1981) sketched out a comparable scenario for public housing tenants in Scotland. From their analysis of housing markets in the US Clarke et al (2003) identified a limited number of frequently observed housing sequences, though noted there is considerable variation in housing trajectories across the population. To a degree, time acts independently of other processes and adds to the complexity evident in housing over the life course. It does so with respect to the period in which events may take place, the variable duration or timing of changes, and with respect to the maturation of the household. These are critical factors as each shapes the housing transitions of individuals and those of the population as a whole. Events that happen at a specific time or period may affect a whole cohort of households, as evidenced by the rise in the number of foreclosures in the US associated with the sub-prime crisis. This event will have a generational impact that will permanently mark the housing careers of those affected. By contrast, the maturation of the household is largely independent of external processes and reflects an internal demography that potentially includes the arrival and departure of children, the ageing of the residents, and the eventual dissolution of the household.

Conceptually, it is important to avoid a monochromatic view of housing market processes and recognise that an individual's experience of housing over a life course will be affected by location (Clarke, et al, 2003), but also by race, socioeconomic status, wealth and position within the labour market. For many households in advanced economies, occupying or consuming housing is an end in itself (Allon, 2008): the quality, quantity and nature of housing occupied is seen to make a statement about the individual's position within society and provide a source of psychological security or comfort (Clapham, 2005a). In any discussion of housing there is, perhaps inevitably, a tension between housing's role in meeting a basic human need and its status as a 'want' – a commodity embedded with social, personal and economic meanings that can serve to encourage increased consumption regardless of real needs. Our understanding of housing over the life course has to acknowledge that housing performs different roles for different groups within society and may serve different roles over the life course of individuals and households. Housing is central to both human 'wants' and 'needs' and for many middle class and affluent households the sequence of homes they occupy reflects their social, economic and other aspirations. For many poorer households, housing is an essential need. For these individuals, movement through the housing market is a matter of requirement not choice and is a consequence of eviction, escalating housing costs, or mortgage default. The dualistic nature of housing as a 'good', in combination with market processes, means that in many regions it is possible to simultaneously have both a housing shortage and excess supply.

Research into housing through the life course has a long history and a promising future as researchers and governments grapple with questions of social constitution and policy dilemmas. The challenge for both individual researchers and the academic community is to develop better understandings and then communicate those insights to as wide an audience as possible. Work in this area needs to be informed by the economic and social environment of the 21st century, and mindful of the differences between places and groups within society. It is also important to shed light, where possible, on key issues of public concern, including critical transitions. These key questions include: Will housing in the 21st century follow the same trajectories as those evident in the 20th century? Or will economic, social and demographic changes usher in substantial transformations in the relationship between housing and households over their life course? In response to large-scale changes in the social, economic and physical environment, will lifetime housing outcomes become more or less equal between individuals and localities? And if they change, what will be the implications for the well-being of individuals and society in the context of mounting evidence of the impact of housing circumstances on employment outcomes, health, social capital and educational attainment? How will governments constitute and deliver housing policy in the 21st century in light of the sub-prime crisis, changes in philosophies of social assistance, competing demands for attention and resources from other policy domains, as well as shifts in demographic structure? How will housing demand and provision over the life course be integrated with other areas of social and economic intervention? Finally, given recent trends in housing scholarship, how can this research work to inform our wider theoretical understanding of housing and housing markets?

## Demographic, economic and political challenges in housing through the 21st century

One of the most basic questions about housing over the life course in the 21st century is whether it will follow the same pathways as those evident in the 20th century? It is a critical question because many of the key actors in the housing market use their explicit or implicit understanding of lifetime housing outcomes to underpin their investment and expenditure decisions. Home builders, real estate developers, social housing providers, rental investors and land development companies all operate with a set of a priori assumptions on the nature and drivers of the housing market. These assumptions are grounded in observations that link stage in the life course to various forms of housing need or demand. Kendig (1981, p 1) was able to articulate late 20th-century Australia's expectations about housing and the life course, recording the view:

> ...that nearly everybody follows the same housing progression or 'career'. It is usually supposed that young adults with their own income leave the family home to rent a flat and enjoy the single life. After marriage, both partners work and economise on rent so they can save a deposit to buy a house in which they will rear their children. Although a few move later to bigger houses before their children grow up or to own their flat after children leave home, it is usually assumed that most households remain in their first owned home into old age, enjoying the lost costs and security of outright ownership.

There is, however, strong evidence to suggest that the social and economic conditions which underpinned that set of housing relationships have changed profoundly. Over the last 40 years there have been substantial shifts in demographic structure and population processes – with the structural ageing of most advanced economies such as the UK, Italy, Germany, Australia, New Zealand and Japan – and declining fertility rates. In many nations the rate of divorce or separation has increased (for example, Australia, US, Canada, Ireland) and there has been a consequent rise in the number of households comprised of one person and of sole parents. Life expectancies have continued to increase within developed economies, with those commonly classified as the 'old, old' (those over 85 years of age), one of the fastest growing segments of the population. Moreover, many older people now enjoy levels of health and well-being that were rare within previous older generations. The growth in the older population has both changed the nature of demand or need for housing, and the relationship between households and their accommodation.

Significant shifts in social attitudes have contributed to the changing relationship between the life course and housing outcomes. In many developed economies rates of female participation in the formal labour market have grown over the past 40 years, with a more recent rise in educational attainment, and consequent career opportunities, for women. Many societies have also become more accepting of alternative lifestyles and values, including gay and lesbian relationships, and these shifts have opened up new housing and lifestyle opportunities for these groups. There have been fundamental changes in attitudes to persons with a disability, with a decline in support for institutional forms of accommodation and a more positive attitude to housing that is integrated within the community (Quibell, 2004). This restructured approach to the housing of persons with a disability creates a new set of relationships within the dwelling stock that at a societal and individual level fundamentally reshapes the relationship between housing outcomes and life course.

Changes in labour markets are another dimension of social and economic life where there have been significant shifts that affect the relationship between life course and housing. In many developed economies labour market growth has been concentrated among persons employed part time or on a casual (non-permanent) basis. These new forms of employment create different opportunities and limitations with respect to access to home purchase and, potentially, the need for greater mobility within the labour market. More generally, economic restructuring in the advanced economies – with the hollowing out of manufacturing in many nations – has directly intervened in the employment careers of individuals and households, which in turn has affected housing outcomes. Shifts within the global automotive industry are indicative of this larger-scale trend with an observable preference for moving vehicle production to the global south and east (Kim and McCann, 2008). For workers made redundant at General Motors plants in Flint, Michigan; the MG Rover factory in Birmingham, England; or the Mitsubishi facilities in Adelaide, Australia, the loss of well-paid, permanent employment may result in forced relocation, a downward shift in tenure, overcrowding or reduced housing quality.

The recent evolution of real property markets has also affected the lifetime housing outcomes of many households. In South East England, Australia, New Zealand and some parts of the US, escalating house prices through the late 1990s and first decade of the 21st century have created a cohort of homeowners with significant housing wealth. While asset values have fallen in New Zealand and some parts of England and the US, considerable wealth remains and provides an asset that some households use to leverage additional housing opportunities or lifestyle aspirations (Ellis et al, 2003). In this sense the property market per se has emerged as a factor influencing the life course of some individuals and households. On the other hand, over the last decade some regions have evidenced low demand for housing and consequent low house prices. In the UK there is a considerable literature on 'low demand' housing estates, with many concentrated in the 'North'. In the US, the 'rustbelt' regions of some parts of the Mid West have experienced depressed housing markets for decades (Glaeser and Gyourko, 2005), while some of the prairie settlements in Canada have stagnated economically and demographically (Leo and Brown, 2000; Leo and Anderson, 2006). In Australia, the restructuring of agricultural production and the workforce has resulted in substantial population declines which have effectively 'trapped' homeowners (Econsult, 1989) whose only asset may be insufficient to support a move to another centre. For households from these regions, the downward movement in the local economy and housing markets effectively limits their housing experiences over the life course.

Over the last decades increased affluence in many developed economies has resulted in a strengthening of the role housing often plays as a site of luxury consumption and this in turn has reshaped the relationship between housing and the life course for a significant section of the population. The development of luxury housing estates and 'gated' communities (Blakely and Snyder, 1999; Atkinson and Flint, 2004) provides tangible evidence of the changing mores and social expectations attached to housing. At another level, the burgeoning of 'second' or 'holiday' homes across Europe, North America and Australasia (Dijst et al, 2005; Gallent et al, 2005) reflects both a new emphasis on the recreational potentials of housing and significantly increased personal mobility. As Paris (2010) has noted, second or holiday homes are both a trans-regional and trans-national phenomenon with second homes in locations such as Thailand, Ireland, Spain and the Gulf States targeted to a global market. For a growing percentage of individuals, therefore, their lifetime experience is not one of home, but of *homes*. This is perhaps best exemplified by the 2008 US Presidential candidate, Senator John McCain, who was originally unable to number the homes he owned before his office confirmed, after some days, his ownership of nine homes for his own use.

Discussion of the luxury nature of some housing consumption brings into focus questions of equity or inequality in housing consumption over the life course. It is important to question whether lifetime housing outcomes will become more or less equal between individuals or localities, both when compared with the past and in the coming decades. Data from the Organisation for Economic Co-operation and Development (OECD, 2009) suggests that advanced economies are becoming less equal over time with substantial increases in income inequality since the mid 1980s in New Zealand, Finland, Germany, Portugal and the US. The UK, Canada, Belgium and Norway recorded smaller, but still significant, increases in income inequality, while income inequality increased in Ireland from the 1980s to the 1990s, but then reduced sharply from the mid 1990s to the mid 2000s to end up with a more equal income distribution overall. In Australia, increased inequality from the mid 1980s to the mid 1990s was offset by a more even income distribution through the following decade, resulting in no measurable change overall. In contrast, across developed economies (OECD, 2009) this trend in income inequality has been heightened by the recession that affected many economies from late 2007. Increased income inequality will result in much less equal housing outcomes over the life course as households or individuals are forced to share accommodation, accept poorer quality housing, do not enter home purchase or fall out of owner occupation. These unequal outcomes are then reinforced by the housing market processes referred to above, as those fortunate enough to own residential property gain access to a significant avenue for wealth accumulation.

More unequal housing outcomes over the life course are not only of academic interest as they can contribute to other dimensions of inequality and limited well-being for vulnerable groups. Work by Mallett et al (2011) suggests that individuals forced to live in precarious housing face greater levels of housing stress and score significantly lower on objective measures of mental health. The greater the frequency of forced moves the larger the impact, and this is further exacerbated if the household is required to move to less secure or inappropriate housing. The cumulative impact of this sequence of household relocations is to undermine the mental and physical health of individuals and further marginalise already vulnerable groups. It is worth reflecting on the fact that the homeownership rate for Indigenous Australians is half that of the mainstream Australian population and that their lifetime experience of housing is often marked by impermanence, forced moves and a lack of control (Birdsall-Jones and Christensen, 2007). Indigenous

Australians have an average life expectancy some 15 years less than that of non-Indigenous Australians and while their housing is not the sole cause of this gap, it is an important part of the suite of social conditions leading to disadvantage. Similar observations about impermanent housing could be made for 'travellers' in Ireland (Helleiner, 2000), low-income tenants in the US and marginalised immigrant groups in Europe.

The role governments play now, and into the future, raises significant questions for our understanding of housing over the life course. In all advanced economies the public sector plays an important role in regulating housing markets, creating an economic framework that guides investment in housing, and, in many instances, intervening directly to meet the housing needs of some groups within society. Governments, and government policies, are a pivotal influence – and often the central focus – of lifetime housing outcomes. Over the last two decades, there have been substantial shifts by governments in how they seek to achieve their social and economic objectives in housing and related fields. A key trend has been the rise of approaches to the development and delivery of government policies and services that are perceived to be derived from neoliberal philosophies of government (Dodson, 2007; O'Neil and Argent, 2007). Importantly, policies that are identifiable as neoliberal are not standardised across nations, or indeed regions within nations, but instead reflect a tendency towards a market orientation. Jessop (1990; 1997; 2002) has identified a number of tendencies within contemporary approaches to government that capture much of what is understood to be the significant developments in how governments engage with the economy and society.

From the perspective of housing policy and lifetime housing outcomes one of the key governmental transformations over the past 30 to 40 years has been the subordination of social policy to economic policy (Jessop, 2002). This trend was especially evident as neoliberalism first emerged (Peck and Tickell, 2002) and involved promoting policies predicated on the notion that the primary problems in housing were economic, in particular market and policy failure, with government intervention said to distort market signals to individuals and to businesses. As neoliberalism evolved it became increasingly clear how untenable aspects of this approach were and that not all social problems could be solved by 'fast tracking' economic growth or participation in the labour market. Governments in advanced economies adopted neoliberalist housing policies in varying degrees: with the UK government promoting the sale of social (council) housing from the late 1970s through to the late 1990s; the New Zealand government de-regulating their financial markets and selling off public housing; and the Netherlands – a nation with a strong tradition of social policy support – changing the relationship between the state and social housing providers in the 1990s (Dieleman, 1994).

In many ways, the shifts in government philosophies of assistance directly impinged upon the lifetime housing careers of individuals and households, especially those on low incomes or otherwise vulnerable. In a number of nations, such as Australia, New Zealand and the US, government-provided housing support is no longer seen as a long-term commitment to the well-being of the household, but instead has been couched as point-in-time assistance during a (limited) period of need (Beer and Paris, 2005). Measures to reinforce this policy direction have included the introduction of limited-term tenure in social housing, greater targeting of access to housing assistance and the effective rationing of assistance. What this has meant is that households who in previous generations may have spent some, or all, of their lives in social housing are no longer able to enter the tenure. This affects the trajectory of their lives and fundamentally reshapes their experience of housing over their lifetime.

The move away from hierarchical forms of government to more porous forms of governance has been one of the key shifts in philosophy of public assistance over the last two decades and one which has reshaped the lifetime experiences of housing in some nations, and has the potential to do so in others. The concept of *governance* lies at the centre of much contemporary theory concerned with the role of the state, and the implementation of urban and housing programmes (see, for example, Kearns and Turok, 2000; Jordan et al, 2005). Jordan et al (2005, p 478) observed that 'there is no universally accepted definition of governance; there is not even a 'consensus on which set of phenomena can be properly grouped under the title of governance'. While there is merit to this argument, much of the literature recognises common elements as typical of governance, including a shift from the formal structures of government to the incorporation of a wider range of interests in decision making and the achievement of programme objectives (Whitehead, 2003). Typically, governance is associated with the rise of partnership arrangements and a reduced ability of governments to directly determine outcomes. Governance takes different forms in different nations and Blatter (2004) notes that within federal systems, such as the US, Canada, Germany and Australia, governance is marked by both horizontal links between agents and institutions, and also hierarchical, competitive and cooperative modes of interaction. Governance, therefore, can lead to complex forms of interaction within federations, with both positive and negative relationships possible. The impacts of governance arrangements are more straightforward in unitary systems of government such as the UK or France, where the national government retains a determinant influence. Importantly, policy approaches and initiatives that are ostensibly decentralised often reveal very little decentralisation of power and resources (Smyth et al, 2004). That is, governments continue to exert a dominant controlling influence, even if they are no longer directly involved in the provision of services or supports.

Governments in a number of nations, including Australia and the UK, have sought to expand non-state forms of assisted housing provision and involve private and other non-government sources of finance and expertise in the development of subsidised rental housing. The introduction of housing benefit in the UK marked a substantial shift away from the direct subsidy of housing supply to subsidising the consumption of rental housing, with the payment of benefit decoupled from the provision of housing by specific forms of landlords. Housing benefit became payable to tenants of non-state landlords, especially housing associations, but also private landlords. Housing associations in the UK, moreover, increasingly made use of private sector finance for capital development projects, while the availability of private finance was underpinned by a housing benefit system that guaranteed the repayment of such loans (Beer and Paris, 2005). In real terms, the shift to governance arrangements in the delivery of housing assistance has meant that not only are low-income households less likely to receive long-term assistance with their accommodation, but the assistance which is available will be provided by a different type of agency when compared with the past. In all likelihood that new form of assistance will come with altered terms, conditions and management practices.

More recently, debates on market-led social policies have been supplanted by a discourse focused on a 'Third Way' of approaching government and politics. The Third Way is seen to have been derived from the work of Giddens (1998, 2000) and was popularised by the incoming Blair Labour government in the late 1990s (Powell, 2000). This philosophy was presented as constituting a new relationship between society (government) and citizens, advocating an approach that was focused on neither the 'market' or the 'state' but, instead, a new Third Way. Key features of the Third Way include a focus on individual responsibility; social inclusion, rather than equality; strengthening education and engagement with the labour market; partnerships between the public and private sector to achieve social and economic objectives; and a commitment to limiting public expenditure – while encouraging those outlays it sees as social investment. While some commentators have noted that the Third Way represents a continuation of a number of previous ideologies of government (Rose, 2001), there can be no denying its adoption by other nations in Europe, North America and Australasia (Green-Pederson et al, 2001; Peck and Theodore, 2001) and across social policy fields, including public health (Muntaner et al, 2000), education (Power and Whitty, 1999) and labour market programmes. Peck and Theodore (2001) note that Third Way policies emphasise the need to boost the productive capacity of societies through micromanagement of labour markets. Their observation lends weight to Powell's (2000) claim that this is a philosophy of the political Right, rather than, as claimed by its advocates, a Centrist policy. It is important to acknowledge that many policy frameworks that could be interpreted as neoliberal in their orientation are entirely consistent with the Third Way.

Third Way perspectives on the relationship between the individual and society have the capacity to shape lifetime housing outcomes in a number of ways, now and into the future. First, this philosophy deliberately rejects an extensive welfare state and the level of public sector involvement in economy and society that characterised some nations in the latter half of the 20th century. From this it follows that in the future few, if any, individuals or households are likely to have a history of housing over their life course that is dependent on the public sector. The types of housing biography that were evident amongst council housing tenants in the UK or public housing tenants in Australia from the 1950s onwards will gradually disappear. Some individuals will remain long term in social housing, but they will be the tenants of non-government housing providers, such as registered social landlords in the UK and non-government organisations in Australia. Second, the emphasis placed within Third Way philosophies on educational attainment and engagement within the labour market will reinforce the determinant role played by position within the labour market in shaping lifetime housing outcomes. Upwardly mobile households from low socioeconomic status backgrounds will have access to more and better quality housing, but those in poorly paid positions will have constrained opportunities and limited prospect of government intervention to improve their circumstances. The emphasis given by the Third Way (Powell, 2000) to the opportunity to participate in society, rather than equality of outcome, effectively rules out many of the redistributive programs previously enacted. Third, the focus on personal responsibility as part of an implicit contract between the citizen and society empowers a managerialist approach to housing that can fundamentally transform housing outcomes for those in social housing. Key features include a greater use within the social housing sector of punitive measures, such as eviction and the regulation of behaviour, as well as the application of tenant incentive schemes (Jacobs, 2008).

Contemporary public policies affecting the lifetime housing outcomes of individuals and households display a number of characteristics that are consistent with both the neoliberal interpretations of government action and the Third Way perspective. What we can conclude definitively, however, is that while the nature of government involvement has changed in appearance, the magnitude of that influence has not. As Jessop (1997) observed, the state has retained its influence through its ability to set the context for social and economic change. It is increasingly strategic in the nature and direction of its involvements, with priority given to those areas of social and economic policy privileged by the Third Way perspective: social inclusion, labour market engagement, educational attainment, and discipline in public finance. At the same time there has been a shift in the preferred model of intervention away from direct intervention to one in which governments enunciate the regulatory and policy frameworks for others. In short, the public sector increasingly seeks to 'steer' not 'row', or it sets out to direct rather than implement. How the Third Way has intersected with the outcomes of the global financial crisis evident from 2007 will be considered in Chapter Three, but it is important to acknowledge that the depth and nature of government intervention owes much to this institutional framework and to the philosophical convergence among national leaders it has helped create.

Importantly, housing per se is not central to the Third Way agendas of government, except in the case of particular groups who are perceived to be socially excluded because of their housing, or lack of housing. A characteristic of Third Way governments is a preoccupation with – often narrowly defined – homelessness (Commonwealth of Australia, 2008a) and the accommodation of groups whose needs cannot be met through the combination of the labour and housing markets. This includes persons with a long-term disability. The lifetime housing outcomes of persons with a disability are likely to be both substantially different to those of the wider population (Beer and Faulkner, 2009) and more likely to be the subject of ongoing policy attention. For these reasons the housing of persons with a disability can be expected to experience a greater depth and pace of change than was evident in the past, and they are likely to be some of the beneficiaries of the new policy levers (Shorten, 2008). The lifetime housing experiences of persons with a disability are considered in greater depth later in this book, but it is important to note that in many nations there has already been a significant shift away from institutional care to integration within the broader community. In addition, there has been substantial reorganisation of the ways in which publicly-funded services and supports are provided, as well as a new emphasis on the rights of disabled persons (Quibell, 2004). At the broadest level, the process of 'de-institutionalisation' has contributed to a widening of the range of lifetime housing outcomes for this group within advanced economies.

In advanced economies the relationship between an individual or household's life course and their housing outcomes has been transformed over the past 30-40 years and, as discussed above, this shift has been driven by a number of powerful processes. The drivers of change have included economic restructuring; developments within the labour market; shifts in social and economic policy; changing social attitudes with respect to gender, disability, and tolerance; movement in housing markets; specific developments in housing policy; and demographic change (Figure 1.1). This catalogue of processes is important as it raises a challenge to conceptualise and, if at all possible assess, the influence of each. Understanding the interplay between these factors is important, as is the way in which there are both commonalities and differences in processes across nations.

**Figure 1.1: Processes contributing to change in 21st-century housing careers**

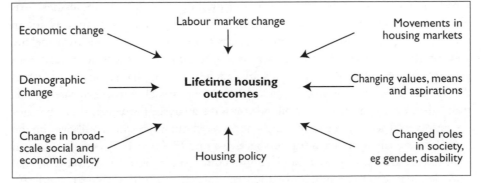

*Source:* Designed by authors of book

## Evidence and theory in understanding housing over the life course

Finally, it is important to ask, how can a renewed focus on housing over the life course inform our wider theoretical understanding of housing and the dynamics of housing markets? Kemeny (1992) noted that much housing research appeared to be atheoretical in its orientation, with a strong emphasis on empirical description and measurement. Clapham (2002, 2004, 2005a) has acknowledged this critique and has argued that social constructionist approaches allow for the development of fresh, and theoretically connected insights into housing and its role within society. Clapham's preferred theoretical orientation has been to the application of a social constructionist framework to the analysis of housing where:

> ...social constructionism is a broad church, with many different emphases within it. Therefore, it is necessary to define the particular approach taken before engaging in the main task of devising a conceptual armoury for the study of housing. The fundamental tenet of social constructionism is that reality is constructed by people through interaction. It is through interaction that people define themselves and the world they inhabit so it is through interaction that the nature of the individual becomes apparent to themselves and to others. (Clapham 2004, pp 94-5)

The detail of Clapham's (2002, 2004, 2005a, 2005b) pathways framework will be discussed in the next chapter, but it is important to consider the broader theoretical shifts impinging upon our understanding of housing and housing outcomes over the life course, including social constructionism. Social constructionism emphasises the subjective knowledge of our understanding of the world and that this understanding is developed in interaction, and competition, with others or other groups (Clapham 2004, p 95). Critically, language and discourse is central to the emergence of socially-constituted and agreed 'meaning', and the subjective meaning actors attach to a phenomenon or state – such as homelessness – is placed at the centre of the analysis. Homelessness, from this perspective, is not an objective state but, instead, is a set of understandings that emerges from debate and interaction between a range of actors stretching from those without a roof through to service providers, policy makers and the media. Jacobs et al (2004) and others have implicitly or explicitly advanced a social constructionist agenda through their use and promotion of discourse analysis. However, there has not been universal acceptance of this approach, with some researchers questioning the value of a social constructionist perspective. Fopp (2008, p 167) noted that in an unadulterated or 'strong' form social constructionism leads to a position where all knowledge is seen to be subjective and that 'not only is it impossible to adjudicate between competing values but it is impossible to arbitrate between competing facts'. Further, Fopp recognised that 'weak' forms of social constructionism, as advocated by Jacobs et al (2004), are faced by an inevitable contradiction in attempting to privilege some forms of knowledge as objective and material, while others are construed to be subjective and socially constructed.

Fitzpatrick (2005, p 2) has argued that critical realism offers a potentially valuable alternative to both 'interpretivist' approaches (as evident in social constructionism) and 'positivist' philosophies with their emphasis on statistically significant correlations between variables. Realist approaches attempt to identify underlying causes (Sayer, 1992) while recognising that outcomes are the product of complex processes and that the impact of many of these drivers are highly contingent upon circumstances. Somerville and Bengtsson (2002, p 124) developed an approach they referred to as 'contextualised rational action', which they characterised as 'accepting that a real world exists independently of our knowledge of it, and it is critical in the sense that we regard our knowledge of that world as wholly fallible and always open to alteration through criticism'. They also redefined the concept of 'necessity' (Sayer 2000) within realist theory to one in which the elucidation of logical relationships was central to the discussion of causality. Somerville and Bengtsson (2002) tied this philosophical position to the concept of 'thin rationality' 'where individual actors are assumed to have some logical consistency in the pursuit of their goals' and that these goals are open to empirical investigation.

Debates around the epistemology of housing research are of fundamental significance in shaping how the research community and policy makers examine and discuss housing outcomes and transitions over the life course. Social constructionist methods emphasise the meanings and values attached to housing by different groups and by individuals at different stages in their lives (Clapham, 2005a). This approach stands in stark contrast to conventional research into housing careers with its empirical focus on enumerating and describing the number and direction of moves through the housing stock. By contrast, a critical realist approach would map out a different pathway of analysis and explanation, with a greater focus on empirical investigations to unearth the motivations of individuals and other actors, as well as underlying causality. To a certain degree, Clapham's (2002; 2005a) work has placed research on housing careers or housing pathways at the forefront of debates on epistemology and the development of housing theory. But as Franklin (2002) noted, grand theory in housing research remains elusive, and scholarly debates continue to move at some pace. Jacobs and Atkinson (2008), for example, observed a range of theoretical concerns of interest to housing and urban scholars, some of which were more practical in orientation while others were derived from core philosophical and sociological concerns. Importantly, there is no consensus on theoretical development in housing research, nor even on the types of issues that should be the subject of such development. In this context, the challenge for *Housing Transitions* is to provide a comprehensive account of housing outcomes over the life course in the 21st century, while simultaneously providing insight into the key processes, perspectives and issues that surround this component of social and individual life. How we contribute to the empirical and theoretical traditions embedded in housing research will become apparent over the subsequent chapters.

### The Housing 21 Survey

Large-scale surveys or data sets are one of the ways researchers have traditionally sought to understand the relationship between the life course and housing. While not consistent with a social constructionist perspective, the attraction of quantified outcomes cannot be denied. Throughout this book we will make use of the results of our own large-scale survey, The Housing 21 Survey, to shed light on the key issues and conceptual challenges confronting our understanding of housing over the life course. The Housing 21 Survey is very much a product of Australian conditions and circumstances, but we would argue that there are substantial similarities between housing conditions in Australia and those evident in the UK, the US, New Zealand, Canada, France, Germany, and other developed economies. In a global economy ruled by free markets and consumption, differences between nations are often a matter of degrees not substance.

The Housing 21 Survey was developed through 2006 and sought to investigate the relative importance of the potential drivers of lifetime housing. The survey was undertaken using a computer-aided telephone interviewing (CATI) method with 2,600 interviews undertaken across all Australian states and territories. Data collection commenced in October 2007 and ended in January 2008 and there was a 38 per cent response rate. The full details of the methods employed are provided in Beer and Faulkner (2009).

# TWO

# Housing over the life course: housing histories, careers, pathways and transitions

Change in the way individuals and households live in, use and consume housing over the course of their lives has been, and remains, a dynamic field of housing research. While Kemeny (1992) and others (Clapham, 2005a; O'Neil, 2008) have decried the failure of housing studies to engage with contemporary sociological theory, researchers from across the globe have quietly amassed a significant body of work that sheds light on the changing relationship between households and the dwellings in which they live over their life course (see, for example, Abramson, 2008; Gram-Hanssen and Bech-Danielsen, 2008; Mandic, 2008). This chapter sets out to review this body of published work and begins with a discussion of the role of risk within contemporary society before moving on to examine debates around housing careers, housing histories, housing biographies and housing pathways. The chapter concludes that there is a need to recast our thinking around this issue and that in the 21st century it is now more appropriate to consider the way individuals move through the housing stock as a set of transitions that embraces both permanent and temporary relocation and the simultaneous occupancy of multiple dwellings. There is also a need to consider the adverse, as well as the positive, outcomes that result from participation in the housing market, explicitly recognising that for many individuals their experience of housing over their life course is not an upward 'ladder' of increasing opportunity and consumption.

## Risk, the life course and housing

Over the last decade or so a number of sociologists such as Beck (1992; 2000) and Giddens (1999) have written extensively on the concept of a 'risk society'. They argue that change within economic and social structures has eroded the certainties of the previous 'Fordist' or industrial society and resulted in a process of 'individualisation' where individuals and households are increasingly confronted by the risks – and opportunities – of a rapidly changing social and economic environment. Giddens (1999) argues that social organisation increasingly avoids risk and seeks forms that are responsive to risk. It is argued that in the past governments and institutions mitigated the level of risk within society through a comprehensive welfare state, strongly developed social institutions (such as family and marriage), and widespread wage employment. By contrast, contemporary society has been marked by a reduction in welfare provision (Beck, 2000), a weakening of some social institutions and traditional roles, and new forms of paid work, including the contracting out of work previously performed by employees. There are links also with contemporary debates around neoliberalism (Peck, 2001; Larner, 2005).

There are many dimensions to 'risk society' theory but only a few will be considered here. The concept of individualisation is important because it suggests that both life course and housing careers will come to encompass a greater range of outcomes as the differences between individuals become more pronounced. Importantly, as Beck (2000) noted, the rise of a risk society gives individuals the opportunity to 'script their own lives'. For some individuals a post-industrial society offers greater choice with respect to lifestyle and living arrangements, as well as enhanced opportunities to accumulate wealth. Others are left exposed within a relatively insecure labour market, where social institutions and government- and community-provided supports are less comprehensive than in the past. Social theorists such as Beck and Giddens have also introduced the concept of 'manufactured uncertainty': that is, recognition that the critical risks faced in the contemporary world are those generated through human action, rather than as a consequence of the natural environment. Importantly, the 'risk society' identified by Beck and others should not be seen as a temporary phenomenon in place until the certainties of the past have been regained. Indeed:

> ...the specificity of the risk regime is that it firmly rules out, beyond a transition period, any eventual recovery of the old certainties of standardised work, standard life histories, and an old-style welfare state, national economic and labour policies. Rather, the concept of a risk regime refers to a key principle of the second modernity, whose 'logic' leads to new forms and images of economy and work, society and politics. (Beck, 2000, p 70)

The impact of a risk society on contemporary housing is evident in many ways. Increasingly, household formation, and the housing consumption decisions of existing households, is shaped by a greater level of uncertainty. Previously young men and women could anticipate finding work, leaving the family home, marrying in their early 20s and raising children in the security of long-term employment (Neutze and Kendig, 1991; Badcock and Beer, 2000). By contrast, young adults in developed economies today tend to delay entry into the labour force as they complete higher education. In addition, there has been a rescripting of relationships with many now partnering later in life and/or establishing a second, third or fourth long-term relationship over their life course. In addition, in the contemporary era long-term relationships may or may not involve marriage; and entry into homeownership may be delayed – or cancelled altogether – because of an insecure relationship, the high cost of housing, or as a consequence of part-time, casual or contract employment. As a number of authors have noted (Williams 1984; Paris 1992), across a range of advanced economies the period from the late 1940s to the mid 1970s was marked by a strong and causal relationship between the growth of manufacturing industry and the expansion of owner occupation. The relatively high and secure wages offered by manufacturing employment provided the foundation for mass homeownership in places such as the US, Canada, Australia and New Zealand. The shift to a post-industrial society – with greater levels of inherent risk for individuals – has profound implications for housing tenure, housing form and housing consumption preferences over the life course.

Both prosperity and economic crisis have shaped housing experiences through the first decade of the 21st century and helped recast the relationship between individuals, households and lifetime housing outcomes. While much current attention is focused on the outcomes and impacts of the global financial meltdown of 2007 and 2008 (Blyth 2008; Schwartz 2008), most developed economies have, with some perturbations, grown strongly since the early 1990s. Both economic expansion and contractions were, in large measure, driven by the 'financialisation' of the economy that directed additional funds into all segments of the economy, including the housing sector, restructured large parts of the labour market, and generated considerable wealth for some within society. The 'spillover' effects into the housing sector have been considerable and for a significant proportion of the population in advanced economies, homes have become sites of luxury consumption rather than places for the satisfaction of basic needs such as shelter, warmth or security. This combination of economic cycles and social realignment has generated new dimensions to the relationship between housing and the life course of individuals, with some of the key developments being:

• greater mobility within the housing stock with people shifting tenure and location more frequently than in the past;
• entry into homeownership occurring later in life;
• an increasing prevalence of owning a second home during the later adult years, either as an investment property, a holiday home or both;
• an increasing impact associated with inheritance, and especially housing inheritance, as current generations inherit from those born in the 1920s, 1930s and 1940s;
• a reduced propensity to enter aged care housing in the later years of life and a greater likelihood of ageing in place;
• greater diversity in housing outcomes as a consequence of the widening of the income distribution, as a result of social change and as an outcome of greater diversity in the ethnic and cultural constitution of many developed economies.

Economic change and the restructuring of labour markets have had a profound impact on the life course of both individuals and households. Work and labour markets influence the ability of households to purchase different kinds of housing services; affect investors' propensities to buy/let/sell housing in relation to other investment opportunities and shape differences between households' capacities. Key issues have included the shift away from 'Fordist' large-scale production with big factories and long production runs, to 'Post-Fordist' production units, flexible production and service provision (Beck, 1992). Much large-scale manufacturing has moved, or is moving, to cheaper labour countries and these processes have affected places including industrial towns and suburbs, which have been transformed or abandoned, while in many nations large public sector housing estates have been sold, become places of concentration of disadvantaged households, or have been demolished.

The idea of a 'job for life' with individuals having single 'careers' through their lifetime has, in many instances, been replaced by serial contracts, interspersed with periods of non-employment, and mobility between occupational groups and types. The transformation of labour markets has had highly differentiated and still changing social effects, including the transformation of manufacturing in advanced economies from a mass employer of largely unskilled male labour to a highly mechanised complex production system with few workers but more highly skilled specialists. This transformation is evident across a range of sectors from automotive manufacturing to biotechnology and food production. The evaporation of opportunities for lifetime manual work has displaced older unskilled men. The labour market position of women has changed as more have entered graduate professions. For many women, as well as men, the new labour market structures offer only part-time, insecure jobs, with serial negotiation and re-negotiation of contracts.

The changing complexion of the life course can be presented diagrammatically as a shifting relationship between household income, expenditure and tenure (Figure 2.1). As the image suggests, contemporary and anticipated life courses have become more complex than 30 years ago, with substantial implications for the relationship between the individual and housing outcomes. There are now more opportunities to accumulate wealth, but there is a new potential for substantial costs at critical phases in the life course. Among the aged, for example, there have been substantial shifts in post-retirement housing. In many advanced economies increasingly older people will choose to 'age in place' rather than spend long periods in specialist aged accommodation (Brink, 2002). While staying within the community presents new opportunities for successful ageing, it also brings with it previously unknown challenges as older persons may enter and leave specialised accommodation several times and may need to draw upon – and pay for – a range of services to maintain them in their home. There is an important geographical dimension to these new interactions between life course and housing outcomes as the set of opportunities and constraints affecting any individual will be shaped by spatially differentiated labour markets, trends within local housing markets, and opportunities for government assistance that vary place by place.

## Housing histories, housing careers and housing pathways

The concepts of housing careers, housing pathways and housing histories first received widespread attention within the academic literature in the 1970s and early 1980s (Pickvance, 1974; Payne and Payne, 1977; Kendig, 1984; Forrest,

—

### Figure 2.1: Changed life histories and changing housing careers

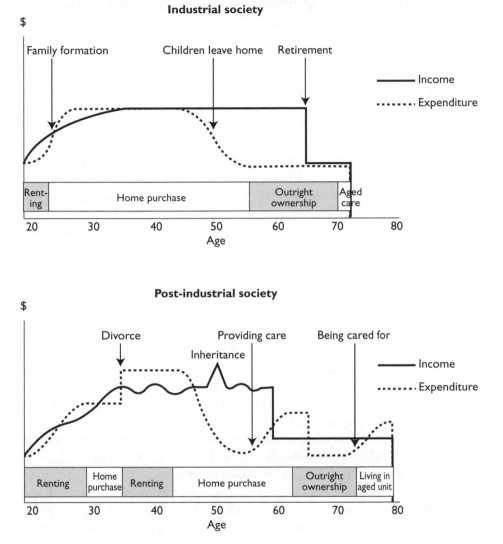

*Source:* Adapted from Williams (2003, p 166)

1987). This body of research noted that there is a strong correlation between stage in the life cycle and the type of housing an individual occupies. Households, it was argued, progress through the housing market in response to their changing demographics, economic and social circumstances. Households were seen to ascend simultaneously three discrete but related ladders: an employment career; a life stage progression (implicitly raising children); and a housing career. The pattern of housing consumption was also seen to reflect local housing market conditions as the specific circumstances in any place – such as the cost of housing, the type of stock available and tenure structure – influenced outcomes. Importantly, this body of work recognised that housing careers or housing histories reflected the balance of constraints and opportunities that directed households into particular situations within the housing system.

## Housing careers

Conventionally, the concept of a housing career has been used to explain the strong correlation between the type of dwelling a household occupied and its stage in the life cycle. Through the 1980s the concept of a housing career was associated with the owner occupied sector (Thorns, 1981; Forrest and Kemeny, 1983; Kendig, 1984; 1990a; Myers, 1999) and for many writers 'homeownership was the peak, the apogee of the housing career' (Clark et al, 2003). Socially and economically aspiring households were considered to possess a housing career that paralleled their career within the work place (Saunders, 1990). A series of moves into progressively more expensive housing generally accompanied occupational success. Dwellings were seen to be exchanged either to improve the level of housing amenity enjoyed by the household, increase opportunities for capital gains through housing, or as a consequence of the movement to a new housing market as a result of a job transfer. Thorns (1981) considered the latter to be a significant influence within the housing market in Christchurch, New Zealand, while Forrest and Kemeny (1983) outlined a typical housing career for owner occupants in Britain in their discussion of the relationship between furnished private rental housing and homeownership. They argued that owner occupants became investors in that section of the rental market as their economic position changed and as they took advantage of the housing circumstances around them. In many respects this conventional view of a 'housing career' implies an upward and ordered trajectory of increasing opportunity, comfort and wealth. Kendig et al (1987) represented this graphically as a ladder (Figure 2.2), with individual households pursuing upward movement through the housing market, while the arrows to the sides respectively indicate both pathways 'forward' and the mechanisms for slipping 'backward'. The figure implies a start point and a destination and also suggests a hierarchy of tenures, as well as a household structure amenable to repaying a mortgage.

Throughout the 1980s research on housing careers was often explicitly linked to the wider debate on domestic property classes (Saunders, 1978, 1979, 1981, 1984) and this connection is illustrated by the work of Farmer and Barrell (1981). Their work focused on the opportunities hypothetically available to middle class British households seeking to maximise their returns from housing. Farmer and Barrell (1981) examined the conditions in Britain's housing and financial markets between 1965 and 1979. They concluded that owner occupants would have received the greatest possible gains from their participation in the housing market if they followed a deliberate career involving the sale and repurchase of a dwelling every three years, at high rates of borrowing. They estimated that households that moved frequently and purchased dwellings at low capitalisation rates received

**Figure 2.2: The housing career 'ladder'**

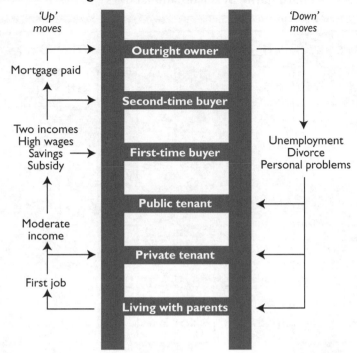

*Source:* Based on Kendig et al (1987, p 30)

a return of 15.7 per cent on their initial outlay. Non-movers and persons who moved infrequently received slightly lower returns of 11.7 per cent and 14.7 per cent. Significantly, Farmer and Barrell showed that, in theory at least, the choice of housing career affected the financial returns arising out of homeownership. Households that adopted a conservative strategy accumulated capital through the establishment of equity in their home. Households who moved frequently accrued benefits through a rise in the capital value of their dwellings.

Badcock and Beer (2000) presented their understanding of housing careers as a set of processes akin to a game of 'snakes and ladders' (Figure 2.3). They argued that 'it is no longer good enough to presume that homeownership is an escalator for everyone, or to assign homeowners to a class position and leave it at that' (p 9), noting that 'not everyone enjoys the fruits of capital accumulation' (p 10). Badcock and Beer's (2000) understanding of, and imagery for, the way individuals interact with the housing market was a reflection of its time, with a greater appreciation of households falling out of homeownership (AHURI, 1998) and the busts as well as the booms of the housing market. In many ways 'snakes and ladders' constitutes an intuitively attractive metaphor for the housing market because it does not imply one pathway or direction, and captures some of the complexities many people face as they seek to balance their housing aspirations with other dimensions of life. However, it is a flawed representation because it

**Figure 2.3: The board game of snakes and ladders**

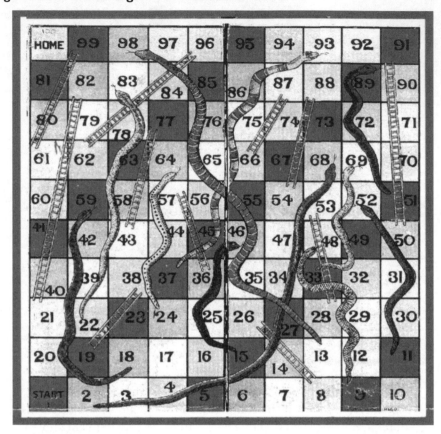

*Source:* Badcock and Beer (2000, p 90)

implies a single start point and destination – 'home' – and because it suggests that all participants eventually achieve a single goal.

## Housing histories

The concept of a housing career provides a useful perspective on the position of individual households within the housing systems of a diverse range of nations. The insights offered into the relationship between household demography and housing outcomes has added greatly to the housing studies literature, but the concept of a housing career can be challenged on a number of grounds. First, the conventional definition of a housing career is limited in that it assumes households move to achieve greater levels of housing satisfaction in their housing or to realise a capital gain. Individuals and households are seen to advance their material position, choosing only to consume less housing during the later part of their life when a substantial dwelling may no longer be appropriate. Second, the concept of a housing career explicitly emphasises choice within the housing market and the individual household's ability to achieve its aspirations. It presents an interpretation of personal experiences which suggests that housing outcomes are a product of the relatively unconstrained preferences of individuals. Each household is seen to be linked causally with a dwelling because that structure has matched their housing and lifestyle requirements. Third, demographic factors alone have been related to the accommodation of the household. Housing and stage in the life cycle have been related in a purposive manner without reference to other influences, such as the values or aspirations of household members, broader social development and position in the workforce.

Forrest (1987) discussed the definition of housing histories and their relationship to the specific processes shaping housing markets. He distinguished the term housing *history* from the alternative notions of housing *career* and housing *pathways* (Payne and Payne, 1977). Forrest (1987) argued that there are sets of housing experiences shared by persons on the basis of class, gender, race and locality. Groups of households, he argued, will experience particular outcomes with respect to their housing on the basis of where they live, what they are able to earn and the accommodation subsidies available to them. In this conceptualisation, actors and influences external to the housing market will, in large measure, determine outcomes, with the household's position within the labour market exerting the single greatest influence. Other factors, such as location, ethnicity and gender, may serve as additional determinants of housing opportunities.

The concept of housing histories recognises that structural influences have a substantial impact on the types of dwellings households occupy and the nature of their occupancy. Payne and Payne (1977) argued from their study of tenure change in Aberdeen, Scotland, that a household's accommodation is a function of the householder's ability to gain access to housing first, and stage in the life cycle a distant second. In their study, the household's economic resources dictated the type of housing they occupied and the researchers noted that there was little movement between public tenancy and owner occupancy amongst their subjects. Life cycle characteristics altered merely the household's position within this tenure framework. Couples who could not afford to purchase a home languished in private rental as public housing was usually denied childless families. The majority of households renting from the council in Aberdeen were only able to move into public housing after the birth of the first, or more commonly the second, child. Similar limiting influences operated within the private sector. Households did not enter owner occupation after the birth of the first child because of the substantial costs associated with raising a family. In short, owner occupation in Aberdeen was a 'closed shop' in which economic resources were the key to access and household characteristics played a peripheral role. A compatible argument can be developed with respect to other processes operating in housing markets. Forrest (1987) noted that a homeowner in the English Midlands was in a very different position from an outright owner in London. The substantial discrepancy in dwelling prices between the two areas meant that a house in the Midlands could not be substituted for a comparable dwelling in London. The spatial characteristics and structure of the British housing market was the limiting influence and one which dictated the ongoing opportunities available to individual households.

The importance of constraints within the housing market cannot be denied. Forrest (1987) recognised that while many housing histories contained a strong career element, 'others are chaotic and characterised by constraints and coping strategies' (p 1624). Kendig (1984) found similar evidence with fully 43 per cent of movers in Adelaide, South Australia in 1975-76 changing their residence for reasons that had little to do with dissatisfaction with their previous dwelling (p 274). Moves compatible with the concept of 'a housing career' did occur, especially among young people. Other influences, however, also precipitated moves between dwellings and localities. Housing careers per se were lost amidst the multitude of social processes shaping the housing market and the trajectory of individuals through that market. Clearly, the notion of a housing career does not provide an adequate explanation of movement through, or outcomes within, the housing market and it is important to incorporate structural factors in our understanding of the determinants of lifetime housing outcomes.

'Housing careers' and 'housing histories' as conventionally understood, are diametrically opposed in some key respects but similar in the focus they place on movement through the housing market, and a link with the life course. The concept of a housing career emphasises free choice within the market and implies an upward trajectory. Households within this paradigm are seen to move to better their situation with respect to tenure or the quality and quantity of housing consumed. Housing histories, by contrast, relate households to the social and/or economic constraints on their housing, especially their position within the labour market. Clearly, both perspectives must be considered and have something to offer our understanding of lifetime housing outcomes. Individuals act according to their free will and attempt to satisfy their personal needs and wants. They act, however, within a range of limiting constraints, which may proscribe the outcomes available to them. Clark et al (2003) acknowledged this interplay between constraints and opportunities and applied a life course perspective to their research into what they characterised as the 'complex process of how households bring their housing consumption into balance with their housing needs' (see also Deurloo et al, 1994). Their research focused on the sequence of housing states occupied by individuals and households over time, as defined by tenure and the quality of dwellings occupied. Importantly, Clark et al (2003) drew a conceptual link between housing circumstance, progress through the housing market (which they labelled housing career), and family status.

The idea of an irregular or spasmodic sequence lies at the heart of Clark et al's (2003) research, as they noted that:

> …the emphasis on sequences and on housing states in this paper serves to rebalance the focus in much of the literature, which pays greater attention to the analysis of *only one* move or *one* change [original emphasis] in the housing career. We know that a complete housing

career can be made up of 5–9 moves with often relatively long stable periods in between these moves. The more limited 'short window' studies of mobility itself probably overemphasise the event of moving and give relatively little attention to the periods of stability. (p 144)

Clark et al (2003) hypothesised that housing careers were likely to be affected by the life stage of individuals and households, with higher rates of movement or other change in early adulthood and greater stability later in life. They also expected to be able to identify pronounced regional differences, with the composition and price of dwellings in different parts of the US influencing the number and direction of moves through the housing stock. They also noted that previous researchers such as Kendig (1981) and Harts and Hingstman (1986) observed substantial variation in housing careers within a population with respect to both the number of moves through the housing market and the final housing occupied by a household.

Clark et al (2003) used data from the US Panel Study of Income Dynamics for the period 1968 to 1993 to examine patterns in the sequencing of housing over life course across continental US. In total this analysis provided them with some 8,663 housing careers to analyse against a matrix of tenure (renting versus owning) and price (high cost or low cost). They found that many of the observed housing careers were, in fact, remarkably simple, with one or fewer changes in state over the 26 years of observations. The authors found that some 26 'typical' housing sequences accounted for the vast majority of housing careers, and just 11 sequences accounted for 75 per cent of the total. They were also struck by the fact that 63 per cent of all housing careers over this period ended with owner occupation and that:

> The many sequences with a dominantly stable situation in the housing market exceed our expectations. The emphasis on the whole housing career...brings forward these long periods of stability in the housing market for many households. (Clark et al, 2003, p 153)

Interestingly, 77 per cent of housing careers showed an ascending pattern with respect to tenure and the price/quality of the housing, but that almost one quarter of two or more stage careers had a descending trajectory and this was consistent with the authors' earlier work (Clark et al, 2000) on overcrowding. Overall, Clark et al (2003) concluded that income level and the growth of incomes were the major drivers of tenure and housing quality over the long term and that 'these variables play a determining role in the development of the housing careers of households over longer stretches of their life course' (p 155). Geography or location was seen to play a role, but it was a more limited impact and one which added nuance to the larger national trends.

Clark et al's (2003) contribution to this literature is important because it emphasises the interplay between structural processes and household dynamics, especially the career trajectories and incomes of household members. At a substantive level, their work provides concrete evidence of the reality of housing careers and the capacity to identify meaningful patterns or sequences amidst a wealth of observations. The fact that there is both a considerable diversity of sequences or careers and a tendency towards a limited number of relatively simple careers is significant, as it reinforces the utility of this concept within housing analysis. In addition, their work acknowledges the importance of location in shaping opportunities for movement through the housing market, while recognising that not all households enjoy an ascending housing career.

Finally, it is important to acknowledge that a housing career is essentially an Anglo-Celtic construct and some researchers have criticised the concept for relating to a specific generation or generations with relatively stable housing circumstances (Watt, 2005). Households and individuals from other backgrounds may have very different relationships with their housing over their life course, and increasing cultural diversity in many developed economies has contributed to a widening of housing outcomes, both at a point in time and over the life course. We also need to recognise that the housing careers of indigenous peoples vary considerably from those of the remainder of the population. Birdsall-Jones and Christensen (2007) have documented the relationship between housing and the life course for Indigenous Australians in Western Australia. Their research showed that the housing careers of many urban Indigenous households were shaped by long-term poverty, incidences of family and neighbourhood conflict, and impeded access to social housing, partly as a consequence of management practices. In addition, research across Australia has shown that cyclical mobility is a feature of the housing careers of some Indigenous households (Taylor, 1997), while others are confronted by problems of homelessness (Allwood and Rogers, 2001), discrimination (Paris, 1992), eviction from public and private rental accommodation (Flatau et al, 2004) and limited housing options. Many Indigenous households have successful housing careers in homeownership or community based housing, though the home purchase rate amongst Indigenous Australians is roughly half that of the population as a whole (Roberts et al, 2005).

## Housing pathways

More recently Clapham (2002; 2004) has argued that research needs to focus on housing pathways that explicitly link the objective analysis of movements through the housing market with the subjective examination of individual experience. Clapham explicitly links this paradigm to both social constructionism (see Jacobs et al, 2004) and Giddens' (1984) theory of structuration. Clapham's (2002; 2004) housing pathways need to be interpreted with reference to these other, very substantial, bodies of scholarship.

In common with some other commentators (Kemeny, 1992), Clapham (2002; 2004) argues that much housing research is both atheoretical and overly focused on government policy. He considers this to be a major failing on two levels: first, governments do not directly influence housing outcomes for the vast majority of the population within advanced economies, and research is inadvertently skewing our understanding of housing market processes and outcomes. Second,

—

housing researchers have distanced themselves from conceptual developments in other areas of social sciences, especially sociology. This latter argument echoes a common theme in Kemeny's (1992) writing. For Clapham the key failing in contemporary housing scholarship is the failure to address both structure (the set of institutional arrangements that shape behaviours in the housing market) and agency (the decisions, values and subjective experiences of individuals and households). The failure to address agency is seen to be a particular gap because, as authors such as Giddens (1990) and Beck (2000) argued, globalisation and the emergence of new technologies and production processes have encouraged individualism and eroded the institutions that previously shaped people's lives (Clapham 2002, p 59). Individuals and individual households are now better placed than in the past to shape their own lives. Clapham (2002) concurs with Giddens' (1991) argument that there has been an:

> 'opening out' of social life in which individuals are more able to make their own lives by actively making choices. This is encapsulated by the concern with 'lifestyle', by which is meant the desire to choose an individual identity, which leads to self fulfilment. (Clapham, 2002, p 59)

Housing, it is argued by Clapham (2002; 2004), is a critical part of the search for a lifestyle that leads to self fulfilment and that housing 'is a means to an end rather than an end in itself' (Clapham, 2002, p 59). Housing is seen as a place of security and enabling for a household (King, 1996), an essential ingredient in the search for Mazlow's 'self actualisation'.

Clapham (2002) recognises that not all households can achieve self fulfilment through their housing. Individualisation carries with it greater levels of risk: risk of unemployment, risk of short-term contracts, and risk of divorce. There is also variable risk according to stage in the life course. Young adults may be at risk of not securing appropriate housing while older people may not find appropriate accommodation when specialist supports and services are needed to assist them with ill-health or disability. Persons with a disability may be at risk of not finding, or not affording, appropriate accommodation in an era when governments no longer provide large-scale targeted investments directed at meeting their housing needs. Within Clapham's pathways paradigm, housing is seen to contain many sets of meanings and it is these meanings that need to be located at the centre of any analysis. This is a significant departure from both the housing history and housing career perspectives discussed earlier, as they focus on measuring change in housing circumstances and assessing the structural influences that have shaped those movements. By contrast, Clapham's (2002; 2004) framework of analysis focuses on how individual households interpret and understand their progression through the housing system.

Housing pathways research, Clapham (2002; 2004) suggests, should be thought of as a 'framework for analysis – a way of framing thought' (2002, p 63) that focuses upon the concept of a housing pathway, which is defined as:

> ...patterns of interactions (practices) concerning house and home over time and space (2002, p 63)

and

> ...the continually changing set of relationships and interactions which it (the household) experiences over time in its consumption of housing.... a housing pathway....seeks to capture the social meanings and relationships associated with this consumption in the different locales. (2002, p 64)

Critically, housing pathways research is seen to embrace all the elements of conventional housing career research, but extends its reach to explore the meanings attached to the home, the relationship with other life events, and interactions within the neighbourhood. Clapham (2002) argues that his approach accommodates the fact that a household's residential circumstances change, even if the members don't move dwelling or tenure. For example, social rental housing no longer carries the same set of meanings as a decade ago, a fact highlighted by the abolition of lifetime tenure in government-owned housing within a number of Australian jurisdictions, and the shift from council-owned housing to registered social landlords in parts of the UK. A housing career perspective would see these households as not having experienced change, while a pathways approach would seek to investigate how their circumstances have shifted as a result of the new tenure arrangements, and would endeavour to investigate the views of tenants on the impact of this transformation on their lives. Similarly, as Clapham (2005a) explicitly notes, 'home' carries a different set of meanings for older people than it did ten, 20 or 30 years previously when they were working. From Clapham's (2005a) perspective, the challenge is to understand how these meanings have changed and what implications that change carries for the individual or individuals.

Clapham (2002; 2004) ties his housing career paradigm to concepts of life planning and identity, with the former drawing heavily on the work of Giddens (1984). In essence, the concept of life planning recognises that households do not consume housing in isolation from other dimensions of life and that 'households undertake life planning in search of identity and self fulfilment' (Clapham, 2002, p 65). A housing pathway follows a life course pathway that includes education, employment, the decision to have children (or not), housing and relationships. Moreover, households recognise this fact and

> ...develop a long term view of where they would like to be in the future and formulate a strategy to achieve this that will frame individual decisions. The existence of a strategy is a guide to the extent to which they engage in what Giddens calls life planning by actively seeking to organise and control their lives. (Clapham, 2004, pp 99–100)

In support of his argument, Clapham (2004) cites other researchers (Anderson et al 1994; McCrone, 2004) who reported that a significant fraction of households in their surveys had explicit and deliberate housing strategies that were integrated with lifetime goals.

Identity is an important part of the subjective inquiry that distinguishes the pathways framework from other perspectives. Clapham recognises both ontological identity – self-identity – and categorical identity, 'the labels which are ascribed to us by ourselves, and by society' (Clapham, 2002, p 65). Housing clearly affects both ontological and categorical identity: we are a 'homeowner', a 'home purchaser', or a 'tenant'; and, the housing we occupy may shape how we perceive our place in the world. Importantly, Clapham (2002) recognises that 'disability' is one of the categories around which discourse and conflict is constructed, with competing views presented by various parties. He notes that:

> ...the discourses associated with physical and mental disability have been actively contested by professions, government agencies and interest groups in what has been called the politics of identity. It is here that the power games outlined earlier are played in which the actors attempt to mobilise their resources to ensure their discourse is the one adopted in public policy and in general discourse. (p 65)

Clapham (2002) therefore urges researchers to investigate the politics of identity associated with particular housing pathways followed by identifiable groups.

Clapham's (2002; 2004) ideas on housing pathways are original and stimulating. The challenge is to translate this framework into concrete research and he suggests researchers need

> ...to employ ethnographic or biographic methods to understand the meaning of individuals and households and the conscious aspects of behaviour. However, the unconscious aspects need to be explored bearing in mind the constraints and opportunities, which structure them and are reproduced by them. (2002, p 66)

The focus of research, he suggests, must be on the factors that are associated with a change in the pathway, with the life plan either being redrafted or edited for external reasons. He also suggests that it is important to generalise from individual pathways to the broader population by focusing on the meanings households attach to their housing; recognising how individuals create their own life plan in association with their lifestyle decisions; and, by recognising the dynamic nature of pathways and how they change over time.

Intuitively, the housing pathways approach is attractive, but we need to recognise that attempts to put into effect social constructionist and/or structuration perspectives are confronted by very real challenges associated with the transferability of the results and the emphasis given to the debates or discourses around housing. Somerville (2002), for example, commends the pathways framework but challenges the need to ground it within a postmodern social constructionist perspective, arguing instead it should be framed within more substantial social theory. Jacobs (2002) points out the impossibility of measuring 'unconscious meanings and actions' (p 75) while King (2002) critiques Clapham for linking housing pathways to social constructionism, a theoretical position, he argues that is now disappearing from other areas of sociological research. King (2002) suggests that a 'postmodern analytical framework' is an oxymoron and echoes Somerville's (2002) contention that structuration theory simultaneously explains everything and nothing.

It is important to ask whether the housing pathways approach adds valuable insights beyond the more conventional discussion of housing careers, whether it can be disentangled from a social constructionist approach, and whether it can be put into operation in a way that results in generalisable outcomes rather than a series of insights into the values and meanings held by a select group of individuals. In large measure we should accept that the housing pathways perspective does add to our understanding of housing processes: its focus on people's perception of their housing circumstances, its concern with the 'fit' between housing outcomes and life plan, and the role of housing in shaping identity is important. It could, for example, be argued that shifts in tenure patterns amongst some groups could be attributed to shifts in their sense – and construction – of identity. Second, it is important to question whether it is possible to fuse a housing pathways perspective with a housing careers perspective. That is, can we successfully integrate the analysis of the subjective meaning of housing when examining more objective measures of movement through the housing stock?

## Housing transitions

The concepts of housing careers, housing histories and housing pathways all add to our understanding of the changing relationship between individual households and housing outcomes over the life course. Determinant factors in this relationship include age, household income, region or locality, the personal and social 'meanings' attached to housing, the presence or absence of children in the household, and the impact of policy frameworks that may influence access to resources such as social housing, subsidised private rental housing or homeownership. The work of Clapham (2005a) on the subjective dimension of housing through the life course has added greater depth to our comprehension of how individuals interact with the housing market. At the same time, there is now a greater appreciation of diversity in housing outcomes, with some individuals and groups following trajectories that differ greatly from assumed social 'norms'. It is no longer possible to identify a 'typical' housing career as lifetime housing outcomes are differentiated by gender, ethnicity, region, nation and social class. This more nuanced understanding of housing outcomes matches increasing complexity within society and the life course of individuals.

The terms housing career, housing pathways and housing history all carry intellectual baggage that impedes the further development of our understanding of the relationship between households and their lifetime housing outcomes. In the past, a small number of researchers (May, 1999; Rugg and Ford, 2004) have used the term 'housing biographies' to reflect the life histories of individuals and their housing. While attractive at some levels, this term implies a subjective, anecdotal perspective on housing over the life course that does not reflect the broader-scale patterns evident in analyses across populations. We consider the term *housing transitions* better reflects the complex and fluid relationship between individuals in developed economies and their housing in the 21st century. It places a focus on ongoing change – potential or real – in housing circumstances and leaves open the possibility of identifying common housing 'sequences' that may shift over time in response to social, economic and cultural developments. It is to be expected that in all nations there will be a limited number of common housing sequences with differences between nations reflecting both cultural values and the impact of government policy settings. Importantly, it leaves scope for both the subjective and objective analysis of change in housing circumstances while having scope to incorporate both structural processes and individual decision making. The term housing transitions does not imply a particular direction or set of dynamics over the life course – a critique levelled at the concept of housing careers – but neither does it privilege the subjective dimensions of housing over quantitative assessment.

A housing transitions framework emphasises the tendency of individuals to make decisions about their housing throughout their life course that are affected by

- their stage in the life course (age, household structure, fertility);
- economic resources (position within the labour market, wealth, access to government assistance);
- health and well-being (presence or absence of a disability within the household);
- tenure (history of prior occupancy in one or more tenures); and
- lifestyle values and aspirations (cultural norms, consumption preferences, relative significance attached to housing).

It is helpful to think of a lifetime of housing transitions as a series of housing decisions about whether to move or not move, the quality and quantity of housing to occupy, location relative to employment and social networks. These decisions are shaped by both opportunities and constraints, with the five dimensions listed above playing a determinant role. A schematic of this perspective on the factors affecting housing decisions is presented in Figure 2.4. It reflects the potential complexity of that decision making environment and the intersection with aspects of individual and household life course. Critically, decisions about housing are undertaken within the context of housing systems that are structured by geography, the balance between social and private systems of supply, and the quality of the housing stock.

Each of these five dimensions – life course; economic resources, well-being, tenure history and values and aspirations – is seen to exert an influence, potentially or in fact, on housing decisions at any point in time. Housing decisions reflect the relative balance and standing of each of these dimensions at that stage in

**Figure 2.4: The housing decision framework**

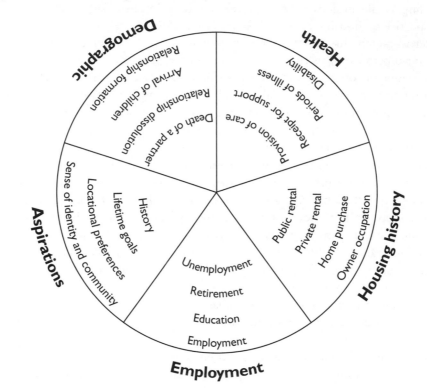

*Source:* Designed by authors of book

the life course and at that point in history. Early in the life course, for example, demographic factors such as marriage and the birth of a child can be an important influence on decisions taken about housing, but position in the labour market, and the type and quality of housing aspired to will be important also. In mid life, demographic factors may have relatively little influence on housing decisions, but tenure may exert a greater influence through the prior accumulation of housing wealth that effectively opens up a greater range of housing options.

The housing transitions perspective acknowledges that many individuals in developed economies are relatively unconstrained by financial impediments and that demographic processes no longer exert the sway they once held. Some individuals and households have far greater capacity to enact their preferences than others and it is not assumed that all start from an equal basis. At the same time, not all housing outcomes are the product of conscious choice, as some individuals have no or few options in their housing. We should not overemphasise the ability of individuals to choose, because while on the one hand a very small minority is confronted by no choice – even the homeless select between a range of options (Beer et al, 2006a) – an equally small minority enjoy unfettered choice. Decisions are therefore made within architecture of often quite rigid constraints. However, even those on very low incomes who lack the resources or capacity to participate in the housing market are likely to have accommodation offered to them on the basis of these five dimensions of housing. The application of formal programmes of Medical Priority Housing in the UK (Dunn 2000) brings into focus the significance of well-being (disability or ill-health) in determining access to social housing, while the importance of stage in the life course for social housing systems is evidenced by the fact that the presence of young children in the household can result in the priority allocation of government-owned housing in Australia. Similarly, prior tenure history (including periods of homelessness) can be a catalyst for housing assistance, and social housing generally includes an aspirational or lifestyle dimension, with a number of jurisdictions around the globe implementing systems of choice-based letting.

From a housing transitions perspective, the focus of analysis is not solely directed to the sequence of housing circumstances occupied by a household over its life course, but instead it also gives priority to decisions taken by a household at a point in time and how those critical junctures are reached. Housing decisions are affected both by subjective factors – the meaning attached to home or housing – as well as more readily measured processes such as change in financial circumstances.

Importantly, the processes of transition through the housing market have cumulative impacts and are affected by all five housing dimensions. For example, the housing decisions of individual baby boomers over the forthcoming decades will, in part, reflect their accumulated experience, and wealth, in the housing market. Those who have been homeowners for the major portion of their adult life will have far greater capacity to meet their lifestyle aspirations – and potentially retire earlier – than those who have lived in rental housing. The cumulative aspect of lifetime housing decisions is reflected in Figure 2.5, which attempts to show how the capacity of individuals to express choice in the housing market varies over time and in ways that reflect a broader life path. The three illustrative cases highlight the way in which an individual has variable power within the housing system and how the culmination of events over the passage of time shapes housing outcomes.

The example of the 'successful' baby boomer highlights the way in which the accumulation of financial assets, in combination with the arrival and eventual departure of children, results in a rapid increase in the capacity to express choice within the housing market in later life. In this instance, the ability of individuals and households to realise their housing aspirations after age 50 is not simply a factor of income at that point in time: it is a reflection of lifetime savings; access to superannuation or pension income; capital gains through the housing market; and the restructuring of the household from a family to a couple-only household. Similarly, the illustration of a person affected by the onset of disability in mid life emphasises the impact of key life events such as disability or ill-health. The figure suggests a lifetime housing trajectory very similar to the successful boomer up until mid life, followed by a dramatic reduction in the capacity to realise aspirations within the housing market. Significantly, we would suggest that even with the onset of a disability, previous life events and participation in housing and labour

**Figure 2.5: The capacity to express choice within housing over time**

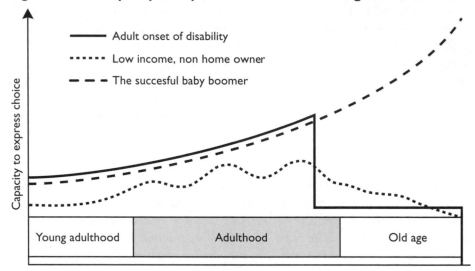

*Source:* Devised by authors of book, based on Williams (2003)

markets continue to be important as the accumulation of resources at an earlier age serves as a cushion or buffer post. As will be discussed later, persons who have acquired a disability in adulthood often have a greater range of housing options available to them when compared with those born with a disability. The final example provided in Figure 2.5 is of a low-income tenant, whose participation in paid employment is insecure and who is marginal financially. Once again, life cycle events such as the birth of children, marriage and separation can be seen to affect movement through the housing market and these processes operate in combination with periods of employment and unemployment. In this instance, the capacity to make choices within the housing market is seen to fall with older age, as hours worked decline, income falls and there is an absence of capital, in the form of housing or other assets, to soften the impact of falling income.

Housing transitions as an integrated concept attempts to bring together point in time decisions within the context of broader social structures and processes that emerge over the longer term, including stage in the life course. In common with Clark et al (2003), the market acknowledges and awards importance to the periods of stability as well as the moments of change, while agreeing with Clapham (2002) that the passage of time means that the relationship between the household and the dwelling is inevitably transformed, even in the absence of a move. This perspective is reflected in Figure 2.6, which shows how complex life trajectories can result in shifts in the influences that shape the housing decisions individuals and households make over the life course. In the first period, when the household is establishing itself, housing decisions are heavily influenced by lifestyle factors and the aspiration for homeownership, as well as the arrival of the first child. Location or consumption aspirations are relatively insignificant, while

**Figure 2.6: Housing decision making over time, the variable influence of life cycle, labour market, well-being, tenure, and lifestyle aspirations**

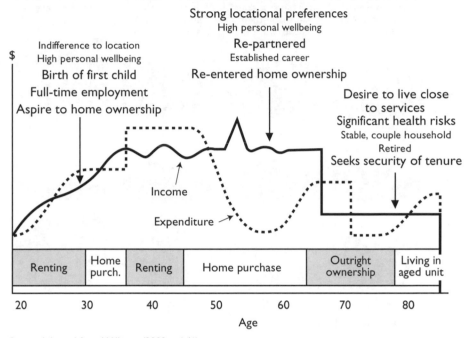

*Source:* Adapted from Williams (2003, p 166)

personal well-being (long-term health and/or disability) exerts virtually no impact. In mid life the individual is shown as attempting to re-enter homeownership, and is able to do so with the benefit of previously accumulated housing wealth. An established career means that labour market factors are an important enabler within the housing market and this, in combination with housing wealth, assists in the movement into a desirable location and/or dwelling. In the third period, health and well-being is seen to exert a considerable influence on housing decisions, with resources previously accumulated through the housing market and the labour market allowing these needs to be met. In this instance health and well-being has both a direct impact on the decision making of individuals – the type of dwelling occupied, the design of the dwelling, access to care and other support services – as well as an indirect influence with respect to locational preferences.

Finally, it is important to consider how housing outcomes through the life course are affected by class or socioeconomic status. Figure 2.7 attempts to capture the housing opportunities and outcomes available to three individuals of differing backgrounds who commence their transect of the housing system with differing capacities in respect of education, labour market resources, health, lifestyle aspirations and values, and experience of the housing market. The position of the three individuals is influenced by their current circumstances, as well as the decisions and events in their past. Long-term outcomes are not equal and

**Figure 2.7: Housing outcomes through the life course**

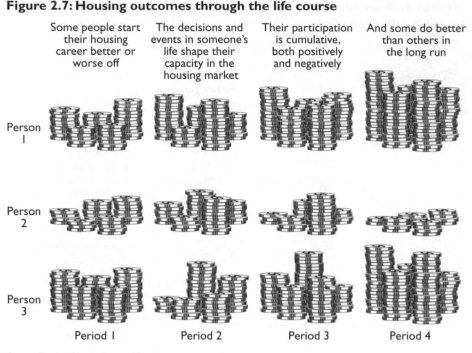

those who enter the housing market with a greater stock of enablers within the housing market are seen to fare better.

## Conclusion

Terminology is always critical in social analysis because the terms we use and the language that we apply to the discussion of those concepts carries implicit meaning and shapes further debate. The term housing career is commonly used in academic work but has been critiqued for its implied uni-directional perspective and the Anglo-Celtic nature of the concept. Some authors have used the term housing histories, housing biographies or even housing trajectories in order to better capture the multi-directional nature of change in housing over the life course and provide adequate recognition of the impact of structural processes in shaping housing outcomes. The term, however, implies a focus on individuals and their outcomes that denies system-wide trends or tendencies. Clapham's (2005a) work on housing pathways has been a useful contribution to this set of debates by emphasising the meanings attached to housing by individuals and how those meanings can change over the life course, even in the absence of formal movement through the housing stock. He highlights the fact that different individuals or groups will attach widely variable meanings to the same housing stock. Most importantly, however, Clapham (2005a) drew our attention to the fact that certain aspects of housing are frequently part of the 'life plan' of individuals and households and that these consumption aspirations increasingly determine housing decisions and lifetime housing outcomes.

This chapter has argued that the term housing transitions better reflects the movement of individuals and households through the housing market over time and across the life course. We believe the term is more helpful than the more commonly used 'housing careers' because it implies change but does not suggest a single source or destination. It is also free of the social constructionist connotations embedded within Clapham's (2002; 2004) account of housing pathways. The term is entirely consistent with the findings of other research, including work by Seelig et al (2005) on the housing consumption patterns of income support recipients. That research found considerable mobility within the housing market, but this activity was marked by an ongoing directionless 'churn' rather than purposive steps up a housing career ladder. A housing transitions perspective also accords with the conclusions of Minnery and Zacharov (2006, p 56) that housing careers or pathways are changing, but not from a relatively simple past to a more complex present and future: instead, housing pathways in the past (as exemplified by a group of 55- to 64-year-olds) demonstrated considerable complexity, in addition to uncertainty and chance. This complexity is likely to remain. From a policy perspective it is worth noting that the transitions framework carries no implications as to long-term housing outcomes – positive or negative – and therefore challenges both the delivery of housing interventions that are sustained in the long term, as well as a reliance on short-term measures that explicitly assume a transition to a 'better' housing state.

# THREE

# Housing transitions and housing policy: international context and policy transfer

*Chris Paris, Terry Clower, Andrew Beer and Debbie Faulkner*

In the late 1980s and early 1990s the American philosopher and political economist Francis Fukuyama triggered considerable debate with his argument that with the advent of Western liberal democracy humanity had reached the 'end of history' as further sociocultural evolution appeared unlikely. Fukuyama's (1992) work has been critiqued heavily, but his ideas highlight the ways in which policies and social practices appear to have converged across nations. Similarly, there are strong international parallels in many aspects of housing policy and the operation of housing markets. The globalisation of financial markets has contributed to the apparent integration of housing markets around the globe, but other contributing factors have included broader shifts in global economic prosperity – at least for the developed world – and deliberate strategies of policy transfer across international borders. It is important to acknowledge that cross-national research plays a valuable role within the social sciences and can lead to robust, transferable conclusions that can be applied in a variety of contexts, and not just those discussed in any one work or research study (Przeworksi and Teune 1970). In many respects the countries discussed in this chapter constitute a 'most similar systems' approach where attention is focused on the differences between otherwise very similar systems. There are strong convergences among the nations discussed here, as each is predominantly English speaking and occupies a 'liberal' position within Epsing-Anderson's (1990) categorisation of welfare regimes.

This chapter sets out to consider the evolution of housing policy in three nations: the UK, the US and Australia. It does so in order to understand the geographical and historical settings for lifetime movements through the housing market. These insights then shed light on the transferability of the understandings we develop between nations and the balance between universal and nationally specific processes in shaping housing transitions. It is important to acknowledge that we need to comprehend the evolution and articulation of housing policies over a relatively long time frame, as past housing policies often have a greater influence on lifetime housing than current government frameworks.

## The UK

Housing provision in the UK changed enormously during the 20th century in terms of quality, the balance of tenures and dwelling types (Lund, 2006; Mullins and Murie, 2006). There was never a settled structure of provision, with regular predictable patterns of access to housing and a single set of routine transitions during life courses. Some trends were sustained over very long periods, especially the rise of homeownership from around 10 per cent of households in 1900 to nearly 70 per cent of households in 2000. Other developments were more variable. Public rental housing, conceived as a secure lifetime form of accommodation, expanded considerably from the end of World War I (WWI) through to the 1970s, when it accommodated around one third of UK households. It was initially a prized form of housing for better-off 'respectable' working families, and grew through the construction of suburban council housing estates from the early 1920s. It also grew through the replacement of inner city slums, starting in the 1930s, and more extensively after 1955 through large-scale redevelopment with mainly high-rise Council housing. Subsequently, the council sector has fallen considerably and other 'registered social landlords' (RSLs), predominantly housing associations (HAs), provide an increasing proportion of subsidised rental housing, but in 2010 this only accommodates about one sixth of UK households.

### Overview of post-war housing policy and provision 1945–79

New housing construction after 1945 was initially dominated by council housing but private sector house building picked up during the 1950s and the peak years of new construction during the late 1960s included high levels of *both* public and private new house building (see Figure 3.1 for England)[1]. Slum clearance, delayed by the need to build up overall supply, surged from the mid 1950s and the inner rings of large UK cities were transformed by the clearance of slums and subsequent construction of public housing, mainly high-rise flat blocks. Much private building was outside the metropolitan areas, in expanding suburban areas and non-metropolitan areas, and in the first wave of new towns around London (Hall et al, 1973).

Cross-party consensus over the aims of housing policy dissolved during the 1970s, and there was a shift towards different policy priorities and mechanisms. The changes marked the culmination of developments that had already begun *plus* some key economic and other changes. The period since the late 1970s in the UK has been one of government withdrawal from direct housing provision, deregulation of many elements of housing markets and finance, and the promotion of homeownership almost at all costs. As a result of the combined effect of slum clearance and new building to higher standards there had been a massive improvement in overall housing conditions by the 1970s. Overall supply had grown considerably and there had been major shifts in tenure. Figure 3.2 shows how private renting had contracted dramatically by the early 1970s, whereas both council renting and homeownership expanded.

**Figure 3.1: House building: permanent dwellings completed, by tenure, England**

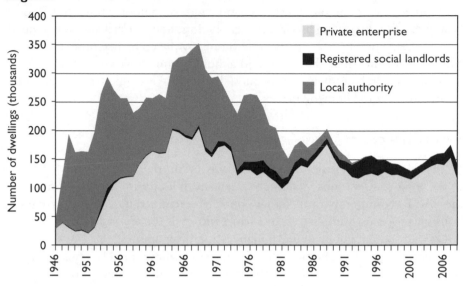

*Source:* Department for Communities and Local Government (2009)

During the 1970s there were three main pathways into housing in the early years after household formation (which was still typically marked by marriage): queuing for council accommodation, while living with parents or renting privately; saving to purchase a home, again while living with parents or renting privately; or, for those with low eligibility for council housing and low incomes, especially

**Figure 3.2: UK dwelling stock, by tenure, 1951–2007**

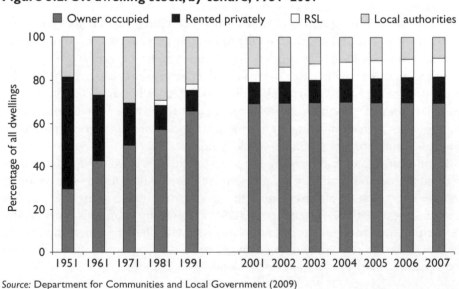

*Source:* Department for Communities and Local Government (2009)

recent immigrants, renting privately in largely run-down and often multi-occupied older housing. Young households with higher incomes, savings or parental help could move directly into owner-occupation and some poorer households could 'leap frog' council waiting lists if they were in slum housing that was redeveloped, leaving them eligible for permanent rehousing by the council. Council tenancies had been 'for life' since the 1920s, and although some tenants were allowed by councils to purchase their homes, most had to leave council housing if they wanted to become homeowners.

## The changing context for housing policy and provision

As in the other countries examined in this book, the 1970s marked the end of the long post-war boom and movement from 'Fordism' to 'post-Fordism' in the UK. In common with the other countries examined here, many changes in housing provision were driven by changes in civil society rather than being a direct outcome of public policy initiatives and programmes.

Some aspects of economic restructuring and labour market transformation were strongly encouraged by governments, especially running down the coal mining industry. But most change was driven by wider processes of globalisation with the relocation of production away from older industrial societies to newly industrialising economies, especially China, India and Brazil since the early 1990s. As manufacturing contracted, growing service sector activity resulted in transformations in labour markets, including much greater female participation in labour markets. Capital and finance markets were transformed from national into international and then global circuits of capital. Globalisation also reshaped the capacities of governments to direct economies and the Thatcher and Major Conservative governments chose to withdraw from direct regulation of economic activities.

Other sociodemographic changes, only indirectly related to economic restructuring and globalisation, have profoundly influenced the numbers and nature of households. These trends are reviewed in an ESRC report (Stewart and Vaitilingam, 2004), which uses a variety of data sources[2] to chart what the Chief Executive of the ESRC described as 'dramatic changes in our society in just the past few decades' (Diamond, 2004, p 5). Such changes have been accompanied by growing diversity of living arrangements that cannot sensibly be captured by one 'life course' or 'household life cycle' model.

Falling birth rates and growing longevity in the UK have followed a similar pattern to many other affluent countries; in 2008 for the first time there were more people over 65 years old than under the age of 16. Average household size has been falling since the 1960s and much additional housing demand is generated by household formation rather than population growth. There have been significant falls in marriage rates, growing cohabitation, increased proportions of children born outside marriage and increased 'blending' of families.

Ferri (2004, p 22) suggested that there has been 'an increasing prolongation of youth and dependency' and striking changes in the advancement of women, especially in terms of educational achievement and workforce participation. More 30-year-olds remain single and 'delays in partnering have led to delays in starting a family' (Ferri, 2004, p 21). Better-educated women have tended increasingly to have their (fewer) babies later in life whereas the growing proportion of sole mothers with poor levels of educational attainment still tend to have their babies before 20 years of age. The number of lone mothers increased from one in eight among those born in 1958 to nearly one in five of those born in 1970. However, 'the most rapidly growing family type is the stepfamily, created when a new partnership is formed by a mother and/or father who already had dependent children' (Ferri, 2004, p 22). Ferri also emphasised the novelty of growing 'social' as opposed to 'biological' parenting 'as more and more men raise other men's children, while, in many cases, their own children grow up elsewhere' (Ferri, 2004, p 24).

The age group now coming up to retirement appears to be in a relatively fortunate position compared with many 30-year-olds. They 'will receive the most generous state pensions of any generation and will also have gone through their working lives in a period of high growth in real wages and real asset prices, both in housing and the stock market' (Banks et al, 2004, p 28). Life expectancy has grown much faster since the 1960s than in the preceding 120 years and most older people 'report good health, little difficulty with functioning or carrying out activities of daily living and high rates of social participation and engagement' (Banks et al, 2004, p 28). A growing proportion own their homes outright: in 2001 around 60 per cent of households aged over 65 in England, Wales and Northern Ireland and 50 per cent in Scotland (Paris, 2008a). Outright homeownership, which insulates owners against most possible housing market shocks, has been growing among all age groups, thus indicating the likelihood of higher levels in future. Not all older households are affluent, of course, and within the UK there has been widespread polarisation of wealth and income (Dorling et al, 2007).

## The changing content of UK housing policy after the 1970s

The election of the first Thatcher government in June 1979 symbolically marked the decisive shift away from the previous period of housing policy and provision, especially regarding the role of council housing (Mullins and Murie, 2006). Although some council houses had been sold to tenants before 1979, this had been a matter of local discretion and many local councils had chosen *not* to sell their housing. The Housing Act 1980 compelled recalcitrant local authorities to sell council houses to sitting tenants so tenants were given a 'right-to-buy' their homes. Successive Conservative governments during the 1980s introduced measures designed to change other settings and operations of housing policy and provision in the UK. The broad parameters did not change substantially after the prime ministerial transition from Thatcher to Major in November 1990, nor were there any significant changes for some years after the election of Blair's 'new' Labour government in 1997.

The growth of HAs through the 1980s, together with mass sales of council housing under the 'right-to-buy', led to changes in the nature of subsidised rental housing. The construction of council housing fell rapidly from the early 1980s, virtually ceasing altogether in the mid 1990s and HAs became the only provider of new subsidised rental housing. The term 'social housing' was introduced during the 1980s to refer to both council housing and HA accommodation and it has subsequently become widely used, though government has created the category of 'registered social landlords' to include all non-government providers of subsidised rental housing (which could even include some private companies). As much of the better council stock was sold, the remainder was stigmatised as a 'residual' tenure, characterised by unpopular dwelling forms, often systems-built high-rise flats, and occupied by an impoverished clientele.

The decline of the council sector was accelerated by changes in housing finance with a switch away from construction subsidies to rental assistance in the form of 'Housing Benefit' (HB). Housing associations continued to grow, despite reductions in grants, through using private finance to expand their production. Stock transfers from councils to HAs, increasingly stimulated by central government funding incentives, resulted in a further shift away from council provision towards ever-larger HAs, (Mullins and Pawson, 2009). The allocation of subsidised rental housing focused increasingly on 'need' following homelessness legislation in 1977 and subsequent developments in central government priorities and local allocations systems. By the early years of the 21st century, most social housing – as it had become universally described – housed workless households and minority ethnic groups.

Conservative governments also sought to revive private renting. The Housing Act 1988 'modernised' landlord-tenant relations by abolishing much of the security of tenure and rent regulation that had been set in place during WWI. There was a modest revival of private renting in the early 1990s, partly stimulated by non-housing policy factors, especially the Business Expansion Scheme (BES) (Kemp, 2009). Further expansion was driven by new lending practices of financial institutions in the late 1990s that stimulated the growth of 'buy-to-let' (BTL) mortgages. The number of BTL mortgages increased from around 44,000 in 1999 to 330,000 in 2006, thus increasing from 4 per cent of all mortgages to 29 per cent during the same period. This growth was associated with a surge of flat development in inner cities across the UK, a disconnection between house prices and household formation, and was a major driver of speculative house and land price inflation in the increasingly volatile deregulated housing finance sector (Sprigings, 2008).

Homeownership continued to grow across the UK throughout the 1990s (see Table 3.1). Although growth in the proportion of owner-occupiers slowed after 2001, the total number of homeowners had increased by nearly two million households by 2007. The relatively static proportion of owner-occupiers reflects

**Table 3.1: UK dwelling stock by tenure**

| | Owner-occupied | Privately rented[1] | Rented from RSLs | Public rental[2] | Total (000) |
|---|---|---|---|---|---|
| | Expressed as percentage of all dwellings | | | | |
| 1991 | 65.9 | 9.2 | 3.0 | 21.8 | 23,550 |
| 2001 | 69.6 | 9.9 | 6.6 | 13.8 | 25,619 |
| 2007 (r) | 69.9 | 11.9 | 8.5 | 9.7 | 26,652 |

*Notes:* [1] includes dwellings with job or business; [2] includes Northern Ireland Housing Executive and other statutory bodies; r = figure revised from previous estimate.

*Source:* DCLG live table 101, as on 10/02/09

the growing number of households overall, with an increasing proportion being accommodated in the private rental sector. The most dramatic changes in terms of the proportion of households by tenure were in the growth of private renting after 2001 and the shifting balance between Registered Social Landlords and local authorities. There is no immediate prospect of a reversal of the changing roles of RSLs and local authorities and it is expected that council housing will be the smallest rental tenure by the time of the 2011 Census.

The combined effect of increased homeownership, the revival of private rental and the increasingly residual status of social renting had created a much more market-dominated structure of housing provision. This has inevitably opened households to greater risk during periods of market recession, especially between 1989 and 1992 when negative equity and mortgage repossessions were widespread across southern England and much of Great Britain (but not Northern Ireland), raising concerns whether growing homeownership was 'sustainable'. Such concerns faded from popular consciousness as house prices began to increase again, rapidly so during the late 1990s and between 2002 and 2007. Instead, from the late 1990s onwards there was growing concern about a problem of 'affordability', especially for first homebuyers. Government became convinced of the need for a 'step-change' in housing production following reports by the economist Kate Barker (Barker, 2004). There had been no significant increase in house building since the mid 1990s, despite growing housing demand. There was some growth in new building between 2002 and 2006 and a marked shift in the mix of dwelling types. Government policies had come to favour new housing development on 'brownfield' sites and builders increased the proportion of flats from about 20 per cent of building in the early 1990s to over 40 per cent after 2002.

### The housing market crash of 2007–09

The period 2006–07 was the high watermark of the tide of rampant deregulated pro-market policies that had been running since the end of the 1970s. The nationalisation of the failing Northern Rock bank in August 2007 became a symbolic marker of the end of an era in housing policy and provision, just as the election of the Thatcher government in 1979 symbolised the end of the post-war housing consensus and the start of a new era (Malpass and Rowlands, 2009). Northern Rock had been an old-fashioned building society, managed prudently, carefully gathering together the savings of working people and judiciously allocating home purchase mortgages within local communities. It became a bank after the deregulatory urges and purges of the 1980s and 1990s and switched investments into the US sub-prime market. It was one of the first UK institutions to be caught in the great housing collapse of 2007–10. This was not unexpected. Many commentators had warned of growing volatility, increasing risks of sub-prime lending, of the disconnection between house prices and incomes, and of an impending 'correction', possibly of an unprecedented magnitude.

UK house prices have been falling since mid 2007, most dramatically in Northern Ireland, which had boomed remarkably from 2004 to 2007 (see Figure 3.3). At the time of writing, there is no objective evidence of any cessation in the decline, despite the bravura of some estate agents. Dwelling completions had also fallen from a peak of 219,000 in 2006–07 to 214,000 in 2007–08 across the UK but in Northern Ireland completions in 2007–08 were down by a third. Dwelling starts have declined much more dramatically: from a peak of 235,000 in 2005–06 to about 204,000 in 2007–08, the lowest since 2002 (DCLG 2009). In England, commencements in the last six months of 2008 (around 38,000) were the lowest ever recorded for the period 1990 to 2008.

The situation at the start of the second decade of the 21st century is one of great uncertainty both in terms of overall housing markets and the future

**Figure 3.3: UK house price change, 1992–2010**

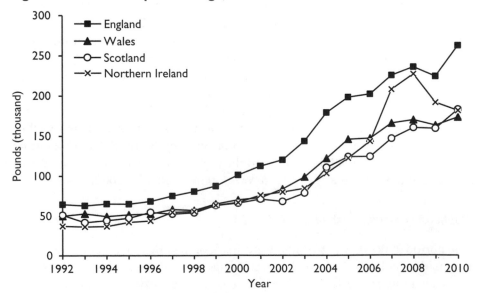

*Source:* Northern Ireland Housing Executive (2009)

housing transitions of many UK households. There is no prospect of a reversal of the long-term residualisation of social housing, despite continuing changes in the pattern of ownership of such dwellings and nomenclature of the sector. The growth of RSLs has reflected central government determination to run down the political role of local authorities in housing provision: council housing may soon be a subject of interest only to historians. The private rental sector has been transformed and become more diverse. It offers a relatively attractive transitional tenure as part of pathways into homeownership. The 'new' private rental sector contains considerably less of older, poor quality stock, though conditions in some parts of the sector are the worst of any in the UK.

Many would-be first-time buyers are currently facing a much more restrictive lending market: banks increasingly require much more substantial deposits than they did between 2000 and 2007, but current interest rates are at an all-time low, so many will not be able to make the move into homeownership. Ferri (2004, p. 21) argued that 'for those born in 1970, prolonged economic dependence and steeply rising house prices relative to incomes mean that homeownership has become an unattainable goal for many'. By 2010, however, the issue had become one of access to mortgages rather than rising house prices. First-time buyers have recently had to compete with buoyant 'buy-to-let' investors (Sprigings, 2008) but investor activity may be reduced, though it is unlikely to go away altogether.

Overall, UK housing provision and policy have changed dramatically since the 1970s but the present situation is one of such turbulence and uncertainty that future housing pathways are hard to predict. There is no prospect of a return to slum clearance or mass public housing construction. There cannot be a repeat of the mass transfer of stock from council rental to homeownership through right-to-buy legislation as that was a once-only event. Future housing transitions will be predominantly through housing market mechanisms, combined with household and individual preferences, choices and life planning.

## The US

Housing policy in the US, in general, has focused on homeownership and assistance to low-income and very low-income households. Though it is readily apparent that some policies supporting homeownership were enacted for different purposes, such as stimulating macroeconomic activity, providing support for politically influential industry sectors, and promoting ideologically based regulatory schemes, homeownership rates have increased, with a majority of households living the 'American dream' of owning their home. In this section we will briefly describe some of these policies, their impact on homeownership, and the series of market and legislative events that sparked the sub-prime lending crisis that spiralled into a near global financial meltdown.

## 1900s–1960s: early policy, the new deal, and post WWII

Perhaps the most unique feature of US 'housing' policy is the tax deductibility of mortgage interest. In general, US homeowners may deduct the amount of interest they pay on their mortgages from their taxable income. This policy was not put in place to spur homeownership, but rather it was a holdover from nascent income tax calculations. The US did not have a tax on personal income until 1913.[3] The income tax did not apply until personal income exceeded US$4,000, affecting about 1 per cent of the population. Over time, the deductibility of mortgage interest payments became increasingly important in housing policy, at least according to realtors and homebuilders.[4] In theory, the mortgage interest deduction allows one to purchase a more expensive home than could be afforded otherwise. However, in practice, only about half of US homeowners deduct their mortgage interest because of the size of 'standard' deductions and the structure of US marginal tax rates. Nevertheless, the several attempts to take this provision out of US tax law have been dashed on the rocks of well-funded lobbying and an almost visceral negative reaction from voters.

A much larger influence on homeownership in the US came through the creation of mortgage insurance programmes (guarantees) administered by the Federal Housing Administration (FHA) in 1934 and the establishment of the Federal National Mortgage Association (Fannie Mae) in 1937. Fannie Mae, which is now the legal name of FNMA, is a government-supported enterprise (GSE) providing mortgage lenders with an opportunity to sell mortgages held, thereby replenishing the bank's capital and promoting new mortgage lending (Carliner, 1998). While the stated policy goal was to promote the availability and affordability of mortgage lending for expanded homeownership, these policies helped boost economic activity through residential construction and consumer purchases related to homeownership (furnishings and the like). Fannie Mae became the first effective secondary market for residential mortgages in the US. It was also during this time that the US federal government settled on its major approach to low-income housing through the Housing Act of 1937, which provided loans to locally operated public housing authorities for the construction of rental units reserved for low-income households (Carliner, 1998).

Concerned about the reintegration of soldiers returning home from WWII, the US Veterans Administration (VA) offered loan guarantees to underwriters of qualifying mortgages, resulting in lower deposit requirements and interest rates. Even though the guarantees were limited to 50 per cent of the loan value, this greatly reduced the risk profile of the loan. Since its inception, the VA programme has guaranteed over 18 million loans (US Department of Veterans Affairs 2009). Rising personal income in the aftermath of WWII, combined with federal mortgage guarantees by the FHA and VA, sparked an unprecedented rise in homeownership rates in the US. In 1940 some 43.6 per cent of all residential dwelling units were owner-occupied but 20 years later, that figure had risen to 61.9 per cent (see Figure 3.4) and has risen only modestly since then.

**Figure 3.4: US occupied housing units, by tenure, 1900–2008**

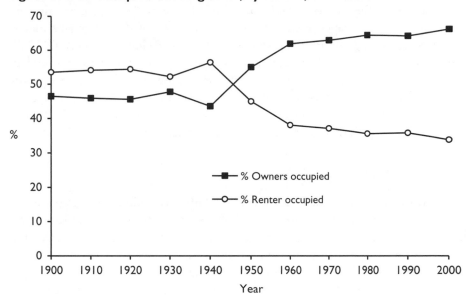

*Source:* US Bureau of the Census historic housing data – ownership; US Bureau of the Census homeownership rates for the US and Regions: 1965 to present

The civil rights era of the 1960s brought important changes in housing policy including anti-discrimination laws focused on race and religion (Fair Housing Act of 1968)[5] and the creation of the forerunner of the 'Section 8' housing program. The Section 8 programme, which was formally named the Housing and Community Development Act of 1974, expanded low-income housing assistance to include payments (vouchers) towards rent in privately owned dwellings. It allowed low-income households to move into middle-income neighbourhoods sparking controversy about the impacts on neighbourhood property values and school ratings. For all of the angst felt by residents in middle-income neighbourhoods that became host to Section 8 households, research has shown that when Section 8 units are not highly concentrated and are located in middle-income areas, nearby residential property values rise (Galster et al, 1999).[6]

By 1968 Fannie Mae had a virtual monopoly on the secondary mortgage market as it had a direct line of credit with the US Treasury; it was exempt from state and local income taxes, and not subject to regulatory oversight by the Securities and Exchange Commission. However, this success came at a price to the federal government in the form of large liabilities posted to government balance sheets. The Johnson Administration, needing borrowing power to finance the Vietnam War, decided to 'privatise' Fannie Mae to get these liabilities off its books (Pickert, 2008). Shortly thereafter, two other GSEs were created to provide competition for Fannie Mae, the Federal National Mortgage Association (Freddie Mac) and the Government National Mortgage Association (Ginnie Mae). Ginnie Mae and Fannie Mae back FHA and VA loans, effectively reducing the interest rates needed to fund these mortgages by pledging the full faith and credit of the US government in the case of default.[7] Freddie Mac served a similar function for 'conventional' mortgages, holding about 90 per cent of the secondary market by 2003 (US Department of Housing and Urban Development – HUD, 2009). Since the late 1970s, federal legislation supporting homeownership could be characterised as circumstantial – directly addressing specific homeownership challenges given a particular set of market conditions. Combined with a series of changes in financial services regulations, the stage was set to move the US housing market down a path that nearly led to global financial disaster in 2007 and 2008.

## Setting the stage for crisis: 1970s–1990s

In a report prepared in early 2010, HUD's Office of Policy Development and Research (HUD, 2010) places the lion's share of the blame for the sub-prime lending crisis on risky lending practices supported by a series of legislative changes directly impacting mortgage lending, automated lending processes, and a lack of regulation in asset-based securities (ABS) markets. The legislative changes span every presidential administration from Carter through to the younger Bush.

In the late 1970s, the US economy was mired in stagflation – high rates of inflation – but little economic growth. Interest rates were quite high, but banking and thrift regulations included interest rate ceilings on residential mortgages, which discouraged mortgage lending. The Depository Institutions Deregulation and Monetary Control Act of 1980, though addressing much broader issues of financial deregulation, included provisions removing interest rate ceilings on first mortgages. By the second year of the Reagan Administration (1982), the housing market was still severely constrained, but now it was mortgage interest rates, which had risen to as much as 18 per cent, that kept many households out of the home-buying market. The Alternative Mortgage Transaction Parity Act of 1982 (AMTPA) nullified state laws that prohibited 'exotic' mortgages such as variable interest rates, balloon payments, and negative amortisation on first and second notes. After addressing regulatory restrictions on innovations in home loans, the US Congress wanted to promote homeownership by increasing the supply of money available for mortgage lending.

In hindsight, the Secondary Mortgage Market Enhancement Act of 1984 (SMMEA) may turn out to have been one of the most influential pieces of financial regulation in the 20th century. This legislation supported the expansion of the market for mortgage-backed securities by allowing federal depository institutions,[8] thrifts, pension funds, and insurance companies to invest in mortgage-backed securities (MBS) possessing high credit ratings from a recognised agency such as Standard and Poor's. Just a few years later, a new tool appeared in the consumer credit market that sparked the flame of sub-prime mortgage lending.

If we think of the AMTPA as the oxygen, and SMMEA as providing the fuel, the FICO credit score, developed by the Fair Isaac Corporation and introduced to the market in 1989, ignited the flame that became sub-prime mortgage lending.

The credit score provided a new, sophisticated modelling tool for predicting the likelihood that a borrower would pay back a loan. This tool allowed lenders to move away from traditional, very conservative rules-of-thumb in lending standards and this opened the door of homeownership to a much broader segment of the population. By the early 1990s, Freddie Mac and Fannie Mae were using FICO scores in both manual and automated mortgage underwriting (HUD, 2010).

Almost immediately, consumer advocates and some legislators became concerned that sub-prime lending could harm lower-income borrowers more than help them achieve the American dream of homeownership. Sub-prime mortgages often had multiple features that increased risk to both borrower and lender. Among the features shown to be especially risk enhancing were adjustable rates (payments increase later in the note to unaffordable levels), prepayment penalties (making it impractical to refinance), balloon terms (unaffordable lump sum payments after a few years), negative amortisation, and the Alt-A class of loans that require borrowers to provide little or no documentation of income or savings, which contributed to mortgage fraud (Ashcraft and Schuermann, 2008; Daglish, 2009; Mayer et al, 2009; HUD, 2010). In the US, mortgage transactions are regulated by the Truth in Lending Act and the Real Estate Settlement Procedures Act. Both required disclosure of information to borrowers, but neither guaranteed that homebuyers actually understood the terms and conditions of financially and legally sophisticated mortgage contracts. In response to these concerns, President Clinton signed the Home Ownership and Equity Protection Act (HOEPA) that prohibited many of these riskier features in 'high cost' loans.[9] However, very few mortgages met the high-cost loan criteria and the Act was effectively useless in regulating the sub-prime lending market (HUD, 2010).

### Breaking the bank

A series of rules put in place by the Office of Thrift Supervision (OTS) in 1996 and the Office of the Comptroller of the Currency (OCC) in 2004 exempting banking and savings institutions from state regulations (HUD, 2010) contributed to the regulatory failure surrounding the sub-prime crisis. Effectively, a bank holding company could buy a mortgage bank and these banking affiliates were not regulated by either the OTS or OCC. Therefore, at a time when the financing of mortgages was becoming more complex, regulatory oversight was effectively being diluted.

The final regulatory issue involved the credit rating agencies. Depository institutions were required to invest only in mortgage-backed securities with high credit ratings. However, there was no regulatory oversight of credit agency practices and standards. Demand for asset-backed securities (ABS) rose dramatically throughout the 1990s and 2000s. In 1985, the ABS market, which includes mortgage-backed securities, was about US$1.2 billion. By 1991 that figure had risen to US$50.6 billion and to US$1.9 trillion by 2005 (HUD, 2010). Demand for the mortgage-backed segment of these securities also exploded, which led to demand for mortgages not from homebuyers, but from investors seeking returns in perceived safe investments. This translated into additional mortgage lending that reached down to homebuyers with weaker credit. According to *Inside Mortgage Finance* (HUD, 2010), the issue of non-traditional loans rose from 7 per cent of all mortgages in 2004 to 29 per cent in 2006. Some writers have suggested that credit agencies faced moral hazards (Khasawneh, 2008; Dorn 2009; Tarr, 2009). Credit agencies' biggest customers were demanding ratings for mortgage-backed securities perceived to be highly profitable, and if they downgraded their ratings, these customers could take their business elsewhere. Without regulatory oversight, there were few influential voices calling into question the ratings being given to MBS products.

As demand for US-based mortgage-backed securities turned global, the secondary mortgage market sought loans in areas with rapid price escalation, exacerbating a real estate bubble that was being fuelled in part by sub-prime lending. Innovations in packaging asset-based securities led investors to believe that they were shielding themselves from risk (DiMartino, et al 2007), with the perverse result that many financial institutions shed other risk-hedging strategies and instruments in favour of MBS products (Nadauld and Sherlund, 2009). The share of the sub-prime lending market rose from a little over 2 per cent in the late 1990s/early 2000s, to more than 13 per cent by 2005 (see **Figure 3.5**). The inevitable bursting of the real estate/financial bubble exposed lending institutions across the globe to losses reaching several trillion dollars. As of January 2010, homeownership rates in the US had fallen back to year 2000 levels.

**Figure 3.5: Sub-prime mortgages as a percentage of all US mortgages, 1998–2008**

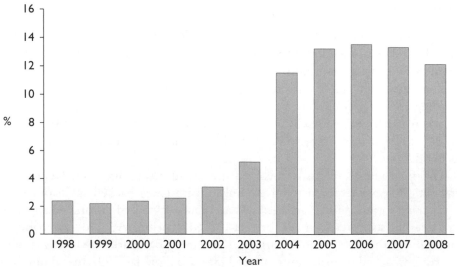

*Source:* HUD (2010, p 6)

The US has promoted homeownership as an essential component of the American dream. With the help of New Deal policies and post-war economic expansion, homeownership rates in the US rose rapidly from the late 1940s through to the mid 1960s. Subsequent decades have seen a levelling off in the growth of homeownership, which has served as an impetus for administrations on both sides of the political spectrum to continue introducing policies intended, at least in part, to expand the ranks of homeowners in the US. However, some of these legislative efforts set the stage for unwise choices for consumers and lenders. Financial market deregulation occurred concomitantly with the introduction of asset-based securities. The demand for mortgage-backed securities drove lending policies that were increasingly divorced from conservative assessments of buyers' ability to repay loans. The subsequent demand for housing created an unsustainable asset bubble. When default rates started to rise, housing prices plummeted in many US markets and the financial system teetered on the brink of collapse. At the end of the day, the modest gains in homeownership rates associated with the policies implemented in the 1980s through to the 2000s have failed to provide the desired boost to homeownership rates, while sparking a financial crisis that removed trillions of dollars from US household wealth – hardly a good trade-off.

## Australia

Housing has long occupied an important place in the Australian psyche, with many suggesting that it represents the 'Great Australian Dream', although Kemeny (1983) characterised it as the Great Australian Nightmare. For many Australians the primary role of homeownership within Australia's housing system is unquestioned; however, its pre-eminent position was a feature of the second half of the 20th century, but not the first. It is true that homeownership was far more widespread in Australia in the 19th century than in the UK, the source of most migrants to the Australian colonies (Beer, 1992). Urban housing in the UK was dominated by widespread tenancy, particularly among working-class households, with fewer than 20 per cent owning their home. Owner-occupancy rates were also comparatively low in Australia up to the 1840s (Troy, 1991), but rose to somewhere between 40 and 50 per cent of houses in Australia's cities from the 1850s onwards (Williams, 1984). Rates of homeownership varied substantially by location, and the number of homeowners tended also to shift in line with national prosperity. Working-class households were more likely to own their home in Australia than in Britain, but owner-occupation was still largely the preserve of the middle classes.

By 1911, owner-occupation accounted for one half of the housing stock nationally. However, only 36 per cent of housing in the cities was owner-occupied, compared with 57 per cent in country areas (Jackson and Bridge, 1988). The older and larger cities of Sydney and Melbourne had lower rates of ownership compared with cities such as Adelaide and Brisbane, where the industrial base was limited. Importantly, homeowners in Australia in the first decades of the 20th century were literally that: outright owners. At the 1911 Census just 4 per cent of dwellings were being purchased via a mortgage, and this reflected the shortage of a well-developed housing finance sector. By 1947 owner-occupation had expanded to 53 per cent of households but the number of households purchasing their home remained at just 8 per cent.

## Overview of post-war housing policy and provision

Owner-occupation grew rapidly after 1945 and its expansion was made possible by its transformation from a tenure dominated by *homeownership* to one predominantly of *home purchase*. The proportion of Australian households buying their homes rose to 36 per cent by 1976. While the housing policies of governments were important, many of the most significant government actions were directed at improving the performance of the economy as a whole rather than at specific housing interventions. The growth of Australia's population and ongoing economic prosperity from the late 1940s to the mid 1970s set the preconditions for the growth in homeownership as the majority tenure in Australia. The number of households in Australia grew from 1.9 million in 1947 to 2.4 million in 1954, with most of this growth among families. There were 0.5 million more births in the 1940s than in the previous decade, and the 'baby boom' continued throughout the 1950s.

State and Commonwealth government policies triggered the growth of owner-occupation in Australia through a range of policies that directly promoted that tenure. The most important initiatives were the War Service Loans Scheme, the Commonwealth State Housing Agreements, and changes to the retail banking sector. The provision of adequate and affordable housing was a priority of the Curtin and Chifley Labor governments, which held power from 1942-49. They introduced the first Commonwealth State Housing Agreement (CSHA), which was signed in 1945. Under this Agreement, the Commonwealth assumed responsibility for the provision of funds with which the states were to develop a public housing sector (Kemeny 1983). In addition, funds were made available for home mortgages through the Commonwealth and state savings banks.

The public sector directly dominated the provision of housing in the decade after WWII. The Commonwealth government provided finance for the private housing industry through the War Service Homes Division, which arranged loans for men and women who served in the Australian Armed Forces. Between 1945 and 1956 the War Service Homes Division provided 113,000 loans, accounting for 10 per cent of new dwelling completions (Hill, 1959). Almost 120,000 government rental dwellings were built in Australia between 1946 and 1956 (Hill, 1959) as the original CSHA envisaged the development of a strong public rental sector to serve as an alternative to privately financed housing. State government finances, however, could not sustain the sector and from 1956 the re-negotiated CSHA emphasised the promotion of owner-occupation with state authorities encouraged to sell their stock, while other funds were directed into cooperative building societies. In 1956 the Commonwealth government provided almost 30 percent of all funds for home ownership.

The importance of state and Commonwealth government policies in this period cannot be overemphasised. Commonwealth subsidies for homeownership were an important part of the expansion of the tenure. Jones (1972) estimated that 36 per cent of all new homes and flats completed in Australia between 1945 and 1970 were funded on terms and conditions that made them much cheaper than if they had been produced by the private sector alone.

The major financial changes which enabled the expansion of homeownership after WWII were centred on the savings banks and building societies. The rapid growth of savings banks was a product of post-war financial legislation. Up until the 1950s government-owned savings banks dominated retail lending, providing over 50 per cent of finance for homeownership (Kemeny, 1983). Regulatory reform in the middle of that decade encouraged the emergence of new retail banks, albeit under heavy regulation. Home loan interest rates were subject to regulation by the Reserve Bank, a power which passed to Cabinet after 1973. The private banks established themselves quickly and the sector grew rapidly. There was a continuing demand for home loans, which saw many banks ration funds. One measure of the success of the private savings banks was their share of the market: in 1945 savings banks accounted for only 14 per cent of outstanding housing advances; by 1972 they were the single largest lender, with 31 per cent of loans (Hill, 1974).

Building societies were a second important source of housing finance in Australia from the 1950s to the 1980s and the sector benefited from fewer regulations when compared with the banks. They also had the capacity to charge higher mortgage rates. Building societies, however, largely disappeared as a force within the Australian housing market in the 1980s as a result of reviews of the Australian financial system. Following the Martin and Campbell Reports into the banking sector (Australian Financial System Inquiry, 1981, 1984), the Australian Government reviewed direct controls on the sector and placed a greater emphasis on market-based approaches. These changes were part of a wider impetus to open up the Australian financial system, and encourage greater efficiency in the operation of capital markets.

Deregulation of the market for housing finance resulted both in a greater supply of funds and the restructuring of the housing finance industry. In the early 1980s, banks provided roughly 60 per cent of loans, building societies 30 per cent, and finance companies 4 per cent. By the early 1990s, banks had 80 per cent of the market for housing finance (partly through the transformation of building societies into banks), with the building societies' share halved to 15 per cent (HIA, 1990).

## Affordability, housing finance and policy

By the beginning of the 21st century Australia's housing market had both changed and remained constant in its structure and functioning. It remained constant in that many of its headline features appeared set in concrete: approximately two thirds of households were in owner-occupation, some 20 per cent of households were private tenants and the public housing sector represented five per cent of the total. However, these broad-scale features masked substantial change: the rate of outright homeownership was rising as the percentage of home purchasers fell; the position of the private rental sector had shifted as it no longer represented a tenure of transition, but instead a long-term option for many low-income households (Wulff and Maher, 1998); and – paralleling the UK experience – the public housing sector had been reshaped into a tenure of last resort for those on the margins of society.

With the beginning of the new century Australia's residential property markets boomed. The triggers for house price growth included the general inflationary impact of the introduction of a Goods and Services Tax (GST), the introduction of a First Home Owners Grant (FHOG), ongoing economic growth, higher rates of immigration and changes to the taxation treatment of capital gains that reinforced the attractiveness of residential property as an investment vehicle. Growth in the demand for housing was not matched by supply, with inadequate land holdings, planning regulations, skill shortages, infrastructure pricing regimes and inappropriate standards all held accountable for the consequent increase in house prices (Beer et al, 2007). By 2006 the Demographia International Housing Affordability Survey reported that Australia had some of the least affordable housing in the developed world, with the ratio of house prices to average earnings in some cities exceeding nine to one (Demographia, 2006). The Australian government was sufficiently concerned to instruct the Productivity Commission (2004) to investigate housing affordability, but decided – against the Commission's findings – that it was simply a matter of property market cycles and that current house price pressures would resolve themselves.

Movements in the housing market after the year 2000 affected both housing finance, as well as the position of individuals and households. Rapidly escalating house prices generated a housing affordability crisis that affected up to 1.1 million households (Yates et al, 2007). And while mortgage holders felt this impact, the greatest consequences were for low-income tenants in the private rental market, many of whom were forced to pay up to 60 per cent of their gross household income for accommodation. By 2006, 26 per cent of low-income tenants in Australia were in housing stress, as were 7 per cent of low-income home purchasers. Many households were effectively excluded from access to home purchase because of the high cost of homes and their inability to save a deposit because of high rents.

Regulatory reform in the 1990s opened the way for the emergence of non-bank lenders within the mortgage market. Beginning with a relatively small market share, the non-bank lenders expanded from 2000 and placed pressure on bank lenders who in turn reduced their prudential margins (Gottliebsen, 2002). By 2006 non-bank lenders accounted for a rapidly growing share of all home loans with a suite of new housing finance arrangements – including low documentation loans – and institutions, such as mortgage brokers, flooding the market. As Berry et al (2009) noted in their work on mortgage defaults in Australia, the number of home loans in arrears increased rapidly from 2000, primarily because of high levels of debt relative to the capacity to service that debt. However, the total percentage of loans in arrears by more than 90 days never exceeded 0.6 per cent of the total. In addition, mortgage arrears were concentrated among 'non conforming' loans, and especially within 'wholesale originators' rather than the banks. In summing up this period, Berry et al (2009, p 20) concluded that:

> over the last decade lenders had relaxed their lending standards in terms of the range of acceptable borrower profiles and the size of loans for home purchase, renovation and extension, and for non-housing-related purposes. The range of mortgage lenders and products had expanded substantially, with increasingly aggressive lending by poorly regulated non-bank entities, i.e. non-ADIs (non-Authorised Deposit-taking Institutions) that are not regulated by the Australian Prudential Regulation Authority (APRA).

Importantly, mortgage defaults have had a distinctive geography, being concentrated in the low-income western suburbs of Sydney where house prices are high and incomes low or modest.

The advent of the financial crisis from 2008 ushered in large-scale changes to the system of housing finance. The non-bank institutions disappeared from the market because of a shortage of credit, buyouts from the banks, exclusion from the financial guarantees provided by the Australian government to the banks, and an aversion to such experiments within housing finance within the market. By 2009 the banks, and especially Australia's 'Big Four' banks, once again dominated the housing finance sector. Lending criteria returned to the 1970s, with banks once again requiring both a substantial deposit – often in excess of 20 per cent – and a secure income stream. Access to home purchase has once again become difficult because of deposit requirements and the conservative lending practices of the banks.

Australia's recent history of housing finance innovation has been both similar and different from the experience of the UK and the US. Australia is a nation that was brought up on property booms and busts (Daly, 1982) and in consequence it retained a strong regulatory framework for its major financial institutions. This strength was further reinforced by a highly concentrated banking sector, and the limited development of alternative mortgage instruments; for example, no large-scale secondary mortgage market has emerged in Australia. In this respect Australia's experience more closely reflects that of Canada. The US sub-prime lending crisis did not create the depth or breadth of problems for the Canadian financial sector evident across the border.

There were market, regulatory, and cultural differences that insulated the Canadian market from the worst of the US sub-prime lending crisis. These included different standards of deposit requirements on mortgages, comparatively low rates of selling mortgages on the secondary market, differing appetites for risk among financial institutions, a comparatively smaller and simpler financial industry and differing cultural perspectives on regulation (Wilson Center, 2009). Canadian lenders continued to require either a 20 per cent deposit on a mortgage or a mortgage insurance policy covering any deficit between the deposit and the 20 per cent mark. This had been traditional practice for conventional mortgages in the US until the 1990s, when it became the trend to allow borrowers to take an immediate second mortgage to make up any deposit shortfall. In common with Australia, Canada has not had government-supported enterprises boosting the sale of mortgages, and thus Canadian lenders have tended to hold onto their mortgages (75 per cent held in Canada compared with less than 50 per cent in the US). This limited the lender-driven demand for mortgages that pushed aggressive lending in the US. Moreover, in Canada banking executives are not commonly issued stock options and other incentives for taking on excessive risk (Wilson Center, 2009). While there are providers of alternative mortgages, including sub-prime mortgages in Canada, the housing finance market has remained dominated by the largest banks, holding more than 90 per cent of assets (Wilson Center, 2009), which is much easier to monitor than the several hundred lenders in the US market. Like Australia, the sub-prime mortgage market simply did not achieve the scale evident in the US. At is peak, sub-prime mortgages in Canada represented less than 7 per cent of the Canadian mortgage market (Globe and Mail, 2009) and as the default rate on these mortgages started to rise in the US, Canadian regulators moved to tighten lending standards (MacGee, 2009).

## Convergent and divergent policy futures

The period since the 1990s witnessed a remarkable shift in the ways in which governments sought to affect housing markets and the quality and quantity of housing individuals consume over their lifetime. In each of the three nations considered here innovation in mortgage financing was either an implicit or explicit tool of governments to promote access to homeownership. Similar stories could also be told for other nations, including New Zealand, Ireland and parts of Europe. Governments bereft of other policy levers saw new forms of housing finance as a low-cost strategy for boosting homeownership while building political support. It was a strategy in tune with its political times and welcomed by an ever-expanding global financial industry. The US followed this strategy most aggressively of the three nations considered here and suffered the greatest consequences when events unravelled. Importantly, the history and culture of each nation was responsible for this divergence. Australia and Canada, as culturally similar nations with relatively long histories of mass homeownership, retained a greater degree of regulation in their housing markets and thereby quarantined the impact of crisis within the finance system. The US, by contrast, sought more radical deregulation, while the UK's housing system was caught between a strongly social housing past, and an emerging, but not yet fully developed, tradition of mass homeownership.

This examination of housing policy and the history of housing finance in the UK, the US and Australia provides the context for understanding the lived experience of housing. The changes described in this chapter have had profound impacts on the life course of many individuals and households and these effects will continue to reverberate for decades to come. Most starkly, some who have lost their homes due to mortgage default since 2007 will never re-enter homeownership, while others will remain in rental housing for a longer period or face precarious housing circumstances over the years to come.

## Notes

[1] Data and figures are drawn from the Department for Communities and Local Government (DCLG) housing statistics live tables; last accessed 10 March 2009.

[2] The study draws on large-scale datasets including census data, three birth cohort studies of 1958, 1970 and 2000/01, the British Household Panel Survey, the Workplace Employment Relations Survey, and the English Longitudinal Study of Ageing.

[3] An earlier attempt at taxing income at the national level had been ruled unconstitutional by the US Supreme Court in 1894. Subsequently, the 16th amendment to the US Constitution was passed allowing the creation of a federal income tax.

[4] One estimate places the average value of the mortgage interest deduction at less than US$2,000 per year.

[5] Laws prohibiting housing discrimination based on familial status and disability were added in 1988.

[6] However, when high densities of Section 8 housing are located in lower-income areas, the presence of the Section 8 properties brings down nearby property values. Galster et al (1999) reported that local focus groups place the blame for lower property values on property managers rather than tenants.

[7] Ginnie Mae also provides backing for mortgages and loans issued under the Rural Housing Service and the Office of Public and Indian Housing.

[8] Federal depository institutions are banks that accept consumer deposits, which are insured by the Federal Depository Insurance Corporation (FDIC).

[9] High cost is defined as having an interest rate 8 percentage points above US Treasury securities of similar duration, or with fees (points, origination fees, etc) exceeding 8 per cent of the loan value.

# The housing transitions of younger adults

The transition from the parental home to independent living is one of the most significant changes to occur in the housing circumstances of any individual. For some, the first living arrangements away from the family are a staging point toward further change, while others move directly from the parental household to housing that will be prominent over much of their lives. There is evidence that the housing decisions and circumstances of younger households are changing: as more young adults stay in the parental home for longer, access to home purchase is delayed, and relationship formation is postponed – especially when compared with the generation of their parents or grandparents. This chapter canvases contemporary trends in first housing transitions and places these movements within the context of a generation that is increasingly mobile with respect to social values, labour market attachment and the locations in which they live.

## Moving out, moving on

Leaving the parental home is one of the reference points in young people's lives to mark the transition to adulthood. A growing literature has examined a number of factors associated with leaving home including the timing of the event, its determinants, its variation across time and space, and the demands such transitions place on the housing system. Over the last two to three decades this research has highlighted major shifts in when this transition takes place and the sequence of housing opportunities pursued by young people. A key outcome has been the recognition that the steps toward independent living are no longer predictable and linear. Moreover, instead of being viewed as a one-off event, moving out of home has become a process of gradual transition. Since at least the 1980s commentators have noted an increasing proportion of young people returning to the family home for an extended period, particularly within a year or two of leaving. This shuttling from and to the parental home effectively prolongs the transition to adulthood. This delay in moving out and moving on, a 'hiatus in the life-course' as described by Cote and Bynner (2008) has resulted in the 18–25 age period being described by the much debated term 'emerging adulthood'.

The early adult years are a period of major upheaval in housing and the life course. As Billari et al (2001, p 340) notes, leaving home is 'one of the crucial nodes of the life course and a crucial event in the transition to adulthood' as it 'generally implies not only household independence but also greater social autonomy for young people.' Such a decision can often be emotionally charged as it is often accompanied by a range of feelings that span excitement, a sense of freedom and hopefulness, through to fear and anxiety (Rochman and McCampbell, 1997). Therefore while greater autonomy is welcomed by some, for others leaving the parental home for the first time can be difficult, particularly if the move is involuntary (Jones, 2004).

A major issue in the literature is the timing or age at which young people leave the parental home. Attention in this topic has been pronounced in Europe (Billari et al, 2001; Guerrero, 2001; Iacovou, 2002; Billari and Liefbroer, 2007; Mandic, 2008) but it has also drawn the attention of researchers in the UK (Patiniotis and Holdsworth, 2005; Cote and Bynner, 2008), the US (Whittington and Peters, 1996), Canada (Cote and Bynner, 2008), Australia (Young, 1987; Kendig, 1990a; Weston et al, 2001; Cobb-Clark, 2008) and, more recently, in Japan (Fukuda, 2009). While in the past leaving home was closely connected to marriage or employment, today young people leave home for a variety of reasons.

The theoretical framework implicitly and explicitly favoured in examining the transition from dependent to independent living is the life course approach, 'in which transitions are conceived to be shaped by the time of birth, circumstances and experiences to which each new generation in each country is exposed' (Cote and Bynner, 2008, p 256). As noted earlier, leaving the parental home is now a more complex transition than it was for previous generations. The age of leaving home has been strongly influenced by a range of structural features that have transformed society in the later half of the 20th century and the first decade of the 21st century. These include trends in marriage, household formation patterns, the demand for higher levels of educational achievement, later age of entry into the workforce (Billari et al, 2001), the changing structure of the labour market, changing housing markets, reformation of welfare provisions, shifts in societal expectations about the transition to independence (Iacovou, 2004), greater individual choice and changing parental expectations and attitudes about young adult behaviour and parental support.

Changes in the structural factors underpinning the transition to independent living have reshaped the decision framework of young people. This has included change to personal income and job status, parental income and employment, financial help received from parents, the circumstances within the parental home – including personal conflict within the family – and, most importantly, gender (Mandic, 2008). Numerous studies (Mandic, 2008; Furlong and Cartmel, 2007) highlight gender differences in leaving home, with women leaving at an earlier age than men. In broad terms, across many developed nations the restructuring of economies and labour markets has made financial independence at an early age difficult, resulting in a situation where remaining within the parental home has become an accepted norm.

## The structural drivers of, and impediments to, independence

The age at which young people leave home is mediated by the way in which these social and economic factors interact. There would also appear to be a strong regional dimension, as European studies have identified a clear distinction between Southern and Northern European countries with young people leaving home at a much later age in Southern Europe (for example in Italy, Spain, Portugal) (Billari et al, 2001; Iacovou, 2002). Mandic's analysis of 24 member states of the EU found that only 17 per cent of men aged 18-34 in Denmark were still living with their parents compared with 67 per cent of men in Malta and 61 per cent of men in Italy (Mandic, 2008, p 627). Mandic's analysis is one of the few studies to examine the enlarged EU and build upon the existing analyses of home-leaving in Western European countries. His finding generally reflects those of previous studies in that 'three distinctive clusters of countries emerged, indicating specific constellations of how structural factors of leaving home appear and interact, resulting in diverse, regionally specific incidence of home-leaving' – a north-western cluster of countries, a south-western cluster and a north-eastern cluster (Mandic, 2008, p 632). The patterns identified reflected the age of leaving home: with home-leaving occurring earliest in the north-western cluster of countries; living with parents was more widespread in the north-eastern cluster; and, independent living was considerably delayed in the south-western cluster. In explaining this variation, Mandic examined structural factors, in particular welfare regimes, and while his explanatory model was, in his own words, 'far from comprehensive', he argued that countries in north-west Europe, including the UK, had the best 'opportunity structures for independent housing', including an extant private rental sector, strong support from the family for leaving home and late parenthood. The north-eastern countries were characterised by early childbearing and 'outstandingly unfavourable opportunity structures in terms of all components of the welfare mix' (p 632). These unfavourable conditions included high unemployment, an underdeveloped private rental sector, limited family support and restricted social welfare. For the southern cluster of countries, a number of factors restricted home-leaving to the latest ages: restricted social housing provision, strong family-cultural supports and very late parenthood. In Italy, for example, where young people leave home at the oldest ages in Europe, marriage is still the strongest influence on the age of leaving home and even when people leave home they usually live very close to their parents (Santarelli and Cottone, 2009).

The timing of leaving home in Britain, the US, Canada and Australia matches the patterns identified for north-west Europe. In the past relationship formation, especially marriage, as well as childbearing and employment were the driving forces for young people setting up a new household. In the 21st century, the reasons for leaving home are more varied. Research from the Housing 21 Survey in Australia was able to shed light on the major motivations for leaving home in the first decade of this century, as well as for earlier generations. While partnership formation remains important for the younger generations, its importance has declined significantly. Whereas 48 per cent of 65- to 74-year-olds originally left home to enter marriage, just 22 per cent of 25- to 34-year-olds left home in order to establish a relationship (Figure 4.1). Similarly, while an additional 26.9 per cent of 65- to 74-year-olds left for employment reasons, only 13.8 per cent of 25- to 34-year-olds left the family home for this reason. The transition to independent living amongst the younger cohorts was driven by a diverse array of processes, including the desire to live independently or with friends (26.2 per cent compared with 4.9 per cent for those aged 65–74), in response to educational opportunities (20.1 per cent compared with 4.6 per cent) and as a consequence of personal circumstances (12.0 compared with 4.4 per cent). In many instances 'personal circumstances' can be interpreted as conflict with parents or other guardians.

### Boomerang children

Returning to the parental home has become an increasing phenomenon over the last few decades across many advanced economies with some commentators labelling this group 'boomerang children' for their propensity to come back to their origin (Molgat, 2002). This phenomenon has had an impact both on how we think about the age at which young people leave the parental home as well as the dynamics of contemporary family life. Some have argued that the parents of such 'boomerang children' are 'baby gloomers' rather than baby boomers, because of the expectation that they will continue to support their offspring. Whatever the impacts at a personal level, the reality cannot be denied. Analysis of cross-sectional data has identified a trend towards young people remaining in

**Figure 4.1: Reasons for leaving the family home by age**

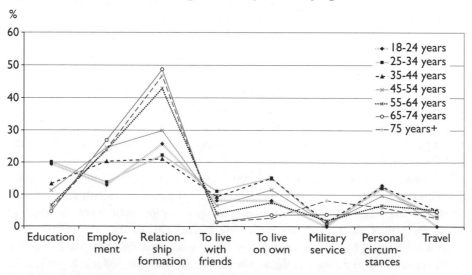

*Source:* Housing 21 Survey

the parental home longer than was the case for previous generations. For example, data for the UK indicates that in 2008 29 per cent of men and 18 per cent of women aged 20–34 were residing with their parents, compared with 27 per cent and 15 per cent respectively in 2001 (Office of National Statistics, 2009, p 17). Similarly in Australia, 23 per cent of young people aged 20–34 were living with their parents in 2006 compared with 19 per cent in 1986 (ABS, 2009a, p 24). Such trends led Côté and Bynner (2008, p 253) to state 'one of the least contested issues in contemporary youth studies is that the transition to adulthood is now taking longer on average than in the past'.

Young (1996) observed that establishing trends on the percentage of young people still living at home with their parents does not necessarily provide a true indication of the age at which young people first left home. Analysis of longitudinal data allows for a more accurate analysis of the timing and synchronicity of leaving home and may tell a different story (Holdsworth and Morgan, 2005). For example, in Australia in 2006–07 the Australian Bureau of Statistics (ABS) conducted a survey to examine more specifically trends in living arrangements of people aged 18 years and over, including experiences of leaving the family home. The examination showed that for males aged 18-34 years the median age of first leaving the family home was 20.9 years and for females the median age was 19.8 years, representing little change over around 50 years (Baxter and McDonald, 2004; Flatau et al, 2004). The ABS survey also indicated that by the age of 28 some 94 per cent of people had left the family home, whether they had returned or not. Moreover, 31 per cent of people aged 20–34 years had left and then returned, and the probability that a young person would return home at least once before turning 35 was close to 50 per cent (ABS, 2009a).

The Housing 21 Survey provided a comparable set of insights into the housing transitions of younger people in the first part of the 21st century. When asked, persons aged 18–24 were much more likely to report that their household had changed composition through a child leaving home than those aged 25–34, once again reinforcing the interpretation that most young Australians leave the parental home in their early 20s. Some 26 per cent of respondents aged 18–24 indicated that the composition of their household had changed through a partner, parent or adult sibling leaving home. By contrast, only 4 per cent indicated one or more adult offspring had returned to the family home. Importantly, while 41 per cent of 18- to 24-year-olds still lived in the family home, only 4 per cent of 25- to 34-year-olds still lived with their parents. Most young Australians leave home in their late teenage years through to their mid 20s (see Figure 4.2). The process appears more concentrated for the 18–24 cohort because the figure does not – and cannot – include the moves of persons still resident in their parent's home. It is worth noting, however, that the departure of young people from the family home stretches over 15 years, and that those who left the family home first had already spent half their life away from the family home by the time the last person departed. We can, however, conclude that the percentage of offspring remaining in the family home until well into their adult years is small: just 12 per cent of respondents to the Housing 21 Survey aged 25–34 left the family home at age 24 or older. While some young adults return to the family home, it appears to be a small-scale and transient phenomenon.

One of the most influential factors contributing to the rise of boomerang children has been growing rates of participation in post-school education. Over the last three to four decades growing proportions of young people have remained within the education system. There has been a marked rise in many nations in participation in higher education. Education can have one of two completely contrasting effects: for some young people ongoing participation in education delays the departure from the family home by postponing the start of their working careers; for others, it precipitates leaving home earlier simply because the university or educational institution they attend is distant from the family home. In the UK, for example, Patiniotis and Holdsworth (2005) estimate that around 75 per cent of students attending higher education 'live away' from home. The pattern in the US is similar, but conversely very few Australian students leave the family home in order to obtain a first degree. This phenomenon adds complexity both to our understanding of the transition away from the family home and the academic debate around its incidence and character. In discussing trends in the US, Furlong and Cartmel (2007) stressed that children leaving home to further their education are only 'moving away', not 'leaving' the family home. The overwhelming majority of students return during holidays and over 40 per cent return to the family home upon completion of their college courses. In Europe, however, students in similar circumstances are treated by researchers as having left home (Mulder, 2000). In some respects, therefore, independent or quasi-independent living associated with education can be thought of as an intermediate step in the transition to adult life. The growing rate of participation in higher education is one of the ways in which the path to adulthood and adult housing has become more complex over recent decades.

For many young people in the 21st century moving out does not necessarily mean moving on – emotionally, intellectually and often physically. Instead of being a one-off event, moving out of home has become a sequence of limited moves that are often time limited, linked to specific opportunities and, importantly, often supported by parental finances. Critically then, it is important to distinguish between leaving home for the first time (moving out), and leaving home for the last time (moving on), and the experiences and directional changes that occur between these two points in the life course.

## The motivations for independence

The housing young people first occupy is commonly dependent on the precipitating factors that triggered departure from the family home. As these initiating factors or circumstances have become more varied over time, so have the housing options sought by, or available to, younger people. Using the experiences of young people in the UK, Ford et al (2002) showed that how young adults left the family home resulted in significant differentiation in subsequent housing. They noted that in the past young people moved into the same housing market as their parents, albeit entering at the bottom of this market, before gradually working their way towards greater permanence and quality. Change in housing markets, in particular affordability, has meant that young people now enter what they term as a 'youth housing market' – 'characterised by shared housing, precarious housing, temporary housing and frequent mobility, and which is clearly distinct from accessing and holding housing in a 'mature' or 'adult' market' (Ford et al, 2002, p 2456). This description can be aptly applied to the housing situation of young people in many countries. For example, in countries such as the Netherlands, Australia, the US and the UK, private renting is frequently the first destination of young people leaving home. Sharing is often the first step in an 'independent' housing career, particularly for those attending university (Mulder and Hooimeijer, 2002). Young people who are working and leave home are also likely to be renting in the private rental sector but are less likely to share accommodation, while homeownership is only likely to be an option for those who leave home to live with a partner, though as a first entry point into the housing market this has become increasingly difficult (Mulder and Hooimeijer, 2002).

Family-specific factors can be important in shaping the initial housing of young people, with Mandic (2008) arguing that in southern Europe and some eastern European countries construction of housing by the family network is an important avenue for independent living for young people. In all countries an absence of family support means some young people leave home under questionable circumstances and the risk of homelessness is considerable. For many young people homelessness, or the risk of homelessness, can be a recurring nightmare.

That homelessness could be part of the lifetime relationship between an individual and their housing would appear to be an oxymoron, but this is the case for increasing numbers of young people in many advanced economies. It is estimated that on any night, some 75,000 young people in the UK are homeless (Wincup et al, 2003), while Australian estimates suggest 32,000 youth are homeless at any time (Chamberlain and MacKenzie 2008, p 27). The drivers of youth homelessness are reasonably well understood and they reflect a combination of social, demographic, legal and housing market processes. Key factors include the incidence of substance abuse; conflict with parents; low and/or insecure parental income; interaction with the judicial system, including periods of incarceration; the inability to secure affordable housing; and leaving guardianship arrangements after being fostered or cared for by the state. Many of these risks have been present for decades but their impacts appear more acute in the 21st century because of ongoing crises in the provision of welfare services and the demise of many low-cost housing options. Moreover, most developed economies now have relatively few jobs that can be filled by young people with relatively low levels of education or skills. Demographic change has also exerted a profound impact. Higher rates of divorce or relationship breakdown across society have contributed to an escalation in the number of 'blended' households, and conflict with step-parents pushes some out of the family home at a young age.

Young people are generally the most mobile group within the housing market, with many moves across many dwellings and types of accommodation. In conceptualising the housing transitions of young people in England at the turn of the 21st century, Ford et al (2002) were able to identify five typical housing pathways, which they classified as chaotic, unplanned, constrained, planned (non-student) and a student pathway. This classification was based on four main factors: the ease with which young people were able to plan and control their move into independent living, the nature and character of the local housing market, access to benefits, and the degree of family support available. These processes have an influence on the long-term housing trajectories of young people. Mulder's (2003) analysis of two retrospective life course surveys conducted in the Netherlands in the 1990s found young people who left home initially to live with a partner or marry were more likely to become homeowners and less likely to share, and this remained significant after eight years. Interestingly, Mulder (2003, p 717) also observed that while highly educated young adults may start off in a less favourable housing situation when they first leave home, after eight years they are more likely to be homeowners than the less well educated and this reflects their greater earning capacity. Rugg and Ford (2004) would also argue that the student pathway allows young people to obtain housing knowledge in a progressive way in a supportive context, where young people can learn about living independently and budgeting within sheltered environments (university halls, for example). They see the student pathway into housing as constituting 'an essential education in housing that enhances the housing and labour opportunities of graduates' (Rugg and Ford, 2004, p 19).

### Entering the homeownership market

Homeownership in many western societies is an expected, almost unquestionable, stage in the sequence of housing young adults occupy and the broader transition to adult life. In many nations homeownership remains a highly desirable goal and, as discussed in previous chapters, homeownership is increasingly central to people's sense of identity and well-being. The purchase of the first home, therefore, is perceived as an important 'rite of passage' or, as Mulder and Wagner (1998, p 687) see it, a crucial step in the life course, arguing that 'the effect of this step on people's housing situation, accumulation of wealth and disposable income can hardly be overstated'.

Since 1945, homeownership rates have risen in almost all OECD countries and in the last 20 years or so homeownership as a tenure has become more popular than rental (Atterhog 2005; Havet and Penot 2010). Chiuri and Japelli's (2003) comparative study of owner-occupancy rates across OECD countries highlights the considerable variation in the age of entry into this tenure. In Anglophone countries such as Australia, the UK, the US and Canada, as well as in Finland, the

Netherlands and Sweden, young people generally enter homeownership in their 20s or early 30s. In Germany, Austria, Italy and Spain, on the other hand, movement into homeownership has tended to occur much later, in the 30s and even 40s.

Movement into homeownership has been explained in terms of family life cycle models, with the timing of homeownership connected to marriage and childbearing as well as of socioeconomic circumstances (employment status, income, and parental resources, for example). Though the relative importance of factors vary regionally, in essence the overwhelming weight of research indicates that married people have a greater probability of becoming homeowners, that higher education is positively associated with homeownership, as is employment and length of employment, and that parental homeownership and resources favour the probability of homeownership. Degree of urbanisation also has an influence on homeownership possibilities, with the likelihood of homeownership decreasing with increasing levels of urbanisation (Mulder and Wagner, 1998, 2001; Hillman and Marks, 2002; McDonald and Baxter, 2005).

In addition to events in the family life course, contextual factors are of significance and may be of even greater importance than individual demography. The decision to enter the homeownership market needs to be examined within the pricing and political framework of the housing market of the time (Mulder and Wagner, 1998; Atterhog, 2005; Kupke, 2007). Factors including the price of housing, homeownership subsidies, interest rates, rental shortages, property taxation, loan deposits and lending regulations and practices can all be influential in the decision to enter homeownership. In Canada, for example, from the early 1980s through to the mid 1990s ownership rates for young households decreased as a result of high interest rates, recession and an unfavourable labour market for young males. By the mid to late 1990s homeownership rates for younger age groups increased as interest rates decreased, employment conditions improved and changes in mortgage regulations made it easier for young people to obtain finance and safeguarded loans (Hou, 2010).

In Australia and the UK, the ability of young people to enter the homeownership market is under increasing pressure, with official data indicating a trend towards declining homeownership for young people. The Office of National Statistics in the UK reports that the proportion of people aged under 30 buying a home with a mortgage declined from 43 per cent in 1997 to 27 per cent in 2009, while in 2008 only 18 per cent of first-homebuyers were aged under 25 years, compared with 30 per cent in 1990 (Office of National Statistics, 2009). In Australia, ABS data indicates a significant decline in the homeownership rate of people aged 25–34 (ABS, 2004a; Yates et al, 2007; Flood and Baker, 2010).

Of necessity, census data reflects conditions at a point in time, does not provide insights into the past housing of individuals, and is analysed from a household rather than individual perspective. In Australia there have been two concurrent debates about homeownership: first, whether the decline in homeownership rates is an actual decline or is simply a reflection of the fact that entry into homeownership has been delayed to a later age; and, second, whether the reason for the fall in homeownership rates is a consequence of a lack of affordable housing or delays in family formation among young Australians (Yates, 2002; Baxter and McDonald, 2005). In relation to the first debate, a life course approach suggests that more Australians have been able to enter homeownership at younger ages over recent decades than was historically the case (Baxter and McDonald, 2005; Beer and Faulkner, 2009). Over the last five decades most Australians who become owner-occupiers did so early in their adult lives with 67 per cent of respondents to the Housing 21 Survey doing so by age 30 (Figure 4.2). These data, however, reflect all of the approximately 1,900 respondents who had entered home purchase regardless of current age. The more important question, however, is the percentage of each cohort to enter home ownership by a particular age, and especially age 34 and age 44, the traditional and emerging thresholds for measuring recruitment into owner occupation.

The Housing 21 Survey permitted the calculation of the age at which the respondent first entered homeownership: for the total population (including persons currently tenants) 51 per cent had taken out their first mortgage on a home by age 30 and 16 per cent of those aged 18–24 were already homebuyers. The more telling set of figures is the percentage of each cohort to become home purchasers or homeowners at a benchmark date, and Figure 4.2 reveals that the results contradict the conventional interpretation that younger cohorts have found it more difficult to enter home purchase than older groups did at the same age

**Figure 4.2: Age at which entered home purchase, all respondents**

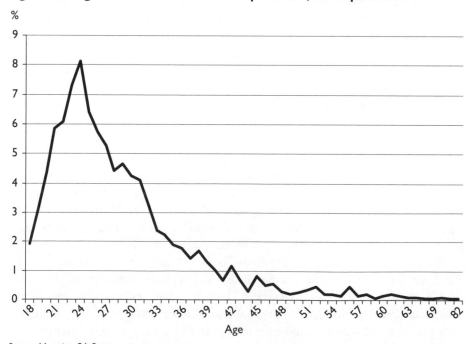

*Source:* Housing 21 Survey

(Figure 4.3). For those aged 25–34, fully 56.7 per cent had entered home purchase by the age of 30, compared with 56.8 per cent of the 35–44 cohort, 52.6 per cent of the 45–54 age group, 53.9 per cent of those aged 55–64, 50.8 per cent of the cohort aged 65–74 and 41.9 per cent of those aged over 75. Similar trends are evident at the other benchmark ages of 34 and 44 years, and it is worth noting that the percentage of households to have entered home purchase by age 44 is broadly comparable between 35- to 44-year-olds and 45- to 55-year-olds, even though the majority of the former group had not achieved that age at the time the survey was conducted. Put simply, the Housing 21 data show that more Australians have been able to enter homeownership at younger ages over recent decades.

The introduction of the First Home Owners Grant by the Australian Government (FHOG) in 2000 played an important role in encouraging many young Australians to enter home purchase. Wood et al (2003) showed that the FHOG 'brought forward' home purchase decisions for a significant number of households. Kupke and Marano (2002) concluded that for those households able to secure the FHOG, the timing of home purchase was determined by access to the grant. However, the FHOG alone does not explain the younger ages for entry to home purchase because of the relatively modest level of assistance provided and the high rates of entry to home purchase amongst those currently aged 35–44 years. While the overall finding appears to be at odds with earlier analyses (Yates, 1996, 2003; Baxter and McDonald, 2005), it is consistent with the outcomes we

**Figure 4.3: Percentage of the population to have entered home purchase, by cohort, at age 30, 34 and 44**

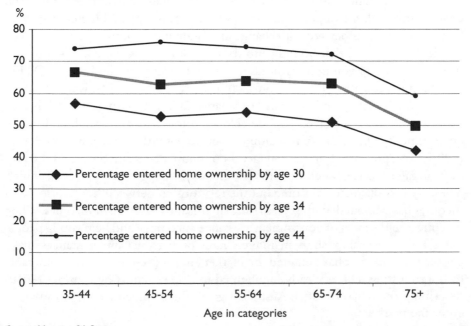

would expect within a liberalising housing market and an increasingly prosperous economy. The older generations were confronted by the need to save for an extended period in order to secure a home loan, had lower household incomes and had higher rates of entry into public housing. Moreover, some groups, such as women, were effectively excluded from entry into the housing market by discriminatory lending and employment practices (Watson, 1988).

It is important to consider why the results on entry into home ownership by age from the Housing 21 Survey appear to contradict earlier research. Critically, the data discussed here report on the age at which the respondent entered homeownership, regardless of their current tenure. A significant percentage of those who have entered home purchase subsequently leave the tenure. Other research has simply considered tenure and age of the population at a point in time and ignored previous tenures. The Housing 21 data show that younger Australians are both more likely to enter home purchase and more likely to exit from that tenure when compared with their parents' or grand-parents' generations. Analysis of the Housing 21 data for people aged 18–34 showed that 25 per cent of tenants had previously been homeowners. This movement between tenures was due to a number of factors including work related moves, temporary renting while looking for another residence or building a home, affordability issues, and relationship breakdown. The results already discussed suggest that for governments concerned to maintain relatively high rates of homeownership in current and future generations, the major policy challenge is in assisting people to retain owner-occupation rather than increasing the rate of entry. The findings also indicate that divorce and relationship breakdown have a comparable impact on housing transitions in the 21st century to that held by marriage in the 20th century but with the opposite impact on tenure. It is a pivotal life course event that is likely to be associated with change in an individual's housing circumstances.

There is no doubt that housing affordability (or the lack thereof) and housing stress are issues for young households in the 21st century in the UK (ECOTEC and Joseph Rowntree Foundation, 2009), New Zealand (Ministry of Social Development, 2009) and Australia (Richards, 2008). Housing affordability in these countries has received considerable attention within research and policy environments. The ability of first-homebuyers to enter the market is, as Yates et al (2007) note, predicated on the interaction of house prices, incomes and the cost of mortgage finance, together with a household's savings and deposit assistance. These factors fluctuate over time but the relationship between house prices and incomes has worsened, with prices rising significantly faster than incomes. While incentives in the form of government assistance encourage and help young people enter homeownership, shifts in interest rates or personal circumstances make people who may not have entered the market but for these incentives vulnerable to housing stress. This is clearly highlighted in a news report by Gardner (2010) describing the outcome of an Australian government incentive of A$14,000 to enter the market:

—

Just weeks after the grant was withdrawn a survey of more than 26,000 borrowers conducted by Fujitsu Consulting has found 45 per cent of first–home owners who entered the market during the past 18 months are experiencing 'mortgage stress' or 'severe mortgage stress'.

Younger households not only have to contend with the growing inequity between house prices and incomes, but their ability to enter the market or maintain their tenure, is compromised by the burden of a higher education debt. Investigation of the impact of student debt on first-homebuyers in Britain concluded that increasing debt levels among students coupled with a new repayment profile and mortgage lender imposed borrowing restrictions delayed first-homebuyer entry into the market (Andrew, 2010). A number of authors in Australia have argued that the Higher Education Contribution Scheme may work to discourage family formation (Jackson, 2002) and act as an impediment to home purchase (Badcock and Beer, 2000; Pearse, 2003) by reducing both the capacity to save for a deposit and by producing a lower mortgage repayment capacity.

## Housing aspirations and expectations

There is limited research on the aspirations and expectations of younger households in terms of housing preferences, tenure, quality and location. In countries where homeownership has been the dominant tenure for decades and in other countries where homeownership has relatively recently gained precedence over renting, homeownership is the tenure of choice for young households (Casells and Harding, 2007; Beer and Faulkner, 2009; ECOTEC and Joseph Rowntree Foundation, 2009). This desire for homeownership changes people's aspirations regarding the quality and location of housing.

In the UK, practitioners and policy makers are increasingly questioning the rationality of homeownership as a lifetime goal. Research undertaken by ECOTEC and the Joseph Rowntree Foundation (2009, p 6) indicates that homeownership remains a strong aspiration, an ultimate objective, among younger people in the UK, despite the increasing difficulty they face in accessing homeownership. There was a realisation among the young groups interviewed that this ambition was becoming an increasingly unobtainable reality. Young people were consequently looking at alternatives, including socially rented accommodation. This tenure was also difficult to enter because of a lack of supply and an apparent lack of flexibility. Shared purchase was seen as an option but remains untested in the UK market. The research canvassed the possibility of long-term occupancy of private rental housing, but noted that while there are some benefits in terms of flexibility and choice of location, high rents, poor quality housing and a lack of security make this tenure unattractive.

In Australia where homeownership has a strong tradition, survey data indicate a strong preference for homeownership. The Housing 21 data suggest that fully 60 per cent of 25- to 34-year-olds who were renting believed they would enter home purchase within the next five years, while the Household Income and

Labour Dynamics of Australia Survey indicated that in 2004, 94 per cent of 15- to 29-year-olds anticipated they would own their own home, many by the age of 30 (Cassells and Harding, 2007). In common with their counterparts in the UK, young Australians are concerned about their ability to achieve this goal in life with 55 per cent reporting that they were somewhat worried or very worried about their ability to buy a home by the age they planned to do so (Cassells and Harding, 2007). Indeed in most Anglophone countries the desire to own a home is greater than the rates of lifetime achievement of this aspiration. In assessing the confluence between aspiration and achievement for Australian households, studies by Merlo and McDonald (2002) and Baum and Wulff (2003) found that expectation of entry into homeownership has a low predictive value. Merlo and McDonald concluded that considerable caution needs to be taken in the use of aspirations in projecting future behaviour.

## The future for young people and housing

Younger people in the majority of advanced economies have and will experience radically different housing sequences through their life course when compared with their parents' or grand-parents' generations. They will be more likely to enter homeownership at a young age and much more likely to fall out of it once they get there. If homeownership was the apogee of a 'housing career' for earlier generations and in previous conceptualisations of the relationship between housing and the life course, now it is much more likely to be a tenure occupied for a defined stage in the life course. Ironically, the evidence suggests that governments, in their eagerness to maintain high rates of owner-occupation, have contributed to the tenure's instability: the programmes and policies intended to support access to home purchase have encouraged at-risk households into the tenure, from which measurable proportions then exit. Of greater concern is the fact that there is no 'natural' tenure, or progression of tenures, for young people in many advanced societies: homeownership is unaffordable for many, social housing is inaccessible and private rental housing is unattractive. It is little wonder, therefore, that many young people continue to return to the family home as they journey through an extended transition to adulthood.

The current generations of young people are also much more likely to experience homelessness, both because of changes affecting their generation, and those affecting their parents' generation—especially the increase in relationship breakdowns and divorce. Over the coming decades many people will have had firsthand experience of homelessness and its consequence, and this will have long-term detrimental impact. As the research discussed earlier has shown, how young people first enter the housing market affects their longer-term outcomes and creates the conditions for housing success or failure later in life.

# FIVE

# Housing in mid life: consolidation, opportunity and risk

In the traditional representation of a housing career a discussion of mid-life housing transitions would almost seem unwarranted. Mid life has conventionally been seen as a period of consolidation and stability in the housing of individuals and households. In the past, at this stage of life, traditional patterns of behaviour, stable employment careers, and the demands of childrearing contributed to limited movements within the housing market. The middle years of life have been associated with the gradual transition from home purchase to outright ownership, accompanied by some limited upward movement through the housing market to better accommodate the needs of the family. Mid life in this representation of the relationship between housing and the life course is seen as the culmination of a household's housing aspirations and needs, where many households maximise their consumption of housing.

There is relatively little known about the housing position of persons in the middle years of their life, as the apparent stability of these households has not made them an attractive subject for research. Over the last few decades, however, the life course has become much more complex, differentiated and de-standardised as a result of economic growth, affluence, more mobile labour markets and in some households, growing instability. These changes have eroded traditional conceptions of stability in housing in mid life and while some households go through a period of quiescence relative to the housing market, a growing minority do not. Events and changes in the family life course have substantially reshaped mid-life housing transitions, resulting in widening differentials in the housing trajectories. Some households have taken advantage of their opportunities to accrue considerable wealth while others have experienced a less favourable life course that has interrupted, or significantly altered, their housing aspirations.

## Family and the consumption of housing

Marriage and the birth of children have conventionally been seen as pivotal markers of the move from rental accommodation to home purchase (Neutze and Kendig, 1991). While societal change has meant that marriage per se and the arrival of the first child are not as universally important in the 21st century as previously, relationship formation and the birth of children remain critical to shaping transitions. Baxter and McDonald (2005) argue that in Australia the most significant factor in predicting a move to owner-occupation is formal marriage, while internationally it has been argued that the birth of children or the anticipation of childbearing is critical (Mulder and Wagner, 2001; Feijten and Mulder, 2002). Evidence suggests that delays in both of these processes, marriage and childbearing, have resulted in the postponement of entry into homeownership (Baxter and McDonald, 2004; Mulder, 2006a, 2006b), but both marriage and the arrival of a child clearly increase the likelihood of a change in housing circumstance (Deurloo et al, 1994; Mulder and Wagner, 2001; Clark and Huang, 2003).

The evidence from the Housing 21 Survey on the impact of the birth of children on housing transitions is mixed. In establishing the primary reason for moving from one dwelling to another over the period 1996 to 2006, relatively few households suggested the arrival of children was their primary reason. Analysis of the Housing 21 Survey data on the relationship between the first entry of respondents into homeownership and the birth of the first child (who at the time of the survey was under 20 years of age) tells a different story. These data strongly suggest that, in Australia at least, the birth of children or the expected birth of children remains highly instrumental in the decision to enter homeownership. Fully 67 per cent of the 610 respondents who had entered homeownership at some stage in their life, and who also had children, did so prior to the year of birth of their first child (Beer and Faulkner 2009). In the five years prior to the arrival of the first child, 36 per cent entered home purchase, while 10 per cent became homebuyers in the year their first child was born and 13 per cent entered home purchase in the five years after the arrival of their firstborn. Overall, approximately 60 per cent of households entered homeownership in the five years before or five years after the arrival of their first child. The year the first child was born was also the single most common year for entering owner occupation. Clearly, the arrival of children remains an important driver of first-home purchase even though relationship breakdown and lower fertility rates have reduced its overall significance. It should also be acknowledged that there is a growing lag between relationship formation and the arrival of the first child, such that many households may enter home purchase in the expectation of children at some stage, even if it is not the primary driver for residential relocation (Beer and Faulkner, 2009).

The qualitative interviews with families with children (54 households) undertaken as part of the research into 21st-century Australian housing careers (Tually, 2008) provides a rich source of evidence on the impact the arrival of children has on housing needs and preferences. The birth of a child or the impending birth of a child was for all of the respondents a significant motivator for change. For many respondents, both those who had formally married and those in an informal relationship, the transition to parenthood prompted them to move into homeownership (Tually, 2008, p 51):

> …the reason we originally wanted to buy was because we wanted to start a family and have them in a secure environment and I think you always want to have a secure home when you've got children so that they can settle somewhere and if you want to get sand pits for them

and things like that, you can do that if it's your own home. You can't always do it if it's a rental property.

People in rental accommodation were also influenced by the arrival of children. For the private renters in the group, having a child or children spurred many to move out of shared housing into a larger private rental property or to move from one private rental property to a larger, more family-friendly, property.

Regardless of tenure and income, children appear to be a motivating force for mobility, especially in the desire to provide stable and secure housing. For those who could afford it, stability meant homeownership, while for renters it meant seeking a larger house and hopefully a landlord who would provide a measure of certainty. These sentiments were clearly enunciated by a lone female parent (Tually, 2008, p 51):

> I think when you're a single person or even…like a couple without children, it's much easier to just kind of pack up and move because you don't have to think about schools or their friends and stuff like that. So I'd really just like to have a stable base.

Households with children also voiced a need for more space (both inside and outside the dwelling) and this appeared to be a significant factor in households seeking alternative accommodation. From their perspective, housing needed to cater for both immediate and future needs. Tually (2008, p 52 ) noted that many interviewees discussed the importance of living in a 'good area', near a 'good school' and public transport, as well as other facilities such as parks, sporting clubs or grounds and childcare facilities. The need for parents to cater for the needs of their children was voiced by one parent who said:

> She governs all my decision making. I suppose I didn't want to live in a flat because I wanted her to have enough space and not that we always use the yard but the older she's gotten so – and also I suppose it affected where – our location. So I wanted to live [in]…an area that had lots of parks around us and was close…to getting to her childcare and all that sort of thing. (Tually, 2008, p 51).

Establishing a household and consolidating one's housing in mid life is challenging for many, as it is the stage in the life course with the greatest commitment of resources. The combined tasks of raising children and purchasing/renting housing places pressure on mid- life households. Research in Australia on the costs of raising children indicates that the lifetime (birth to age 21 years) costs of raising two children represent around 23 per cent of a household's income (Percival et al, 2007, p 20). In addition, many of the mid-life population – whether buyers or renters – have more than 30 per cent of their income committed to housing. For homebuyers this situation improves in their late 40s and at older ages as the real cost of their mortgage falls; as a group they begin to achieve outright ownership and their children begin to forge their own independence. Risks, however, remain as the proportion of people aged 45–54 achieving outright homeownership has declined over time (Tanton et al, 2008) and the return of children to the family home after initially leaving for a period (Young, 1987) has added complexity to established household structures.

Achieving stability in one's housing situation in mid life is affected by a range of factors, specifically attachment to the labour force, household income, family composition and tenure type. Some mid-life households have built considerable wealth in housing and non-housing assets (Headey et al, 2008). However, as the cost of housing relative to incomes has increased over time (Yates et al, 2008) some low- and moderate-income households have been excluded from this avenue for wealth creation.

## Housing shocks and successes

For some people, mid life represents the pinnacle of their position within the labour market and the high point in their lifetime of housing consumption. It can be a period of high incomes, growing wealth, falling household expenditures as children begin to leave home and an expanding horizon of opportunities for investment and consumption. For others, mid life is a period of vulnerability, some of which is anticipated and some of which arrives as a shock. These interruptions, or housing shocks, can occur for a number of reasons including unemployment, retrenchment, illness, the onset of disability and, increasingly, partnership breakdown leading to separation and divorce. These shocks often have adverse outcomes for households, in particular those who 'fall' out of homeownership. Both sets of processes need to be understood if we are to fully comprehend housing transitions in the 21st century.

From his work in the Netherlands, Feijten (2005) observed that once people have become homeowners they tend to stay within this sector except if disrupting life events such as separation or unemployment force them to make a 'backward' or 'negative' move to rental housing. The Housing 21 Survey explored the degree to which respondents had moved from homeownership to rental housing and the reasons behind that change in tenure. Amongst the respondents aged 35-54 years (1,104 persons) 9.8 percent were renting, although they had previously been outright homeowners or in the process of purchasing a home. The rate was slightly higher for women at 10.3 per cent compared with men at 8.9 per cent, but in both instances roughly one in 10 people within this age group had fallen out of homeownership. The reasons for currently being in the rental market varied: for some the rental market was a planned temporary transition while they worked to improve their long-term housing position but for the majority it appears to have been an unplanned, and almost certainly unwelcome, move. It is a phenomenon that reflects social and economic change and may foreshadow a longer term trend. Certainly this was the inference drawn by Berry et al (2010, p 66) from their study of mortgage defaults; they argued that 'more Australians are going to be affected by involuntary exit from home ownership more often in their lives than in the second half of the twentieth century'.

## Partnership dissolution

Demographic processes continue to shape the relationship between housing and the life course through the 21st century, but in this century the impact of household formation is equalled by the influence of household dissolution. The breakdown of relationships, whether formally married or de facto, is a common feature of western societies. The probability that a marriage will end in divorce has been increasing over time. For marriages in Australia that began at the start of the 21st century, there is an expected probability that one third will end in divorce (ABS, 2007a, p 3) and mid life is the stage of life with the highest rates of marriage breakdown (Bracher et al, 1993; Hewitt et al, 2005). Official divorce, statistics, however, are not a true reflection of partnership dissolution as many formal marriages result in permanent separation and never proceed to divorce, or it is many years before divorce proceeding are instigated (Hewitt et al, 2005). In addition, official statistics do not capture the formation and dissolution of de facto relationships. As marriage rates have fallen in Australia and other developed economies, cohabitation rates have increased, and de facto relationships are associated with higher rates of relationship breakdown (Hewitt et al, 2005; Qu and Weston, 2008) and therefore greater levels of risk for the partners. Partnership dissolution has a considerable impact on many facets of life, including a measurable influence on housing transitions. It has become a key driver of households 'falling out' of homeownership.

The Housing 21 Survey sheds light on the impact of relationship breakdown on the housing of contemporary Australians. Some 35.1 per cent of males and 40.8 per cent of females aged 35-54 years who were renting because they had fallen out of homeownership did so because of marriage/partnership breakdown. The males were evenly divided in the reasons they fell out of homeownership between 'partner received dwelling' and 'couldn't afford mortgage costs associated with dwelling', while 75 per cent of women who left homeownership did so because they could no longer service the mortgage. These findings reflect those of international studies (Feijten and Mulder, 2002; Feijten, 2005; Feijten and van Ham, 2007) showing that, for one partner at least, separation causes an immediate housing move while for the other the challenge is to maintain housing stability in the face of high costs and diminished resources. Generally, this lagged effect is gendered because of women's more marginal attachment to the labour force and consequent lower incomes. In the Netherlands, Feijten (2005) tested the probability of separated persons leaving homeownership. He found that within three months of separation the odds of moving from owner-occupation were high for both men and women. Over time, however, the trends diverged. In the second and following years post separation there was hardly any difference in homeownership trends for separated men and male homeowners. By contrast, the probability of moving remained strong and significant for women. The probability that women would leave owner-occupation was almost 4.5 times higher than for men in the second and subsequent years post separation (Feijten, 2005, p 67).

In Australia, Flatau et al (2004) used econometric modelling to predict the probabilities of a household being in owner-occupation after separation and divorce. Their findings indicated that for people aged 35–64 years divorce results in a 9 percentage point lower probability of homeownership when compared with the continuously married. Separation has an even greater negative impact on homeownership prospects. Separated individuals have a 21 percentage point lower probability of attaining or retaining homeownership when compared to the continuously married.

Divorce brings with it the risk of substantial financial hardship. Those most affected are generally women and, as Smyth and Weston (2000) argued, this is the case despite the introduction of income support measures and changes in the labour market. As women are more likely to be responsible for the care of children, their labour force participation, and therefore earning capacity, is limited when compared with fathers. The distribution of a household's assets post divorce also differs between males and females, with women in Australia losing access to superannuation savings for retirement. A study by Sheehan and Hughes (2001) on the distribution of a couple's assets post divorce showed that on average women receive two thirds of the household's basic assets (family home, bank savings and the like) but only one fifth of the non-basic assets (such as superannuation). Similar findings were reported by Kelly and Harding (2005). They found women received the house but relatively few other assets such as superannuation. This meant that divorce, financially, had relatively little impact on men but resulted in a significant reduction in the income of women.

Research in Australia (Smyth and Weston, 2000; Flatau et al, 2004) and internationally (Lewis, 2006) demonstrates that re-partnering – effectively the establishment of a new household and a new stage in the housing of an individual – was an important pathway out of poverty for many divorced people, especially women. Flatau et al (2004) found that remarried couples had the same likelihood of homeownership as continuously married couples. While at an individual level this is a positive outcome, remarriage rates in Australia and many other developed economies are not rising (ABS, 2007a), and those who were previously divorced and subsequently remarried are slightly more likely to divorce than those who had not previously been married (Carmichael et al, 1996).

Qualitative research in Australia has shown that there are a number of possible pathways for people affected by divorce or separation: moving in with family or friends, remaining in the owner-occupied family home, using the proceeds of the sale of the family home to downsize to another home, moving from owner-occupation into private rental, moving into social housing, and experiencing homelessness (Gwyther, 2007; Tually, 2008). Those 'forced' out of homeownership often see a significant decline in the quality and quantity of their housing and may occupy housing that does not meet all their family's needs (Feijten and Mulder, 2005). Consequently, separation and divorce often lead to a change in housing aspirations and a realignment of housing priorities in both the short term and longer term (Tually, 2008). While many still aspire to homeownership, a significant proportion quickly recognise that it is beyond their reach. Many women consider that homeownership is a housing option permanently shut off to them. As one respondent, a separated mother of two commented:

> Homeownership…It's not the be all and end all, I admit that. As long as you've got something to keep you warm at night, a roof over your head. That's the most important thing, but as far as meeting those goals that you set for yourself in life. Having my name on a mortgage document and eventually having the papers in my hand will mean a lot. Having the deeds to the house…knowing that my children have got something at the end of the day. (Tually 2008, p 44).

### Retrenchment, unemployment and underemployment

Employment largely determines the income and wealth of households and therefore acts as a determinant of housing outcomes both with respect to tenure and the realisation of housing market aspirations. Unemployment and retrenchment in mid life can significantly interrupt the lifetime housing experience and the realisation of long-term housing aspirations.

While unemployment and retrenchment can occur at any age, mature-aged workers are disadvantaged within the labour market with a much lower rate of re-employment compared with younger job seekers. Mature-age workers are over represented in the long-term unemployed and underemployed. In comparison with younger persons, many older workers spend one or more years finding employment (ABS, 2010). Often, when they do find employment it is at a lower level of seniority and pay and/or they may have fewer hours of work, the work they may be able to secure is of a casual or short term nature, and the salary may be less than their previous position. The difficulties of re-entering the labour market are ascribed to a mismatch between the skills demanded in a 21st-century labour market and those held by the employee. Mature workers are also confronted by ongoing discrimination in the workplace (Encel, 1993). Job search experience surveys conducted by the ABS in Australia (for example ABS, 2005, 2007b, 2009b) indicate that the dominant reason given to people aged 45 years and over why they were not successful in a job application was that they were 'considered too old by employers'. This occurred three to four times more frequently than being told that they 'lacked necessary skills or education'. Mature-age workers are very susceptible to the 'discouraged worker effect' that leads to many leaving the work force involuntarily in the guise of early retirement (Encel, 1993).

Losing one's job may not initially exert an impact on housing outcomes. As savings diminish with long-term unemployment, or underemployment, a household's susceptibility to housing stress increases, compromising immediate housing options as well as future housing aspirations and retirement prospects. One-income families with a mortgage are particularly vulnerable, while two-income families whose commitments are predicated on those two incomes may also face hardship if either income earner becomes unemployed (McDonald and Brownlee, 1992).

A survey of 54 low- to middle-income families in a rapidly expanding outer area of Melbourne affected by the recession of the late 1980s and early 1990s highlighted the hardships mid-life families face when retrenchment is common and unemployment levels are high. McDonald and Brownlee (1992, p 12) reported about the difficulties of sustaining day-to-day life:

> Several families talked about cutting back on food, clothing and basic necessities. Sixteen families, who were buying a home or renting privately, were having great difficulty making mortgage or rent payments. 'It is just very hard to meet the mortgage payments, leaving us with hardly enough money for other things', one respondent said. Six families said that due to unemployment they may have to sell the family home.

Unemployment is one of the major triggers of mortgage default. Berry et al's (2010, p 24) study of mortgage default in Australia found of 87 mortgagors who had been subject to claims of possession on their property during 2008, over 60 per cent indicated the initial trigger of mortgage delinquency was 'loss/reduced income/work'. Overall, mid-life households (couples with children, single-parent families, blended family households) are over-represented amongst those in mortgage default (Berry et al, 2010).

### Illness and disability

Unexpected illness or disability within a household serves as a significant housing shock. The impact on housing may not be immediate but be expressed over the longer term. Illness and disability brings extra costs to the household in terms of the direct costs of healthcare and/or equipment as well as the indirect costs associated with a loss of income or reduced income. In addition, illness or disability to one household member may jeopardise the employment capabilities and career advancement opportunities of other household members, typically a partner, as they take on caring responsibilities.

As an interviewee involved in a qualitative study commented:

> Your whole life changes, everything changes. If anybody wants to see a big change they go from earning a wage to a disability and you know that's what you've got and you've got no more, there isn't I'll nip down to the bank or I'll take out a loan, that's it. (Tually, 2008, p 64)

For others in this study the onset of disability, combined with low incomes or limited earning capacity, resulted in priority access to social housing. This outcome is consistent with international experience, with Smith et al (1997) reporting on the outcomes of an explicit programme of medical access to social housing. Tually (2008) observed that some tenants in social housing had been forced to sell their homes because of illness-related financial hardship. For many of those interviewed, private rental was untenable as the illness/disability resulted in a substantial loss of income at a time when they faced significant medical costs. Accordingly, as Tually summarised, 'they all considered social housing was the best and most appropriate housing option for them' (Tually 2008, p 64).

Clearly there is a range of life events that can result in significant interruptions to a household's housing. The degree of vulnerability households face and the housing options available to them are closely tied to labour force status, income earning potential, accumulated savings and the nature of the housing market. Depending upon the state of the housing market in their region at that point in time, it can be very difficult for those who have suffered a housing shock to re-enter homeownership or continue on the housing pathway they once aspired too.

## Success in the housing market

For some households mid life represents the apogee of their housing career – in the traditional sense of a housing career. It is a period in their lives of relatively high incomes, of potentially more rapid accumulation of wealth and of relatively few non-economic barriers, such as health or disability, to increasing housing consumption. At this stage in their life course many households occupy larger and more expensive housing than at any other period in their lives. Housing also becomes an important setting for successful careers and the lifestyles that support them. McDowell (1997) discussed the ways in which proximity to 'The City' was central to success as a high-earning banker in London. Owning a home close to the centre of London gave access to the social networks, luxury retail outlets and grooming businesses that are central to the image of success amongst bankers. For other high-income-earning occupations, homes are simply one of the stepping stones they pass over during the course of their glittering career, and for some geographically and economically mobile workers housing may offer prestige value but little other sense of 'home'.

For the majority of middle-class households in the developed world there is a high likelihood that income will peak and expenditures begin to decline in mid life. By mid life a significant proportion of households, particularly those aged 45 years and over, have considerable wealth. For Australians, much of this wealth is tied to, or dominated by, housing investment (Headey et al, 2008) and this tendency has gathered pace over the last decade. While at ages 35–39 the majority of people in the home ownership market are mortgagors, by the ages of 50–54 and 55–59, 48 per cent and 63 per cent respectively had achieved outright ownership. The combination of greater prosperity (rising employment and incomes) and reduced fertility has raised disposable incomes for many sections of the population and given households greater choice within the housing market. Many have chosen to exercise their greater power by purchasing more housing and/or housing of higher quality. In Australia it has been suggested that it is the willingness of mid-life owner-occupier households, in particular those with high incomes, to borrow

—

and spend more on housing that has been responsible for the growth in house prices in Australia since 1996 (Ellis et al, 2003; Productivity Commission, 2004).

As children age and equity increases many mid-life households re-evaluate their housing. Many households consider the option of renovating their current residence or upgrading to a larger and/or better located home, more suitable to the evolving needs of the household. For at least the last 20 years, new housing construction on the fringe of Australia's cities has been dominated not by the building of new affordable homes for young households, but instead dominated by the second-, third-, fourth-, fifth- or sixth-time homebuyers in their late 40s through to their 60s building their 'dream' home. In some instances these are five or six bedroom homes, with four or more bathrooms and parking for up to six vehicles. It is little wonder that the average size of new homes constructed in Australia has been increasing steadily. At the same time, those who do not build their dream home renovate and extend to a comparable degree (Allon, 2008). Data from the 2005–06 ABS Survey of Income and Housing indicates that around one quarter of recent homebuyers (built or purchased a home in the three years prior to the survey) aged 35–54 years were, as the ABS classifies it, 'changeover buyers'. Couple families with children accounted for 35 per cent of changeover buyers (ABS, 2008a, p 321). Families who upgrade are able to use the considerable equity they have built up in their current dwelling, which acts as a substantial deposit on a more expensive home. This substantial downpayment means many are able to make the changeover with a manageable mortgage and some do so without any borrowings at all (ABS, 2008a). The 2005–06 Survey of Income and Housing for Australia showed average housing costs were lower for changeover buyers and such buyers were less likely to have a mortgage than first homebuyers (ABS, 2007c).

The Housing 21 Survey focused on the housing transitions of respondents for the period 1996 to 2006. It asked respondents to list all their movements through the housing market – that is, the relocation from one dwelling to the next – and asked them to identify the primary reasons for the move. For home owners aged 35-54 the primary reasons for moving were 'bought house', accounting for at least 25 per cent of responses, followed by 'moved to better home/location' (around 20 per cent). Movements through the housing market for 'employment or study reasons' came third. These findings concur with the latest Australian data on housing mobility available from the ABS. For couple households with dependent children, 13.4 per cent stated the main reason for their last move was 'employment reasons', 20.6 per cent stated it was 'purchased own dwelling' while the most popular choice at 27.7 per cent was because the family 'wanted a bigger or better home' (ABS, 2009c). Trading up in the market has become an important driver of housing transitions in the late 20th century and early 21st century.

In addition to the trend to moving house, there has been substantial growth in the renovations and additions market, as middle-aged couples seek to extend or renovate their properties rather than move. In the late 1970s, when housing represented 6 per cent of Gross Domestic product (GDP) in Australia, investment

—

in home renovations represented just over 2 per cent of GDP. Now Australians are spending as much on alterations and additions to their homes as they do on new housing, with each accounting for 3 per cent of GDP in 2009 (Lowe, 2010; Stutchbury, 2010). The Housing 21 Survey asked respondents questions on renovations they had undertaken. For households aged 35–54 years, 26.7 per cent stated that they had undertaken renovations, and the main reason given for renovating (73.4 per cent) was that the house was not appropriate to their needs; they needed more room or an extra bedroom. An additional 11 per cent stated that they intended to renovate the house when they bought it. Of those that had not renovated their home at the time of the survey an additional 30.7 per cent indicated they intended to do so. Astoundingly, then, over 57.4 per cent of home owners aged 35–54 captured in the Housing 21 Survey had renovated their home or intended to do so.

To undertake renovations many households restructure their loans and this practice has become an increasing phenomenon over the last two decades. While it may be expected that households refinance to service their initial or original loan, increasingly restructuring has taken advantage of the equity built up in the family home. This equity is put to a range of uses, including renovations, providing additional cash for consumer goods and/or for other forms of investment, such as property or shares. Investigations in the Housing 21 Survey into the refinancing of loans found that 51 per cent of those aged 35–54 years (273 of 535 persons) had refinanced their loans at some stage with the majority (72.2 per cent) doing so to receive cash or increase the outstanding balance of the loan. Respondents were quizzed on the two main uses for the money and the most significant reason was to undertake 'additions, improvements or repairs to property', followed by 'other purchases' (16.8 per cent) and 'to consolidate debt' (10.6 per cent) (see Figure 5.1).

Besides investing in the family residence, increasingly Australians, like the residents of many other nations, are investing in other real estate. In 2008 the ABS reported that approximately 20 per cent of Australians owned holiday homes and investment properties (both residential and non-residential) for rent (ABS, 2008a, p 279). For the population aged 35–54 years in the Housing 21 Survey, 23.7 per cent of households owned holiday homes or other investment properties. While for a limited few this ownership arose through inheritance (1.2 per cent), or the property was a previous home (5.0 per cent), a future home (3.1 per cent), or a holiday home (7.7 per cent), for the overwhelming majority the reason for owning property other than the family home was purely for investment (77.7 per cent).

Clearly it appears that for many mid-life households the accumulation of equity afforded to them by homeownership has resulted in further expenditure on housing consumption, even if part of their commitment could be viewed as investment (Reserve Bank of Australia, 2005). In the 21st century, homes have become much more than just a place of shelter and security. The changing role and meaning of housing is clearly expressed by households in the middle years of life, when lifetime earnings peak; not only do these households consolidate

**Figure 5.1: Mid-life households and the use of money from refinanced loans**

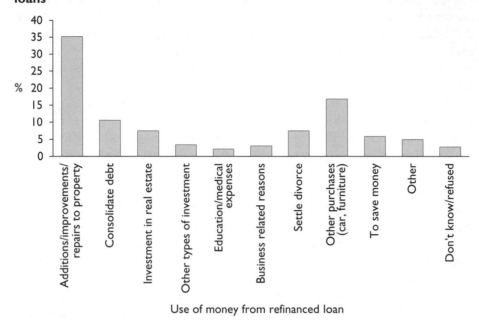

Source: Housing 21 Survey

the ownership of the family home but they also 'over-consume' housing as a mechanism for investment.

Housing success among mid-life affluent households has a measurable impact on the housing market in many developed economies and it also generates previously unseen social and economic processes. Tomaney and Bradley (2007) have shown that increasingly regions need to be able to offer an attractive housing stock to affluent workers in the global knowledge economy if they are to enhance their prospects for economic success. Tomaney and Bradley (2007) tied their analysis of North East England to Florida's (2002) ideas on the creative class and emphasised the way in which an absence of housing attractive to this mid-life group could serve as an impediment to both investment and the relocation of key staff.

## Housing affordability in mid life

Over the past decades, as housing prices have increased more rapidly than incomes, housing costs have consumed an increasing proportion of household income (Yates et al, 2008). In consequence, housing affordability has been a serious issue in many nations, including Australia, the UK, and Ireland. In Australia the majority of households in housing stress are private renters but a significant number are purchasers. Overall housing costs as a proportion of household income in Australia have increased by over 30 per cent since the late 1970s to 15 per cent. Average figures mask differences between tenure types. Average housing costs for outright owners in the highest income quintile in 2003–04 averaged just 1 per cent while for private renters or purchasers in the lowest income quintile average costs were close to 50 per cent of gross household income.

In many nations and many regions access to home ownership requires two incomes. The absence of affordable housing affects all age cohorts, including those in mid life. In Australia, homeownership rates are falling and are projected to continue to fall for mid-life households (Table 5.1). While Yates et al (2007) suspected that some in the early phases of mid life may be delaying entry into homeownership, they agreed that it was unlikely many would purchase housing for the first time once past 40 years of age. Declines or delays in entering the homeownership market put increasing demands on the private rental system. Over the past decade rents have increased and higher-income households have, according to Yates et al (2007), displaced lower-income households from the more affordable housing stock.

The decline in homeownership rates among mid-life households has significant implications as the residents of these households age. Australia's welfare system is predicated on the assumption that older people will own their homes (Yates and Bradbury, 2009), and in this respect Australia is typical of a number of nations reliant upon asset-based welfare systems. In addition, private rental accommodation is commonly seen as unsuitable tenure for older low-income persons (Faulkner et al, 2007; Morris, 2007).

Responses to attitudinal questions within the Housing 21 Survey suggest that the affordability of housing, especially entry into home purchase (via a deposit) and the ability to meet mortgage repayments is shaping housing aspirations and expectations. For mid-life households in the rental market interviewed in the Housing 21 Survey (104 households where interviewees were aged 35–54 years) 40 per cent indicated they had not purchased a home because they could not afford the mortgage repayments. Another 21 per cent had not entered the homeownership market because they could not save a deposit. Homeownership remained a significant aspiration for renters, with 62.7 per cent stating it was important or very important to own a home some day, while another 11 per cent considered it somewhat important. Many of those who stated that homeownership was of little importance or unimportant were disheartened about the prospect of

**Table 5.1: Census and projected age-specific homeownership rates, Australia**

| Age group | Census date | | | Projection |
|---|---|---|---|---|
| | 1981 | 2001 | 2006 | 2046 |
| | Percentage of homeownership | | | |
| 35-44 | 75 | 69 | 68 | 67 |
| 45-54 | 79 | 78 | 77 | 68 |

*Source:* Adapted from Yates et al (2008)

ever buying a home. When asked why they saw owning a home as not important they replied they couldn't afford it or their future was too uncertain. Of those renters who considered homeownership to be worthwhile, however, many (80 per cent) were concerned about their ability to buy a home. Asked if they expected to buy a home in the next five years, only 30 per cent remained optimistic.

Whether purchasing or renting, housing stress is considerable for many mid-life households. Yates and Gabriel's (2006) analysis of a national Income and Housing Survey from 2002–03, showed that more than 40 per cent of all households in housing stress were couples with children and sole-parent families. Similar findings were recorded in a 2005–06 Survey of Income and Housing, where 33.8 per cent of sole-parent families were paying more than 30 per cent of their income in housing costs (Tanton et al, 2008, p 16). This situation, particularly for sole-parent families, is not expected to improve. Projections produced by Yates et al (2008) show that in Australia the percentage of lone-parent families in housing stress will increase rapidly over the next 30 years.

Sole- or lone-parent families have considerable difficulty establishing stable housing. Such households are compromised by the need to find housing suitable for children, have considerably less wealth than other similarly aged family types, are more likely to be living in public or private rental accommodation, and tend to be reliant on a government pension or allowance. As Table 5.2 highlights, one-parent families with dependent children differ significantly in all measures of economic wealth and housing stability, with 40 per cent living as private tenants. Overwhelmingly this depiction of lone- or sole-parent families is about the disadvantaged position of women, as 83 per cent of such households are headed by women (ABS, 2007e).

The Housing 21 Survey allowed an in-depth examination of sole-parent families. Sole-parent households constituted 5 per cent of Housing 21 Survey households (97 females; 26 males). Sole-parent families in the survey were financially disadvantaged relative to other households with a much greater reliance on a government pension or allowance than couple families (61.3 per cent compared with 8.2 per cent respectively) and this was particularly the case for women. For those sole parents within the workforce, women worked many fewer hours than men, with 36 per cent of female sole parents working less than 24 hours a week and 62 per cent working under 34 hours per week. By contrast, 34 per cent of males in this category worked more than 49 hours a week. The difference in workforce participation results in significant variations in household income for men and women. Women's annual household income was concentrated in the lower income categories while male sole parent's income was clustered at the top of the range. Two thirds of female sole-parent households in the Housing 21 Survey reported an income of less than A$41,599 per annum and 46 per cent were living on less than A$25,999 per annum. Over 40 per cent of male sole parents enjoyed household incomes greater than A$62,499 per annum (Beer and Faulkner 2009, p 71). The gap in household earnings was also reflected in the wealth of male and female sole-parent households. Fully 15 per cent of female-headed households in

—

**Table 5.2: Selected economic and housing characteristics of selected household types, Australia, 2005–06**

| Household characteristics | Unit measure | One-parent family with dependent children | Couple family with dependent children | All households |
|---|---|---|---|---|
| **Financial assets** | | | | |
| (Value of: accounts with financial institutions, shares, trusts, debentures, bonds, own incorporated business} | $000 | 21.6 | 123.0 | 108.5 |
| Superannuation | $000 | 26.1 | 100.2 | 84.5 |
| **Non-financial assets** | | | | |
| Value of owner-occupied housing | $000 | 141.1 | 376.2 | 286.1 |
| Value of other property assets | $000 | 42.2 | 130.1 | 90.7 |
| Value of other non-financial assets (contents of building, car etc) | $000 | 49.4 | 339.2 | 85.6 |
| **Gross household income** | | | | |
| Median income per week | $ | 724 | 1,637 | 1,040 |
| **Source of income** | | | | |
| Government pensions and allowances | % | 50.9 | 6.9 | 26.1 |
| Wages and salary | % | 43.6 | 80.9 | 59.3 |
| **Tenure and landlord type** | | | | |
| Owner without mortgage | % | 12.8 | 17.0 | 34.3 |
| Owner with mortgage | % | 27.0 | 61.8 | 35.0 |
| Renter State/Territory Housing Authority | % | 14.8 | 2.0 | 4.7 |
| Private landlord | % | 40.1 | 16.3 | 22.0 |

*Source:* ABS (2007d)

the Housing 21 Survey had wealth – exclusive of housing – of less than A$10,000 and 50.6 per cent had assets of less than A$50,000. Male sole-parent households, by contrast, had much greater wealth, with just 7 per cent holding wealth apart from housing of less than A$10,000 and three quarters holding assets in excess of $A50,000 (Beer and Faulkner, 2009, p 71). The Housing 21 Survey allows a greater exploration of the housing circumstances and aspirations of sole-parent families than is available elsewhere. Female-headed sole-parent households were more likely to have children resident in the household and women sole parents were more likely to live in a house (83.5 per cent) than male sole parents (75.9 per cent). Both groups were slightly over-represented in semi-detached housing and flats/units relative to the general survey population. The greater concentration of female-headed sole-parent households in separate households is an outcome of the distribution of assets following the breakup of a relationship and the need for housing to accommodate children (Beer and Faulkner, 2009). Sole-parent households of both genders were over-represented in rental housing and under-represented in homeownership. Of female-headed sole-parent households who had moved from home purchase into the private rental market, 67 per cent indicated that they did so because of a relationship breakdown. Most female sole parents fell out of homeownership because they could not afford the mortgage, while just one female sole parent moved to private rental because their ex-partner received the dwelling. By contrast, just one male sole parent left owner-occupation because he could not afford home purchase (Beer and Faulkner, 2009).

Among sole-parent households in the rental sector, men placed greater importance on entering home purchase, with 67 per cent reporting that they felt it was very important for them to buy a home, compared with 47 per cent of women sole parents. Male sole parents also had a far higher expectation that they would be able to buy in the next five years, with 73 per cent in this group, compared with just 32 per cent of women. Female sole parents were more likely to be concerned about their capacity to afford to enter into homeownership, with 40 per cent reporting that homeownership was unimportant to them simply because they could not afford the mortgage. Women sole parents were more likely to have applied for public housing than men, and of those who applied just over one quarter were on the public housing waiting list (Beer and Faulkner, 2009).

While most sole-parent households felt that it was unlikely or very unlikely that they would move in the 12-month period post interview, data collected on the number of times respondents had moved home since 1996 suggests sole parents are mobile. Female-headed sole-parent households were much more mobile than male sole-parent households; a reflection of the insecurities of the private rental market, as well as their changing household circumstances.

The Housing 21 data show that male and female sole parents had differing attitudes to their housing decisions and careers. For example, female sole parents were less likely to believe that their housing choices had been part of a longer-term plan (59 per cent for male sole parents and 50 per cent for female sole parents). Women in the Housing 21 Survey were more likely to report that their relationship had affected their housing, while men considered their financial circumstances had been more important. By contrast, male sole parents placed a greater emphasis on entering homeownership as a lifetime housing goal. These results suggest that the stronger financial circumstances of most male sole parents have given them greater capacity within the housing market when compared with female sole parents and therefore differing aspirations. Women sole parents in the Housing 21 Survey, while viewing home as an investment, also saw home purchase as a risk. It is clear that the low incomes of female sole-parent households have significantly shaped their attitudes to housing as both a desirable and a 'risky' investment (Beer and Faulkner, 2009).

Clearly housing affordability is an issue currently touching mid-life households. It affects both their current housing circumstances but also future housing

—

prospects and aspirations. These outcomes would be transferable to many developed economies around the globe, and unless governments can find a way to improve the sustainability of their housing systems these results will have significant consequences for the well-being of such households into the next stage of the life course – older age.

## Housing in mid life: success, challenges and transitions

This chapter has highlighted the diversity in housing sequences amongst current mid-life households. In many respects a dichotomy exists between those who have suffered an interruption to their housing at a crucial juncture in their life course compared with those who have followed a more conventional sequence of housing transitions. For the former group, housing in mid life is an issue of risk and shocks, with changes in personal household demography spilling over to long-term implications for their housing aspirations and their capacity to meet those goals. There is a significant gender dimension to the distribution of 'risky' mid-life housing, with women who are sole parents at considerable risk. By contrast, in Australia and many other developed nations, homeowners who remain in stable relationships consolidate their position in the housing market during this stage of life and many are able to enhance both their consumption of housing and their opportunities to accumulate wealth.

# SIX

# Housing transitions in later life

Stereotypically, old age has been viewed as a time of reduced income, incapacity, frailty and dependency. This perspective has directed the development of policies and planning for an older population and resulted in a focus on the provision of retirement incomes and the delivery of care. Often, little attention has been directed to other aspects of life, such as the suitability of housing and the functioning of the communities in which older people live. This common image of old age is at odds with contemporary trends, as the citizens of advanced economies live longer than ever before, enjoy a better quality of health, are wealthier, more active and more aspirational than previous generations of older people. These trends will only accelerate over the next two to three decades. Older age in the 21st century will be very different from older age in the 20th century and there is consequently a pressing imperative to move away from a view of old age as a period of frailty and dependency and instead focus on understanding the needs and wants of older individuals. For many in older age, housing decisions are likely to be governed by consumption factors and choices rather than ill-health, disability and social isolation. Overall, the housing market positions and transitions of those in later life are changing, and this transformation is increasingly important for the whole of society as the housing demanded by the older population will drive housing markets, housing policy and welfare support measures.

## Conventional and emerging housing transitions for older households

For much of the 20th century older people who had left the workforce were either seen as not having a housing career or were considered to be at the end of their engagement with the housing market, with only retrograde movement in prospect. The circumstances of the time-limited lifespan after retirement, few resources and therefore modest aspirations, generally meant housing in older age was a matter of staying put and effectively ageing in the family home. Housing and care of older people was the domain of the family and those with no or limited resources had to rely on charitable organisations and state institutions where the quality of accommodation and care was of variable quality (McNelis and Herbert, 2003).

In the 1950s and 1960s in Australia, the US and the UK other options emerged, mainly to cater to those in need: retirement homes, independent living units, cottage homes, sheltered housing, assisted living, and convalescent or nursing homes. In Australia in 1954 the Commonwealth government entered into aged care through the Aged Persons' Homes Act 1954. Dargavel and Kendig (1986) believe this Act was instrumental in establishing the basic foundation and directions to guide the development of aged housing and aged care in Australia. As noted by McNelis and Herbert (2003, p 8), the objective and purpose of the Act was the provision of independent housing for older people, 'in particular homes at which aged persons may reside in conditions approaching as nearly as possible normal domestic life, and, in the case of married people, with proper regard to the companionship of husband and wife'. The Act sought to achieve these objectives through the provision of capital subsidies to voluntary/not-for-profit/charitable organisations. By 1969, however, the subsidies were being used increasingly to fund residential care – hostels, nursing homes and personal care – at the expense of the provision of independent housing. Rapid growth occurred in the establishment of residential facilities such that by the late 1970s Australia had many more nursing home places in relation to population size than comparable countries (Hogan, 2003; Fine, 2007). This trend in residential care facilities in Australia was mirrored in countries such as the US and the UK (Rowles, 1993; Peace, 2003). An outcome of the availability of residential care places was that, in Australia at least, some older people found themselves in hostels and nursing homes mainly because their housing was inappropriate rather than because of their need for acute care (McIsaac, 1997; Faulkner, 2001).

The growth of residential care homes was supported intellectually by a focus within gerontological theory on decline, dependency and disengagement among older persons (Rowles, 1993; Heywood et al, 2002) leading to the general belief that these residences 'were the normative final destination for the elderly' (Rowles, 1993, p 68). Housing developed for older people was customarily thought of as housing for people with special needs (Hanson, 2001, p 29). These developments reinforced a negative image of the elderly as 'vulnerable and needy' and requiring relocation to specialist services and housing. These beliefs, however, persisted at a time when the overwhelming majority of older people in Australia (over 90 per cent) and throughout the developed world, continued to live in their homes in the community (Howe, 2003).

In the mid 1980s the demographer Hugo (1986, p 33) examined the social and economic implications of population ageing in Australia and commented that 'Today there is considerable debate and concern in Australia about the lack of intermediate accommodation available to the aged between two extremes: the detached three-bedroom house in which the aged originally raised their children, and some form of institution'.

In Australia growing interest in housing for the older population arose out of a series of reforms that began in the mid 1980s, in particular the House of Representatives Standing Committee on Expenditure (1982) *In a Home or at Home: Home Care and Accommodation for the Aged*. This report calculated the escalating cost to government of continuing to provide residential care and how this contrasted with people's wishes to remain at home in the community. This report resulted in a rapid move away from residential care to community care and contributed to growing interest in ageing in place. The term 'ageing in place' arose from humanistic research in the 1970s and 1980s that investigated the deep attachment that older people have with home – a place of special meaning – providing people with not only a physical but emotional sense of self identity (Davison et al, 1993; Dupuis and Thorns, 1996;).

Ageing in place has become the cornerstone of policy for the older population in Europe, North America, Japan, Australia and other countries with a rapidly ageing population. It has led to a reorientation of the way housing and social policy for the older population is conceived (Pastalan, 1997; Bochel et al, 1999). The policy recognises the desire of older people to remain in familiar environments and is seen to optimise opportunities for well-being and healthy ageing. Brink (1990, 1998, 2002) also notes that ageing in place policies are also attractive to governments because they reduce public sector outlays on specialist aged housing. Indeed, Brink (1990, 1998) argues that such policies are inevitable in an ageing society, given the potentially high cost of alternative policies (James, 2009). Regardless of the fiscal drivers for the recasting of policy, housing constitutes an important part of the complex and interrelated factors that influence well-being. However, this policy framework was not supported by a substantial evidence base; relatively little research on the housing of older people existed at the time either in Australia or internationally (Tinker, 1997). This absence was highlighted by *The Mid Term Review of the Aged Care Reform Strategy Stage Two* (DHHLGCS, 1993, pp 133-4). The review found that 'surprisingly little primary research has been carried out into any aspects of aged persons housing over the last decade'. In particular it highlighted the absence of evaluations of residents by housing type, measures of resident satisfaction, costs of different housing options and a lack of understanding of housing transitions. Since that time there have been much greater research efforts into the housing issues, needs and aspirations of the older population, as well as policy attention directed toward ageing and housing.

As is the case for many countries, Australia's population is undergoing fundamental change with the ageing of the population. Over the coming decades older people will make up an increasing proportion of Australia's population such that by 2056 people aged 65 years and over will represent between 23 and 25 per cent of the country's population (ABS, 2008b)[1]. In addition between 2001 and 2026 in Australia, older people will account for between 53 and 57 per cent of the projected increase in the total number of households (calculated from ABS, 2004a). Similar increases are expected or are coming to realisation in other developed nations and even China has a rate of population ageing that matches that of Australia. Like all age groups the older population are not a homogenous group: they have different lifetime experiences, characteristics, abilities, needs and behaviours that result in a diversity of views and expectations about the suitability of housing and the communities in which they live. The choices people make regarding their housing are heavily dependent on the options available to them, including the housing types available and the capacity to take advantage of the choices on offer. Tenure is one of the most significant factors influencing older people's ability to make choices.

## Homeownership, home purchase and rental housing in older age

*Homeownership and purchase*

Homeownership remains a near-universal aspiration in many nations, including New Zealand, the US, the UK, Ireland and Canada. In Australia, one of the outstanding features of the housing characteristics of the older population is the very high level of homeownership and the stability in this level over the last two decades (Howe, 2003). At the 2006 Census, 83 per cent of the population aged 65 years and over were homeowners, with 75 per cent outright owners. This is one of the highest rates of homeownership in the world (Yates and Bradbury, 2009). The baby boom generation (those aged 50–64 years at the 2006 Census) have followed this trend with 83 per cent owning, or currently purchasing, their home.

Homeownership is generally viewed as an advantage in older age as it provides security of tenure, reduced housing costs in retirement, and the means to alter through the housing market a person's housing situation to suit their needs. However, there is considerable diversity in the situation of older homeowners and this diversity will intensify with the entrance and passage of the baby boomers into, and through, older age. Australia's current aged population have considerable wealth when compared with the rest of the population. Those aged 65 years and over have almost double the wealth of the population aged 15–64 years (Kelly, 2003, p 8). Most of this wealth is tied up in the family home and they have limited alternative forms of wealth accumulation available to them, especially if they are no longer attached to the workforce. In consequence, the current generations of the aged population are heavily dependent on a government pension (78 per cent of older Australians) (Kelly, 2003, 2009; AIHW, 2009). Being asset rich but income poor influences the ability of older people to maintain their homes, or modify them according to need. The situation for the baby boomers, however, will be more variable. Like the previous generations of older people, the home will be the major asset for many, but there will be greater variation within the baby boomer cohort with respect to assets and income (Heady et al, 2008, p 16).

Economic theories such as the life cycle and permanent income hypotheses (VanderHart, 1995) suggest that homeowners will use their accumulated assets to support themselves in later life. As the home generally forms the major asset then it is expected that older home owners will become renters or downsize. Wood et al's research (quoted in Flatau et al, 2003, p 15) suggests that older homeowners would be financially better off if they became renters. The evidence in Australia and overseas, however, suggests that older people do not draw down on their housing wealth (Crossley and Ostrovsky, 2003; Dolan et al, 2005; Olsberg and Winters, 2005). Possible reasons for the reluctance of older people to consume housing wealth vary from country to country but include high transaction costs associated with moving, uncertainties within the rental market, the lack of readily available information on products, mismatch between saleable price

—

of the family home and the purchase price of a smaller home in the same area; the conservative nature of older persons and the desire to pass on this wealth to children or grandchildren (Olsberg and Winters, 2005; Bridge et al, 2009). For the current generation of older persons in Australia another possible reason may be their attachment to their current homes (Davison et al, 1993; Faulkner, 2001) but it is more likely to be linked to the asset tests associated with the Aged Pension and Veterans Affairs Pensions. The value of one's home (principal dwelling) is exempt from the assets test associated with income support payments (pension) but the net returns of the sale of a home are subject to this test and would affect the eligibility for these payments.

Survey research in 2005 (Olsberg and Winters, 2005) suggested community attitudes to the use of housing wealth were little different amongst the first wave of the baby boomers, those aged 50–59, when compared with earlier generations. In the early to mid 2000s there were indications that equity release products were being increasingly considered by older people (Sheen, 2002), but the global financial crisis has seen a reversal in this trend, with a decline in products and providers and increased wariness amongst consumers (Bridge et al, 2009).

There is a strong probability that the current pattern of high rates of homeownership among older age groups will decline in Australia, and may well fall in other nations such as the UK, the US and New Zealand. Yates et al (2008, p 43) suggest that by 2045 homeownership rates among those aged 65 years and over will have declined from 82 per cent in 2006 to 72 per cent. This decline will result in increased pressure on the rental sector and older Australians, for whom homeownership has served a hedge against rising living costs in retirement.

## Rental housing

Rental accommodation is significant for a small proportion of the older population in Australia. Depending on landlord type and individual circumstances, rental housing can be either a suitable housing option or an inappropriate type of housing for people as they age. Around 13 per cent of the population aged 65 years and over in Australia live in rental accommodation: 35 per cent in government-provided housing, nearly 8 per cent in community/cooperative/church-provided housing and the remainder (57 per cent) in private rental housing. Within the older population the proportion renting has been relatively stable over time. One of the characteristic features of the majority of older renters in Australia, however, is that it is not tenure of first choice, but instead it is one of necessity.

As always, projections vary, but Jones et al (2007, p 39) estimated that the number of low-income older people requiring rental accommodation will more than double from 195,000 persons in 2001 to 419,000 people in 2026, while the number of low-income households is expected to rise from 154,000 to 336,000 over the same period. It is projected that much of the demand will be in lone-person households, which will themselves double in number between 2001 and

2026 to 243,000 households. Two thirds of these lone-person households will be sole women (Jones et al, 2007).

McNelis (2007a) provides a different series of projections based on eligible demand from older people for social housing. Eligible demand, he suggests, can come from three different sources: households in public housing, households in other rented dwellings, and households living in non-private dwellings. McNelis assumes that all older persons renting or in non-private dwellings constitute eligible demand as the proportion of this older age group on high incomes is relatively low (p 55). Consequently, he projects a significantly higher number of households will require rental housing than Jones et al's study. Under his criteria, in 2001 eligible demand for rental housing from older persons was 249,315 persons in 209,210 households. This is projected to increase to 436,058 persons aged 65 years and over in 365,914 households by 2016 (p 54). Clearly, no matter which projections are used, the overwhelming outcome is considerable growth in the demand for, and pressure placed upon, the rental sector.

The increase in the number of older renters is not simply a consequence of the overall ageing of the population and the passage of the baby boomers into older age. It is, and will continue to be, the consequence of a number of processes including choice, the inability to enter the homeownership market earlier in the life course and unanticipated changes in personal and financial circumstances. Though the number of renters aged 55 years and over captured in the Housing 21 Survey was small, 82 per cent had previously been in the homeownership market. The reasons given for leaving homeownership were both voluntary and involuntary, with relationship breakdown accounting for over one quarter of responses.

## Social housing

Social housing has traditionally been provided in Australia as a long-term alternative to private ownership and it has been an important avenue of accommodation for single older people, especially women. It has been able to provide housing that specifically caters for the needs of older people. Many older persons who are currently resident in this tenure entered the system as part of a young family and over time have aged within the public housing system. Data from Australia's 2005 National Social Housing survey show that 75 per cent of tenants aged 75 years and over had lived in public housing for more than 10 years with nearly two thirds of the group aged 65–74 years having lived within the public housing system for more than 10 years (McNelis, 2007a). Many of these tenants had also lived in the same house for most if not all of this time (59 and 50 per cent respectively had lived at their current address for more than 10 years), and when asked where they saw themselves living in five years, the majority believed it would be within public housing (74 per cent of those aged 65–74 and 62 per cent of those aged 75 years and over).

Older social housing tenants in Australia view their housing very positively and surveys indicate tenant satisfaction is high or very high among older people

(Faulkner and Bennett, 2002; Faulkner et al, 2007; McNelis, 2007a). There are a range of reasons as to why this tenure is so well regarded, including the affordability and security the tenure offers, as well as the availability of maintenance and modification services when needed. The high degree of satisfaction enunciated by the respondents also reflects, in large measure, their gratitude for secure and affordable housing. Older tenants acknowledge that their tenure in public housing has had a positive impact on their well-being. The 2005 National Social Housing Survey found 65 per cent of 65- to 74-year-olds and 61 per cent of those aged 75 years and older believed public housing had improved their overall quality of life (McNelis, 2007a). Despite their high levels of satisfaction with this tenure type and their age, the Australian ideal of homeownership still persists, with over one third of tenants aged 65–74 and nearly one quarter of those aged 75 and over indicating in the National Social Housing Survey that they would like to buy their current home.

Social housing as a long-term option for older low-income residents is under pressure in Australia. At present, public housing meets well under half the eligible demand from older persons. Over the last few years state housing authorities in Australia, as in the UK, Ireland and New Zealand, have been selling publicly owned assets. In Australia, since 2001 there has been a 20 per cent decline in publicly owned stock (Atkinson and Jacobs 2008; Department of Families, Housing, Community Services and Indigenous Affairs, 2009) and a reorientation of policies in relation to access. It is now unlikely that social housing will be able to maintain its current levels of provision, let alone account for the expected increase in demand. While there are other social housing options, the reality is that many older low-income people in the coming years will have to seek other options, particularly the private rental market.

### Private rental housing

While private rental housing in Australia may provide greater choice for some, very few older tenants benefit from this broader housing stock as their incomes and assets are inadequate to provide choice within the market. Unlike public rental tenants, whose rents are set at a maximum fixed percentage (25 per cent) of their income, private tenants are at the whim of the market, a market in Australia that is tight and becoming tighter. Many older people are confronted by accommodation that is inaccessible, inappropriate, unaffordable and/or insecure. Security of tenure is a significant problem for older renters as it means they are vulnerable to frequent relocation and the associated social and emotional disruption. It is difficult to provide a continuum of care in such circumstances and consequently aged persons living in the private rental sector have long been identified amongst those in greatest housing need (Kendig, 1990b; Roberts, 1997).

Research by Faulkner et al (2007) into older private renters in Elizabeth – one of Australia's most deprived areas – highlights the daily struggle some householders face financially and socially. For example, older renters in Elizabeth paid a substantial proportion of their limited income each week in rent – up to 60 per cent – leaving them with little for bills and other daily living expenses. Most did not have strong family and friendship networks and social isolation was a pressing issue. What relationships they did have were jeopardised by the instability inherent to their tenure. Mobility was a constant fact of life. Period of residence in the current house for most participants in the study varied from just six weeks to 15 months and many had moved five or six times over the previous four years. Relocation because of the end of a lease, because of increases in rent or abusive neighbours was a financial burden and source of stress. While government rent assistance helped offset the impact of private rental costs, it is, according to Yates and Bradbury (2009, p 16) 'often inadequate to protect households from after housing poverty'.

## Income, wealth, and bequests

Despite the focus of world ageing agendas on 'positive ageing', 'healthy ageing' and 'active ageing', the impact of an ageing population on individual nations and the world as a whole has often been framed in negative and alarmist terms. Commonly it is presented as a crisis that will result in the collapse of public pension systems, overwhelmed healthcare systems and create intergenerational conflicts (Merette, 2002). However, the impact of the ageing of the population is likely to be mitigated by a number of other factors, including the wealth holdings of the older population.

In Australia there have been concerns about the capability of the government to provide the healthcare, aged care and welfare services necessary to sustain the level of personal well-being expected by the population. Concerns about Australia's ageing population and its impact on the government's fiscal outlook into the 21st century have resulted in the release of three Intergenerational Reports (Commonwealth of Australia 2002 2007, 2010). The findings of the 2010 report, *Australia to 2050: Future Challenges*, raised concerns for the then Prime Minister, Kevin Rudd, who worried about Australia's ageing population because 'public finances will be burdened with the increased costs of looking after the needs of older Australians – in health, aged care and age pensions …[and] tax revenues won't keep pace with those rising costs' (Rudd, 2010).

### Income and wealth

### Retirees

As with other developed economies, Australia's population aged 65 years and over has considerable wealth relative to other age groups, with much of this wealth tied up in the family home. The majority of the population aged 65 years and over have retired from the workforce. In 2007 this equated to 85 per cent of the aged population (AIHW, 2009) and this group have few other assets. In consequence, around 78 per cent of those aged 65 years and over receive an aged pension or a similar means-tested payment from the Department of Veterans Affairs. Unlike many European nations not all older persons in Australia are eligible for income support, as access is contingent on demonstrable low income and limited income-producing assets. One reason for the reliance on government benefits is the low level of superannuation[2] funds available to this group. In 2007 only 46 per cent of those aged 65–69 and just 21 per cent of people aged 70 years and over had superannuation. This compares with 87 per cent of people aged 25–54.[3]

In Australia, establishing estimates of the wealth of people is reliant in the most part on survey data. Research by Headey et al (2008) on the structure and distribution of household wealth in Australia using 2002 data indicates that at the time the median net worth of the population aged 65-74 was A$318,000 and this declined to A$244,500 for those aged 75 years and over. Within each of these cohorts there was considerable disparity. At the 10th percentile of the distribution for people aged 65–74, net worth stood at just A$19,900 and for those aged 75 and over a net worth was just A$15,300. At the other end of the spectrum – the 90th percentile – the corresponding figures were $1.1 million and A$768,000.

Kelly (2009) examined the income and non-housing wealth of older Australians and found that if the home is excluded the average savings of older people diminished considerably. This research found that in 2009 the average non-housing wealth for the population aged 65 years and over was A$146,600 and was greater for couple households at A$190,100. The lowest figure was for lone-female households at just A$98,900 (Kelly, 2009, p 13)[4] and slightly lower again for those no longer in the workforce: A$107,500 for men and A$81,600 for women. These data are averages and mask within cohort differences. The assessable assets of those receiving government support payments are considerably less. In 2008 the average value of assessable assets for people receiving the full pension was just over A$32,000 and for those receiving a part pension A$133,000 (AIHW, 2009). Incomes displayed a similar pattern, with those receiving a part pension having an average accessible income of A$9,988 per year and those receiving a full pension just A$983 per year.

The age of eligibility for the Aged Pension in Australia has changed over time and will continue to do so in the coming years. In June 2008 the age of eligibility for women was 63.5 years, increasing to 65 years by 2014, and for men it was 65 years. Government policy is that the eligibility age will rise to 67 years by 2023 (AIHW, 2009). Until recently the full rate pension for a single person was set at 25 per cent of male total average weekly earnings. An inquiry into the cost of living pressures on older Australians (Commonwealth of Australia, 2008b) and a subsequent comprehensive review of the pension in 2008 (Harmer, 2009) concluded that 'the rate of pension for single people living by themselves …is too low' (Harmer, 2009, p xiii) to provide 'a basic acceptable standard of living, accounting for prevailing community standards' (Harmer, 2009, p xii). As a result of this review the government increased pensions to 27.7 per cent of male average weekly earnings in September 2009 (Macklin, 2009). Clearly inadequate incomes on limited assets shape the housing decisions of older persons in Australia and other nations.

### The baby boomers: wealth in old age?

In Australia the baby boom generation is commonly seen to be comprised of those born between 1946 and 1965, although debate around the precise boundaries continues (Beer et al, 2006a). Importantly, while baby boom generations have been identified in many developed economies, their size and timing has varied. The baby boom generation emerged earlier in the US than in Australia, and continued for longer in New Zealand (Hugo, 1986). Regardless of their precise timing, baby boomers are seen to represent a sea change in demographic profile and to have transformed economies with their greater numbers, social experimentation and enhanced wealth. Potentially, baby boomers will reshape aged housing across the developed world over the coming decades, with the cohort's leading edge already exerting a considerable impact.

The baby boom generation comprises around one quarter of the population in Australia and holds most of the nation's household wealth (Kelly and Harding, 2007). In common with the generations before them, much of their wealth is invested in homeownership, but in addition they are more likely to have other asset sources they can access. Kelly and Harding (2007) detailed the income and wealth characteristics of Australia's baby boomers and argued that while this generation is more comfortable with debt and hold higher debt levels than previous generations, baby boomer households appear to be the wealthiest households in Australia. Based on 2004 data each baby boomer had, on average, accumulated A$381,100 compared with A$292,500 for all Australians. The average household headed by a baby boomer in 2004 had a net worth of A$650,000: 42 per cent of this household wealth was held in housing with another 17 per cent in superannuation. As with those aged 65 years and over there are significant disparities within the cohort, with Kelly and Harding (2007, p 180) finding 'the poorest one-quarter of baby boomers possess 4.4 per cent of the group's net worth while the wealthiest one-quarter enjoy 60 per cent of the boomers' A$1,648 billion net worth'. Headey et al (2008, p 16) found similar results with data from 2002, suggesting that while those aged 55–64 were the wealthiest cohort the disparities between households was enormous. The net worth of the bottom 10 per cent of the cohort was just A$17,100 and the net worth of those in the top 10 per cent was $1.5 million.

In contrast to the current population aged 65 years and over, a greater proportion of the baby boom generation will be better able to support themselves through old age. In addition to superannuation and other investments, the assets of the baby boomer generation have been boosted considerably by ownership of a second property. Much of the blame for the present housing affordability problem has been directed at the baby boomer generation and older, wealthier people.

A large proportion of the debt increase comes from older and wealthier people buying bigger houses in better areas, or purchasing investment properties. That exuberance has had a ripple effect on housing prices everywhere, including among those who can afford it less. (Hewett, 2007, p 21)

Figure 6.1 provides evidence from the Housing 21 Survey of the extent of ownership of property other than the principal dwelling. For the population aged 75 years and over, ownership of a second home was low and indicative of the traditional reason for owning a home – as a place to live. Many also do not have, and would not have had through their lives, the disposable income and opportunity to invest in another property. The proportion increases significantly (nearly 80 per cent) for the population aged 65–74, but it is for those people aged 55–64 years that housing has become a consumer item, not just a place of residence. Nearly 31 per cent owned a property other than their residence.

It is clear from the Housing 21 Survey that the overwhelming reason for baby boomers to own a property other than the principal dwelling was as an investment. These data support the notion that financially able baby boomers moved into the property market in the late 1990s and early part of the 21st century in order to boost their wealth in preparation for retirement.

**Figure 6.1: Ownership of property other than the principal dwelling**

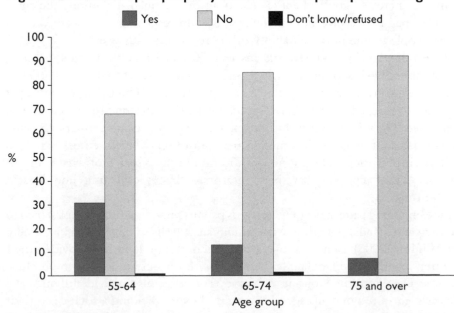

*Source:* Housing 21 Survey

### Bequests

Bequests to children or grandchildren are a long-standing tradition in many nations and have a considerable impact in countries with a history of mass homeownership. This practice has involved a sense of obligation on the part of parents and 'rightful' expectation of inheritance on the part of children. Though there is limited research, there are a number of indications that a growing percentage of older people are changing their attitudes and 'spending the children's inheritance'. As one person noted in a qualitative interview for the Housing 21 Survey:

> I think the difference there is that now you do it for yourselves, you don't do it for the kids, because you know they will grow up and they will get on and they will manage, and eventually they will leave home, so who cares? Very much, you spend your kid's inheritance, and I think it's the only way to go, because if you've brought the kids up properly, they won't need the inheritance. (Minnery and Zacharov, 2006, p 46)

In part, these changes reflect the greater range of lifestyle opportunities and choices available to older persons – including growth in luxury accommodation for aged persons, expansion of privately provided services to the older population and increasing longevity. In a more mobile and affluent society, fewer children and grandchildren will develop an expectation of inheriting the 'family home'. These changes also reflect a market reality: whereas once older persons may have retired owning a property valued at one or two times average annual wages, rampant house price inflation has meant that many older outright owners now own an asset of considerable value. These opportunities for an enhanced quality of life, as well as constraints – such as increased longevity; lack of adequate financial planning; increased government expectations of self-financing among the aged; and user pay policies for health, community and residential care – are causing older people to question their ability or desire to bequeath assets.

Research involving 6,000 Australians aged 50 years and over in 2004 (Olsberg and Winters, 2005) showed that when asked 'Do you expect to use up all of your assets while you are alive?', 28 per cent expected to do so. This belief was strongest amongst those aged 50–59 years, with 35.2 per cent expecting to need to use all their assets. The findings varied by housing tenure (70 per cent of renters expected to have no assets left) and income (83 per cent of self-funded retirees expected to have surplus assets). There is no qualification in the research of what is meant by 'assets' but it appears to have been interpreted by respondents as liquid assets, not housing.

One emerging pattern is a trend towards parents providing financial assistance to children and grandchildren while the parents are still alive. The research by Olsberg and Winters (2005) found that over one third of respondents had provided their children or other younger family members with financial assistance to purchase a home. Data from the Housing 21 Survey confirms this trend, identifying over 20 per cent of respondents aged 55 years and over providing assistance to their children. While those in a better financial position are more able to provide help, even those with few assets had assisted their children, as many believed their children would be unable to enter the housing market without their help. Other respondents provided financial assistance so that their children could purchase investment properties.

## Housing and locational preferences

The impact of an ageing population in the 21st century requires planning for substantial shifts in the lifestyles, aspirations and demands of older people. The stereotypical view of old age as a time of dependence and care is not an accepted view of older age held by the incoming groups – the baby boomers – into later life. The lifetime experiences of the young old and the baby boomers (greater education and employment opportunities, changing family structure, greater affluence, increased consumerism, greater mobility and varied housing experiences, for example) coupled with increasing life expectancy, an extended period of retirement, and new opportunities, have spawned a generation of older people unlike any previously known. The social, demographic and economic changes that have accompanied the baby boom generation have provided the means and desire to structure their own identity through lifestyle choices, and, as Clapham (2005a) has argued, housing is a critical part of this search for fulfilment. For this generation of older persons, housing 'is a means to an end rather than an end in itself' (Clapham, 2005a, p 213). This changes the nature of housing transitions in later life and has significant implications both in defining ageing in place as well as a number of other policy arenas.

As Phillipson (2007) highlights, older people and the baby boomers are increasingly able to make choices about where they want to live, how they want to live and with whom they want to live, as well as the lifestyles they wish to lead. This is not new, but 'the idea that substantial groups of older people are able to control and shape their environment *is* relatively new' (Phillipson, 2007, p 330). The traditional sequencing of housing in older age assumes that older households have limited aspirations for future housing, and mobility has been assumed to be low and infrequent. Current research suggests this is changing. Research by Olsberg and Winters (2005, p vii), from a survey of 7,000 Australians aged 50 years and over, found that the baby boomers (respondents aged 50–59 years) were the least likely of all the respondents to wish to age in place and were comfortable with moving. Olsberg and Winters (2005, p ix) concluded that 'for them the notion of ageing in place was likely to conjure up images of immobility and old age, something which is not yet part of their cultural vocabulary'. A high degree of mobility among those people on the cusp of the baby boomer years (people aged 55–64) was also evident from the Housing 21 Survey (Beer and Faulkner, 2009). In the decade prior to the survey a surprising 41.5 per cent of people aged 55–64 had moved at least once, with 25.7 per cent moving three or more times. In both studies the younger age groups (baby boomers) were the most likely to indicate they were likely to move again. Clearly the residential mobility patterns of the baby boomer generation will be different from those of earlier generations but exactly what the new residential strategies of the older population will be is yet to be determined (Bonvalet and Ogg, 2008). Already for those older people seeking particular lifestyles post retirement, the terms 'sea change', 'tree change' and even 'tee change' have become associated with the movement of those approaching retirement to seaside locations, rural scenic locations and golf courses.

Like all age groups in society the older population is not homogeneous. They have different lifetime experiences, characteristics, abilities, expectations, desires, needs and behaviour. Consequently, there are a wide range of views about housing as people age, and a wide array of factors that are likely to influence housing choice. However older people's aspirations and expectations evolve with society's changing expectations, desires and aspirations. Consequently, while they are a very diverse group, detailed research in South Australia indicates there are some commonalities in what older people are looking for. Often they are looking for housing with two to three bedrooms, which is well designed, easy to manage, adaptable if necessary, affordable and incorporates environmental design features. This housing would preferably be in small clusters of 10 to 20 houses located within the communities in which older people are familiar, whether this is an area they have always lived or a place that is more aesthetically pleasing, such as the hills or coast. It would be close to public transport, key shops and other services. The overriding preference of older people is to remain in their own home in the community with which they are familiar for as long as possible (Beer et al, 2009).

The development of housing specifically to cater for the needs of older people has a long tradition in the UK, Europe, the US, New Zealand and Australia. In the UK much of the development has been around the provision of integrated housing with care and support, so-called sheltered and extra sheltered housing. In Europe, the US and Australia the focus has been on the development of retirement villages. In the US retirement villages tend to be provided by the private sector, whereas in Australia retirement villages have generally been the province of government and the not-for-profit sector, catering to the needs predominantly of low-income households. Recently, however, there has been a rapid increase in private and public for-profit corporations that recognise the potential of catering to the changing aspirations of the baby boomers and the financial means of this group. Profit margins within the retirement village industry are best achieved by targeting wealthy baby boomers and offering luxury retirement village accommodation. While such developments are affordable to a section of the baby boom population, the increasing polarisation of wealth among the older age groups means that many miss out on this style of housing.

## Support services in advanced ages

Policies in Australia and many other nations support the desire to remain within the community but with increasing age this wish becomes, for many, problematic because of the increasing need for some type of help or support. In Australia, around one third of people aged 85 years and over lives in some form of cared accommodation (AIHW, 2009, p 89). One of the realities of ageing is the probable need for people to contend with some form of disability in their advanced ages. These disabilities restrict activities of daily living and raise questions about the suitability of their accommodation arrangements.

Population surveys measuring levels of disability within the Australian population clearly indicate the significance of disability with increasing age (AIHW, 2003, 2009). In the survey of disability, ageing and carers undertaken in Australia in 2003 (ABS, 2004b), 51 per cent of the population aged at least 60 reported a disability that lasted or was likely to last for at least six months and restrict everyday activities. Of people aged 60 years and over, 19 per cent had a profound or severe core activity limitation, but this was much more prevalent at the oldest ages, affecting 58 per cent of those aged 85 years and over.

In 2006 the Australian Census included questions on the need for assistance in day-to-day activities due to a profound or severe disability. The data showed that the proportion of the population needing assistance increased considerably with increasing age: just over one fifth of those aged 75–84 needed assistance. The rate doubled for those aged 85 years and over, to 47.4 per cent. Disability levels were higher for women than men from the age of 65 years onwards. At age 85 and over 57.5 per cent of women needed assistance because of a disability compared with 43.5 per cent of men (Hugo, 2007).

As the overall health status of a population improves there are questions about trends in the incidence of morbidity and disability, particularly within the older population. Within some OECD countries, there is evidence to suggest a decline in disability prevalence among older age groups. Mathers (2007) suggests that at present there is no clear evidence of this trend in Australia. He notes that even if age-specific rates were to fall over the next 10–20 years, it is likely that prevalence and severity rates will increase with the ageing of the population as a higher proportion of the population will be in the oldest age groups where disability levels are greatest. Health and disability, therefore, are likely to exert a considerable influence on housing decisions.

The Housing 21 Survey enquired about the provision of care and assistance on a regular basis by any member of the household to any person who has a long-term health condition, is elderly or has a disability. Households where the respondent was aged 55 years and over were more likely to be providing care on a regular basis than households where the respondent was aged 18 to 54 years. For households where the respondent was aged 55 years and over, 17.6 per cent of households were providing care compared with 11.3 per cent of households where the respondent was aged less than 55 years of age. For persons aged 55–74 provision of care was evenly split between caring for someone in the household and caring for someone outside the household. In many instances this would be caring for elderly parents living elsewhere. By the age of 75 years more people provided care for someone in the household than for people living elsewhere, and this responsibility generally fell on women. In addition, and increasingly with age, many older people with a disability (particularly women) lived on their own and were therefore reliant on the provision of informal care from family or friends or formal support services. This group was most vulnerable to moving to residential care.

The availability and provision of informal care is central to the ability of many people to remain living in the housing of their choice. It also underpins Australia's community care system (AIHW, 2009). The availability of informal care, however, is expected to diminish as the baby boomers age (Percival and Kelly, 2004). Informal carers are increasingly in the workforce and are themselves ageing and hence may become less capable of intensive caring responsibilities. In addition, baby boomers have fewer children to take on care responsibilities and these children are likely to live at greater distances from their parents than has been the case for previous generations (Hugo, 2003; Percival and Kelly, 2004).

As the baby boomers move into the older age groups greater numbers of older people will need to purchase services privately if their needs are going to be met. Many will need to rely on publicly funded services. There are a number of programmes currently in Australia (**Table 6.1**), the largest of which is the Home and Community Care Program (HACC) that provides 'a comprehensive coordinated and integrated range of basic maintenance and support services for frail aged people, people with disability and their carers' (Department of Health and Ageing, 2008). This programme is supported by a similar one operated by the Department of Veteran Affairs to service veterans, war widows and widowers. Recognising the need to provide greater levels of care similar to that available in low-care and high-care residential facilities (previously known as hostels and nursing homes), more flexible care programmes were introduced by the federal government in the 1990s. These programmes – the Community Aged Care Package, Extended Aged Care at Home package and Extended Aged Care at Home for Dementia package – provide more intensive support and are designed as a community-based alternative to residential care.

These publicly funded programmes are targeted at those most in need and are already overstretched. A Report on Government Services by the Productivity Services (2006) found that the needs of over one third of people aged 65 years and over who required assistance with at least one everyday activity in 2003 were not met. In addition, organisations are already finding it difficult to recruit and retain staff to provide existing services.

While the more intensive packages are highly valued (Table 6.1) they are in limited supply and this means many older frail people, particularly women, have no choice but to enter a residential care facility if they require support regardless of their desire to do so or not. As of 30 June 2008, 150,481 people aged 65 years and over in Australia were permanent residents in aged care homes and The Australian Nursing Federation predicts an increase of 56 per cent in such residents by 2020.

Residential care, while a necessary part of the care system, is seen as a last resort by older people. This point of view and the targeting of community care services to those in greatest need is leading to a push for the development of supported

**Table 6.1: Community and flexible care programmes: services provided, and clients aged 65 years and over receiving programmes, 2007–08**

| Programme type | Services provided | Funding organisation | Number of clients |
|---|---|---|---|
| Home and Community Care (HACC) | Domestic assistance, meals, other food services, transport services, home or garden maintenance, activity programmes (home or centre based), social support, personal care, counselling (care recipient and carer), goods and equipment, home modifications, respite care, linen services, nursing (home and centre based), allied health/ therapy (at home or centre) | Federal government (60 per cent), state and territory governments (40 per cent) | 638,218 |
| Veterans' Home Care | Domestic assistance, home or garden maintenance, personal care, respite care | Department of Veteran Affairs | 77,284 |
| Veterans' Community Nursing | Personal care, nursing | Department of Veteran Affairs | 32,625 |
| Community Aged Care Package (CACP) | Domestic assistance, meals, other food services, transport services, home or garden maintenance, activity programmes (home or centre based), social support, personal care, respite care, linen services | Department of Health and Ageing | 33,411 |
| Extended Aged Care at Home (EACH) | Domestic assistance, meals, other food services, transport services, home or garden maintenance, activity programmes (home or centre based), social support, personal care, counselling, respite care, linen services, nursing (home and centre based), allied health/ therapy (at home or centre) | Department of Health and Ageing | 3,354 |
| Extended Aged Care at Home for Dementia (EACHD) | Domestic assistance, meals, other food services, transport services, home or garden maintenance, activity programmes (home or centre based), social support, personal care, counselling, respite care, linen services, nursing (home and centre based), allied health/ therapy (at home or centre) | Department of Health and Ageing | 1,314 |

*Source:* Adapted from AIHW (2009, p 120)

type accommodation in Australia, a housing option that has been available in the UK, the US and parts of Europe for some decades. While the government has paid considerable attention to the development of a community-based aged care system, the development of supported or integrated housing with care and support has been neglected (Jones et al, 2010).

## Older persons and their housing in the 21st century

This chapter has reviewed, predominantly in the Australian context, the housing circumstances and housing transition patterns of the current older population and of the baby boomers about to be classified as older persons. While in the past the older population was considered to be a reasonably homogeneous group with limited demands in terms of their needs, expectations and aspirations in late life, the movement of the baby boomers – a group who have been described as 're-writing' life histories and ushering in substantial social, economic change – into the older age groups is causing a reorientation of older people's housing transitions. The leading edge of the baby boomers is differentiated from previous generations entering retirement age by their much greater asset base, especially housing wealth, but also superannuation. This means that unlike previous generations, a significant proportion of this group has the means to engage in consumer-led retirement lifestyles involving much greater mobility and a willingness to change housing to meet preferences.

It is clear that the older population of the 21st century will require and expect a range of housing options and support systems that enable them to live independently, in the communities of their choosing, no matter what their economic circumstances. An ageing population inevitably focuses attention not only on the suitability of housing but the communities in which members of the community live.

### Notes

[1] In 2007 the population aged 65 years and over comprised 13 per cent of Australia's population (ABS, 2008a).

[2] In Australia the term superannuation is used to refer to private retirement savings. The same savings – and their consequent income stream – would be referred to as a pension in the UK. Modest compulsory superannuation was introduced for all persons in Australia's paid workforce in 1990.

[3] Prior to 1992 the availability of superannuation to employees was reliant on the employer having such a scheme. In 1992 the government instituted compulsory superannuation, the Superannuation Guarantee. Under government legislation employers are required to contribute superannuation for employees. The level of contribution began at 3 per cent of an employee's earnings and this was then incrementally raised to the current 9 per cent. (Kelly et al, 2002). Research indicates that government spending on pensions into the

future would be reduced by 2.3 per cent over 30 years if the superannuation guarantee was raised to 12 per cent (Kelly, 2009).

[4] Personal savings are defined as the estimated sum of the value of cash deposits, shares, superannuation and net business assets (Kelly, 2009).

# SEVEN

# Housing and disability: a 21st-century phenomenon

Conventional accounts of housing careers and even housing pathways present, in some ways, a monochromatic view of households and the housing they occupy. The concept of a housing career holds cogency for young, middle-class household members of Anglo-Celtic backgrounds born in the 1950s, but sheds little light on the more complex realities of households in the 21st century. One of the areas where this gap is most acute is in our understanding of the relationship between disability, households and housing. In most developed economies over the last 30 years there has been a profound move away from institutional housing for persons with a disability to accommodation within the broader community. In some instances this accommodation has been appropriately funded, but in many cases it has not. The relationship between disability and housing is not a niche issue: in Australia 22 per cent of households have one or more household members affected by a disability (Beer and Faulkner, 2009), and similar rates of prevalence are evident in comparable nations. The AIHW (2003, 2007) estimates that some 6 per cent of the Australian population is affected by a profound disability – defined as 'a severe or profound core activity limitation' where the individual requires assistance with meeting his/her daily needs. Under current population estimates, this equates to 1.3 million persons, and if similar rates of prevalence apply in the US and the UK, 21.6 million persons and 3.6 million persons respectively are affected.

The impact of disability on the housing sector in the 21st century is not simply a matter of scale; the care and other needs of persons with a disability are profoundly reshaping the relationship between households and their housing. In the latter part of the 20th century 'home' was an important place for caring for children. In the 21st century 'home' will be increasingly important for the provision of care for adults. The Housing 21 Survey found that 13 per cent of households provided care for a person living within their home and 9 per cent provided care for a person living in another household. Critically, disability does not simply reshape the housing of the affected individual; instead it recasts the housing opportunities, movements and costs of all members of the household and often the outcomes of family members or care providers living elsewhere. To add to this complexity, the housing circumstances of individuals affected by different types of disability vary considerably and those with a sensory disability, mobility impairment, psychiatric disability or cognitive impairment all move through the housing market in different ways. This chapter considers the ways we should conceptualise the housing transitions of persons with a disability and their households, before moving on to consider the evidence on both the housing of persons with a disability and the housing of family members who provide care.

## Housing transitions and disability: conceptualising the relationships

In many ways the concept of disability is problematic within a discussion of housing transitions and there are two fundamental challenges. First, it can be argued that while individuals may have an impairment, it is society – and the inappropriateness of its institutions, built forms, transport arrangements and so on – that creates disability. Second, the discussion of disability and housing creates an expectation that impairment results in a relatively uniform impact on both housing outcomes and movement through the housing market, with all persons affected by disability sharing a single set of housing outcomes and affected by uniform processes. The reality is that disability is not uniform and the housing market impacts vary significantly according to the source, nature and severity of the disability (Figure 7.1). Each can be thought of as a significant determinant of housing achievement for persons with a disability, with an individual's position on each axis shaping their landscape of housing opportunities and constraints and acting independently of the broader set of factors shaping housing outcomes for the population as a whole. For example, a person with mobility impairment acquired through an accident for which they can be compensated (such as a work-related injury or a motor vehicle accident) will have a very different housing

**Figure 7.1: Conceptualising disability and its impact on housing careers**

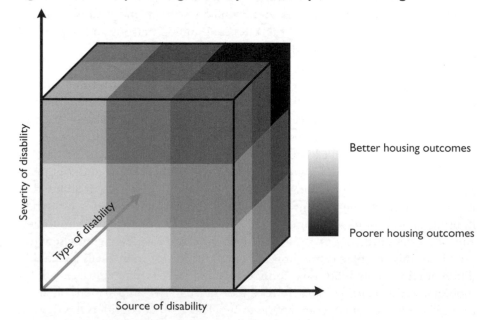

*Source:* Housing 21 Survey

career when compared with someone who has had identical mobility impairment (such as paraplegia) since birth.

The impact of disability on housing transitions varies considerably according to the severity of the impairment: a person in a wheelchair may have a very different set of housing needs from a person who relies on a walking frame. In addition, some disabilities, such as a mobility impairment associated with polio, worsen over the life course, so that potential and actual housing needs change. To further complicate the analysis, many persons have more than one condition; they may, for example, have both a hearing disability and an intellectual disability, or they could have suffered a stroke and experienced both the loss of mobility and cognitive function. Importantly, we have to acknowledge that housing transitions vary considerably for persons with a disability, and that while there are common elements between and across disability groups, an individual's housing transitions will be determined by the nature, scale and source of the disability.

Prior to moving to consider the ways in which disability shapes housing transitions in the 21st century, it is important to examine how households as a whole are affected by disability. The household rather than the individual is the primary unit of analysis in the overwhelming majority of housing research, because it is the household as a whole that occupies the dwelling; it is the household which takes decisions to move or relocate; and, it is the household as an entity which pays for accommodation. There is substantial discussion in the published research around the impact of disability on the housing careers of family members (Beer et al, 2006a) and this work has noted that parents with care responsibilities face higher housing costs and greater transport expenses as a consequence of disability; that one or more adult members of the household is often unable to engage in paid work due to their care responsibilities, thereby reducing household income; and that care givers will often choose housing that meets the needs of the person with a disability, rather than optimise their own preferences. Lower household income reduces the level of choice within the housing market and may truncate housing aspirations. Society, however, relies upon the efforts of unpaid carers to meet the needs of those affected by disability (Jenkins et al, 2003). Importantly, we can conclude that it is the housing career of the household as a whole that is affected by the presence of a disability.

## Indicative housing careers by type of disability

As discussed earlier, disability or impairment type significantly affects the interaction between the individual and/or household and the housing market. Figures 7.2 to 7.6 provide indicative housing transitions for persons and households affected by disability. The figures draw upon the outcomes of focus groups undertaken by Kroehn et al (2007) and are meant to illustrate outcomes rather than provide a definitive account. A more detailed discussion of housing transition by type of disability will be provided later, alongside an examination of the factors shaping housing for persons with a disability. The figures have deliberately been drawn to

**Figure 7.2: Indicative housing career for a person with mobility impairment acquired through injury**

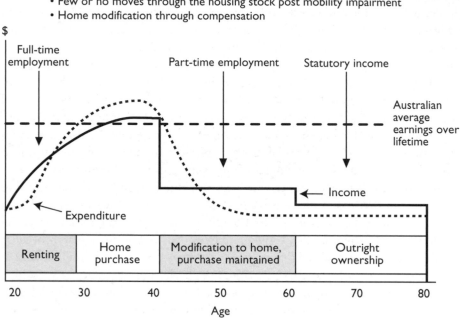

**Mobility impairment through injury**
- Few or no moves through the housing stock post mobility impairment
- Home modification through compensation

*Source:* Devised by authors of book, based on Williams (2003)

provide a point of contrast to the housing transitions of the mainstream population. A line indicating average earnings over the lifetime has been added to highlight the income constraints affecting persons with a disability and their households.

The housing career of a person affected by mobility impairment as a consequence of an accident is presented in Figure 7.2. In the figure the housing career is seen to track the trajectory for the mainstream population, after which income falls, expenditure falls and the individual maintains their position within the housing market through modification of the home they are purchasing – paid for by a compensating body such as a motor accident compensation authority or work-related insurance – and then remains in that dwelling through to old age. Implicit within the figure is a high degree of immobility because of the challenge of finding an accessible dwelling in combination with limited income.

Figure 7.3 offers an indicative housing career for a person with mobility impairment present since birth and differs substantially from its predecessor even though the disability is the same. The figure highlights the potential significance of the source of disability with both the end point and stages in the housing career varying significantly. Key issues include: lower lifetime earnings because of an inability to secure well-paid employment and periods of un- or underemployment; a longer period living in the parental home, when compared with societal norms;

**Figure 7.3: Indicative housing career for a person with mobility impairment present since birth**

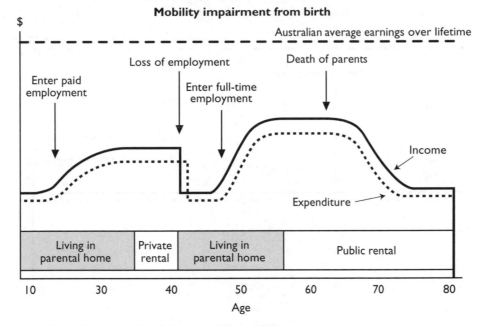

Source: Devised by authors of book, based on Williams (2003)

a return to the parental home in adult life due to the absence of appropriate and affordable alternatives; the impact of the death of parents who have had substantial care responsibilities; and housing outcomes that terminate in public rental housing rather than owner occupation.

The two figures, therefore, emphasise the way in which the source of disability affects housing career and demonstrate the ways in which disability per se can be seen to shape housing outcomes through the life course. There is not a single set of housing transitions for persons affected by mobility disability but there are common drivers in terms of lower income and the need to live in an accessible dwelling. These factors have a demonstrable impact on housing outcomes.

Figure 7.4 offers a different perspective on the housing careers of persons with a disability, focusing on the housing of persons born with a cognitive impairment. In this instance the individual has a flat employment history and set of housing transitions: living with their parents until late middle age (when the parents either die or are unable to continue to provide care) and then living in a community facility. The individual's income is low throughout their life, with employment provided through a specialist facility or activity centre. There is only the one significant transition through the housing market and it is precipitated by demographic processes outside the control of any individual and one which generates substantial angst for many care givers, as well as significant challenges for policy makers. Persons with a developmental disability may have a housing

**Figure 7.4: Indicative housing career for a person with a developmental disability**

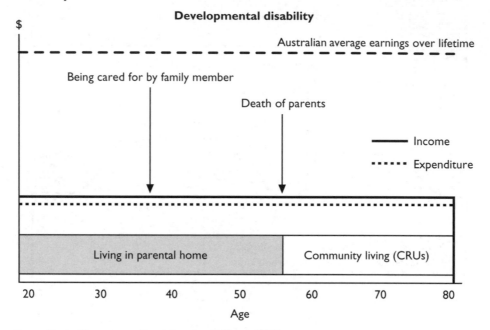

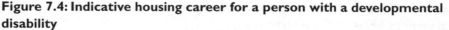

*Source:* Devised by authors of book, based on Williams (2003)

career that is largely determined by the housing opportunities family members are able to provide. The inability of family members to continue to offer care, through death or their own ill-health, can force a transition in the housing of this group. Family members with care responsibilities are aware of the need to plan for the housing of their family member for when they are no longer able to care for them, but find it difficult because the alternatives are unattractive.

Persons with a psychiatric disability are likely to have a much more variable housing career than persons affected by other disabilities (Figure 7.5). The episodic nature of much mental illness results in both periods in and out of employment, as well as significant transitions through the housing market. Unlike the previously discussed disabilities, persons affected by a psychiatric disability are likely to report periods of homelessness, and incidences of living in caravan parks or other insecure accommodation. There is also a high probability of eviction and/or ongoing transition from one tenure to the next. Figure 7.5 reflects the lag-effect periods of mental illness have on the transitions an individual makes in the housing market. Importantly, homeownership is not represented as the outcome of the housing 'career' for this group, instead social rental housing is suggested.

Finally, Figure 7.6 illustrates the likely housing career of a person affected by a sensory impairment, and in this instance it draws upon the experiences of the deaf. They are represented as having both a stable housing career and stable employment, though the latter is not necessarily well paid. Significantly,

**Figure 7.5: Indicative housing career for a person with a psychiatric disability**

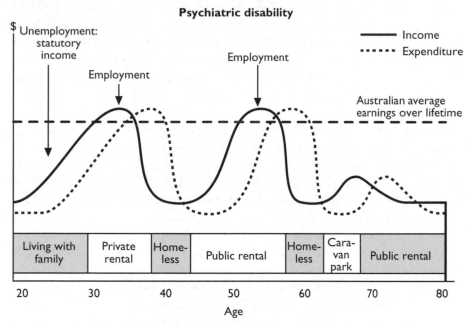

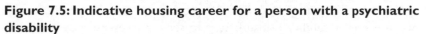

*Source:* Devised by authors of book, based on Williams (2003)

**Figure 7.6: Indicative housing career for a person with a sensory impairment**

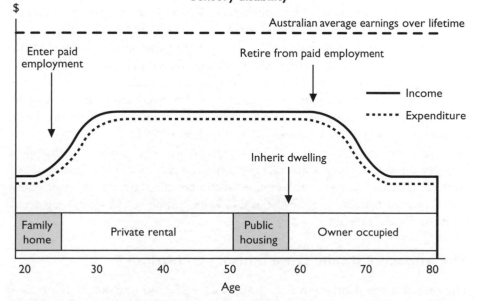

*Source:* Devised by authors of book, based on Williams (2003)

in Australia persons born profoundly deaf often live within the private rental market because their disability is insufficient to secure access to social housing and they are unable, for a range of reasons, to enter home purchase easily. Those unable to hear have relatively restricted employment opportunities; this limits their income and therefore their capacity to repay a mortgage. The figure suggests that homeownership is eventually achieved through the inheritance of a dwelling. The figure also assumes that family members provide significant assistance to the person with a hearing impairment, even though the hearing-impaired enjoy a high level of independence.

The five figures present an abstract 'ideal type' based in large measure on insights garnered from qualitative data collections. The diagrams suggest both similarities and differences across circumstances, and also indicate drivers of housing transitions for persons with a disability that are very different from those evident for the population as a whole. Key issues include the fact that in four of the five figures persons with a disability are seen to have less variability in their housing transitions than the population as a whole. This inertia is a consequence of the limited options available to many persons with a disability and their limited capacity to express their housing needs within the market place. Low incomes – and potentially truncated working careers – result in a limited capacity to express choice. This immobility is significant because individuals with a disability have little opportunity to adjust their housing to meet their current needs or as they proceed through stages in their life course.

A second critical concern is the need to recognise that persons with a psychiatric disability may have complex housing careers that reflect episodes of profound ill health and associated difficulties in maintaining employment. Importantly, persons with a psychiatric disability are more likely than other groups to experience periods of homelessness or inadequate housing as part of their long-term sequence of housing circumstances (Commonwealth of Australia, 2008a). This may, in part, reflect difficulties in remaining in the family home, sustaining relationships or remaining well. A third concern is that social housing is much more prominent in the housing of persons with a disability than for the general population. Persons with an impairment or long-term health condition are more likely to gain access to this tenure because of the considerable disadvantages confronting them, including low income, discrimination and higher living costs. These figures do not offer a definitive account of the housing careers of persons with a disability, but they do suggest themes that deserve further exploration. They raise issues of policy importance because the stability of the housing circumstances of many persons with a disability suggests that it should be possible to engage in long-term planning for their needs.

## The impact of disability on housing transitions

The presence of a disability has the potential to affect an individual's transitions through the housing market. The Housing 21 Survey asked all respondents a suite of questions that related to disability and the provision of care for persons with a disability. Through these questions it was possible to identify all households where one or more persons had a disability or long-term health condition, and where one or more household members provided care. Of the 2,698 households who participated in the Housing 21 Survey, some 595 households (22 per cent) reported that one or more household members had a long-term health condition, disability or impairment. This rate of self-reported disability is consistent with both the 2006 Census (Hugo, 2007) and earlier ABS collections on the prevalence of disability. In the Housing 21 Survey in most instances only one household member had a disability, but in 74 cases two persons were reported as disabled and in three instances there – seven per cent of the total population and 30 per cent of households living with a disability – respondents reported that a household member needed assistance with self-care, mobility or communication. This figure is compatible with the AIHW's (2003) estimate of the incidence of disability to the extent that it represents a 'core activity limitation'. Some 381 respondents reported that they or a member of their household provided care and assistance to a person with a health condition or disability. Of this group, just over half (53 per cent) were assisting a person living within their household, while 54 per cent reported that a household member was assisting a person living outside their household. In approximately 10 per cent of cases, household members assisted both a person within their household and a person living elsewhere.

The presence of a disability within a household can have a profound impact on housing careers. Over 40 per cent of disability-affected households in the Housing 21 Survey reported that health and disability factors had a very important impact on their lifetime housing decisions, and this insight applied only to households where the respondent was under 65 years of age, thereby controlling for age-related disabilities and health conditions. Overall, households where one or more persons had a disability tended to be smaller than households where no disability was present, with two-person households accounting for 43.4 per cent of the total. The smaller number of conventional 'families' would account for this difference. Analysis of the Housing 21 data revealed significant variation between the tenure of households where the respondent was under 65 years of age and one or more persons had a disability, on the one hand, and the tenure of households where no member of the household reported a disability, on the other. The former households were, in percentage terms, less likely to be home purchasers, and more likely to be outright homeowners. At the same time, households where a disability was present were more likely to be renting or paying board.

Importantly, the source of tenancy varied between households affected by disability and those where disability was not reported. While 22 per cent of respondents to the Housing 21 Survey were tenants within the public rental sector, fully 39 per cent of households where a disability was present rented from a government agency, compared with 16.1 per cent of the population of households where disability was not recorded. These data are consistent with information on new housing allocation released by the AIHW (2007). Persons with a disability were also over-represented in community housing.

Just fewer than 50 per cent of private rental tenants from across the general population rented from a real estate agent, compared with 24 per cent of households where a disability was present. Overall the tenure data suggest a significant dependence on the social housing sector when one or more persons have a disability. This outcome reflects contemporary allocation policies and the tight rationing of the social housing stock (Parkin and Hardcastle, 2004).

### Housing affordability and disability

Households where one or more persons are affected by a disability tended to have both lower mortgage payments and lower rents than the general population. Significantly, while the lower rents paid by households affected by disability reflected the more modest cost of housing in the public rental sector, mortgage payments did not.

It is important to acknowledge that lower incomes and lower housing costs than the general population may result in a greater incidence of unaffordable accommodation for households where one or more members has a disability. The data presented in Figure 7.7 and Figure 7.8 suggest that housing affordability is a major challenge for households affected by disability, especially within rental housing. Just fewer than 15 per cent of households paying rent and where one

**Figure 7.7: Housing affordability for tenants aged less than 65 years, by presence of a disability**

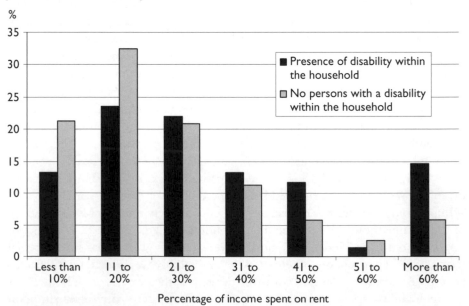

*Source:* Housing 21 Survey

**Figure 7.8: Housing affordability for home purchasers aged less than 65 years, by presence of a disability**

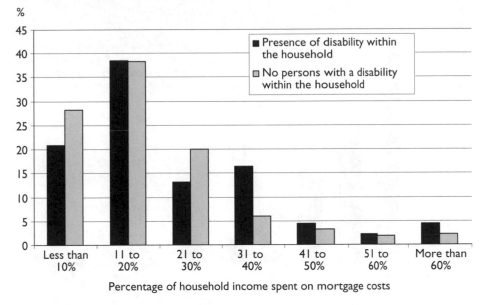

Source: Housing 21 Survey

or more person was affected by a disability or long-term health condition paid more than 60 per cent of their gross income for their housing.[1] Fully 36 per cent of households affected by disability and accommodated within rental housing (including public rental housing, which is capped at approximately 25 per cent of household income) paid more than 30 per cent of their income for housing.

### Disability and movement through the housing market

For a range of obvious, and also not so apparent, reasons, movement through the housing market is much more difficult for households affected by the presence of a disability than for the general population. The Housing 21 Survey showed that households where one or more persons was affected by a disability had much lower relocation rates than the general Australian population (Figure 7.9), with fully 40 per cent of households affected by disability not moving or only moving once over the decade prior to the survey, compared with 30 per cent of households unaffected by disability. Many households affected by disability have simply been priced out of the housing market and this was reflected in a lower rate of take-up of the Australian government's First Home Owners Grant (FHOG) among persons with a disability than for the population as a whole (Beer and Faulkner, 2009).

Overall, many persons with a disability were 'trapped' residentially by a complex set of processes that limit their capacity to relocate to better or more appropriate

**Figure 7.9: Number of times moved, by presence of a disability, all households, 1996–2006**

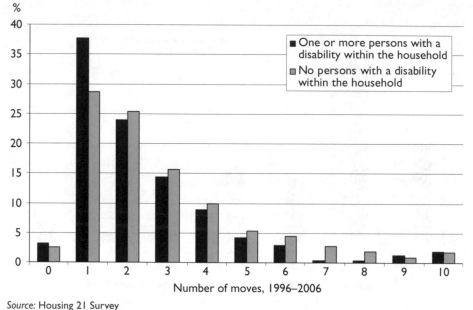

Source: Housing 21 Survey

housing. For example, a female interviewee living in inner Melbourne noted that her current dwelling did not meet her aspirations or those of her partner. However, she was reluctant to move because she did not believe she could find a dwelling in a more attractive neighbourhood that was affordable, offered access to public transport equal to that available from her current home and was accessible for a person in a wheelchair. She also noted that she had modified her current home to make it appropriate for her disability. Any relocation would require an equivalent additional investment in the new dwelling and she expected such expenditure would be beyond her means.

Finally it should be recognised that the relative immobility of households affected by disability should be a matter of policy concern because, as Baker (2007) notes, residential relocation is one of the most important ways in which a population adjusts its housing to better meet its needs, including its health needs. A population unable to move through the market because of unaffordable housing may be forced to live in accommodation that does not suit its circumstances or adversely affects its health.

## Housing transitions by type of disability

As discussed previously, the type of disability and when and how it was acquired can significantly affect a household's housing career. This section examines the variability in the housing careers of people with a psychiatric disability, mobility impairment, cognitive impairment and sensory impairment. The Housing 21 Survey provides some indications of the way in which disability shapes housing outcome, but it provides no indication on any of these four dimensions. To overcome this gap, a specialised disability survey was undertaken in Victoria, focused on three regions: Gippsland, as an example of a non-metropolitan region; the region in and around Darebin, an inner metropolitan area; and Melton/Brimbank, as an example of an outer metropolitan region. In all instances a modified version of the Housing 21 Survey was applied in order to facilitate comparison with that national data collection instrument. The survey instrument had to be truncated considerably for those with a cognitive disability, and in other instances the questionnaire was modified to reflect the potential impact of disability on housing experience. Some 417 interviews were completed with persons with a disability and with carers in the target groups.

## Psychiatric disability

Psychiatric disability can have an enormous impact on every aspect of a person's life. The episodic nature of the illness, resulting in high levels of unemployment, dependency on government-provided income support, and consequent low incomes restricts choice within the housing market. Moving house for this group is a recurring theme and many find it difficult to maintain good relationships with others, including family members. In consequence, they do not have strong networks of support, as is often the case for others with a disability. Saugeres (2008) found many with a psychiatric disability could not turn to their families for support. The lack of interaction with family and friends, poor engagement with welfare agencies and often an inability to make responsible decisions, makes this group particularly vulnerable to social isolation and poor housing outcomes. This in turn had the potential to heighten the impacts of their illness and place them at jeopardy of homelessness. Their lack of financial and human resources makes them particularly vulnerable to living in situations of risk – abuse as well as vulnerability to drugs and alcohol.

A total of 77 persons with a psychiatric disability responded to the specialist survey of persons with a disability, with most respondents aged 25 to 55 years. Some 55 per cent of respondents lived by themselves and a further 31 per cent lived in a household with just one other person. Half lived in a flat, unit or caravan park, while 39 per cent lived in a separate house; 71 per cent were renting. These results are partly a function of the way in which participants were recruited – with several accommodation and service providers collecting the data on our behalf – but are also likely to reflect a more general trend among the population affected by psychiatric disability. Fully 61 per cent of tenants (and 42 per cent of all respondents) rented from the social housing sector, with a further 22 per cent renting from real estate agents and 5.6 per cent from a parent or other relative. Over 27 per cent of respondents with a psychiatric disability had applied for social housing at some stage and 13 per cent were currently on the public housing waiting list. Over 55 per cent of tenants reported that they rented because they could not afford mortgage payments; only 8 per cent of respondents were homeowners and 9 per cent were paying off a mortgage.

Some 20 per cent of persons affected by a psychiatric disability lived with at least one other person with a disability. However, 40 per cent of persons with a psychiatric disability lived by themselves and this is a much higher rate of lone-person living than for the Australian population as a whole. Some 47 per cent of persons with a psychiatric disability had never married or formed a permanent relationship, 13 per cent were separated from their partner, and 19.5 per cent were divorced. Only 16 per cent of respondents were currently married and 4 per cent were living in a de facto relationship. This is a very distinctive household structure and one which inevitably generates housing transitions that are not shared with the broader community. Incomes for this group were very low, with 34.5 per cent of respondents with a psychiatric disability reporting a household income of less than A$12,999 per annum and 90 per cent reporting a household income less than A$26,000 per annum.

## Mobility impairment

Data collected through the disability-focused survey provides quantitative insights into the housing transitions of people with mobility impairment. Approximately half the respondents had mobility impairment for all or most of their lives, with the remainder acquiring impairment in adulthood. Persons with mobility impairment were much under-represented in home purchase, with just 14 per cent buying a home, compared with 39 per cent outright owners and 37 per cent renting. Some 4 per cent lived rent free and a further 4 per cent lived as a dependent with parents. Fully 56 per cent of tenants with a mobility impairment rented from a state housing authority and a further 6 per cent rented from a cooperative or equivalent organisation. Just 18 per cent of tenants with a mobility impairment rented from a real estate agent and 35 per cent had applied for public rental housing at some stage of their life. A total of 32 per cent of tenants with mobility impairment had been owner-occupiers at some stage in their life and this group has had a high rate of departure from owner-occupation. Just under half of tenants with a mobility impairment reported that owning their home one day was important or very important to them, but 20 per cent said it was unimportant. However, 90 per cent of tenants with mobility impairment did not expect to enter homeownership in the next five years, and the contrast with the expectations of the general population of tenants is stark.

Just over one quarter of respondents with a mobility impairment had undertaken major renovations of their home because 'the house was not appropriate to needs' (eight respondents), to 'avoid the costs of moving' (one respondent) and 'to adjust the house for a person with a disability' (nine respondents). Clearly, the challenges of living in the housing stock drove many households to modify their dwelling. Half the respondents reported that their current dwelling fitted their needs very well, and a further 28 per cent said it met their needs well. However, 19 per cent believed that their home did not meet their needs well at all. Participants were more concerned about how well their present home would meet their needs into the future, with 19 per cent indicating that they did not believe their home would meet their needs very well in five years, and 9 per cent indicating that their home would not meet their needs at all. Respondents indicated that insufficient finances, the absence of continuing employment and the lack of suitable housing options prevented them from moving to more appropriate housing. Significantly, 42 per cent of households affected by a mobility disability had not moved dwelling in the decade to 2006 and 71 per cent had moved once or not at all over the decade. These data reinforce the argument that households where mobility impairment is present have a limited capacity to move through the housing market and secure housing that better meets their circumstances.

Mobility impaired respondents to our survey reported attitudes to housing through their life course that differed from the general population: they were less likely to attach value to the material/asset dimension of housing, but were more likely to value highly the physical environment of the dwelling and the access it offered to services. Among the mobility impaired, only 31 per cent rated as very important the capacity to live close to work, but 63 per cent considered living close to services and support a very important feature of housing. In addition, 78 per cent of the mobility impaired acknowledged that their disability had been a very important determinant of their lifetime housing goals and 66 per cent felt that their health had been very important in shaping their housing decisions.

### Cognitive impairment

A total of 29 persons with a cognitive disability participated in the disability survey and they ranged in age from 22 to 61 years, with a mean age of 40 years. Members of this group had either a developmental disability or a cognitive impairment acquired later in life. Just fewer than half this group lived in a house; 16 per cent lived in a flat, unit or apartment; 20 cent lived in a community residential unit (CRU); and 7 per cent lived in other supported accommodation. Of the respondents affected by a cognitive impairment, 70 per cent paid rent or board, 40 per cent lived with their family, 20 per cent lived with friends, and a further 20 per cent lived with other unrelated adults. Only 13 per cent lived by themselves. Many reported very stable housing careers: only 22 per cent had lived in their current dwelling for less than five years and 6 per cent had lived in the same dwelling all their life. Just over 55 per cent of respondents had not moved at all within the last 10 years, and 96 per cent had moved three times or less over the last decade. These data support the conclusion that this population group typically experiences a very stable or 'flat' set of housing outcomes. For them transition through housing is largely a matter of lived change within the same dwelling and/or household.

Respondents reported very favourable attitudes to their current housing, with few looking to move and most valuing their home for the people and relationships embedded in that place. Only 12 respondents worked and they mostly worked one or two days a week only. Family members were nominated as the most important care givers in their life, with staff from support organisations the second most important source of care and assistance. Cooking, assistance with transport and help with craft activities were the most important forms of assistance reported.

### Sensory impairment

A total of 52 persons with a sensory disability participated in the focused survey, with almost 90 per cent of interviewees affected by vision impairment. The population interviewed was an older group, with 47 per cent aged over 75 years and 72 per cent aged over 54 years. Outright homeownership was the largest single tenure amongst the sensory impaired, accounting for 47 per cent of the total, with 11 per cent paying off a mortgage, followed by 33 per cent in rental housing. Just 5.5 per cent had been given life tenure of their property by a relative and 3.6 per cent were living rent free. No other disability group reported similar levels of direct family assistance with housing. Only a small percentage of persons with a sensory disability had renovated their property or intended to do so in the foreseeable future.

Exactly half the persons with a sensory disability who were renting their property rented from the social sector, with 25 per cent renting from a private agent, 18 per cent renting from a relative and 6 per cent from a community group. Of the 16 sensory impaired persons renting their housing, nine had previously been owner–occupiers and seven of these were now renting rather than purchasing a dwelling because of the difficulty of affording mortgage repayments: 85 per cent of this group did not expect to enter home purchase in the next five years.

Most persons with a sensory disability believed their present home suited their needs well (38.8 per cent) or very well (57.1 per cent). They anticipated that their housing would continue to meet their needs over the next five years. That said, one quarter of respondents indicated that they would like to move to a different home, though few expected that this would happen. Finances and the lack of ongoing work were the major impediments to relocation. Overall, the sensory impaired, consistent with their age profile, were a stable population, with 61 per cent not moving at all over the previous decade and 24 per cent moving once only.

Persons with a sensory disability placed a great emphasis on the location and/ or environment of their housing. A total of 41 per cent of respondents considered location had been very important in shaping their lifetime housing goals and 34 per cent believed it had been important. For all disability groups, the ability to gain ready access to services is one of the key drivers of their lifetime housing decisions. Persons with a sensory disability also recognised that their impairment had shaped their lifetime housing goals, with 39 per cent assessing it as a very important influence and 32 per cent as an important influence. Significantly, 73 per cent believed they had been very successful or successful in achieving these goals.

## Carers

Family members who provide support for people with a disability have housing careers shaped by their care responsibilities. Providing care can have a significant impact on families and individuals with respect to their social networks and mental health (Edwards et al, 2007), financial resources (Hughes, 2007) and other relationships (Spicer, 2007). Carers participated in the disability-focused survey and 80 per cent were female. This gender imbalance reflects the unequal distribution of care responsibilities, with women much more likely to take on the role of unpaid carer than men. The respondents were also aged between 45 and 74, with 55–64 the modal age. Most lived in households of two or three people and 22 per cent reported the presence of children under the age of 18 in their home. A total of 74 per cent of respondents described their household as a family, but 14 per cent were sole parents and this reflects the relatively high rate of relationship breakdown amongst households where a disability is present. Couple-only households accounted for 9 per cent of the total, while lone-person households accounted for 2.5 per cent. A total of 24 per cent of respondents provided care to their partners, but children were the greatest recipients of care, with 36 per cent of respondents providing care for a son or sons and 31 per cent caring for one or more daughters.

Carers were concentrated in owner-occupation, with 65 per cent being outright homeowners and a further 20 per cent home purchasers. Just 13 per cent were tenants and 2 per cent lived rent free. This tenure distribution is consistent with the age distribution of the carers included in the survey and highlights the fact that the provision of unpaid care is strongly associated with homeownership. It is interesting to speculate whether a decline in the homeownership rate has the potential to trigger a fall in the rate at which family members are willing and able to provide unpaid care for their relatives or partners. Just fewer than 15 per cent of carers received assistance with the purchase of their home, and while 6 per cent of carers received government assistance, 7.6 per cent received assistance from family with the purchase of the home. A loan from a parent or other relative was the most common form of assistance received, but other forms of assistance included loan guarantees, gifts from parents and inheritance of a house. Family assistance is an important part of the housing career of family members with care responsibilities in Australia.

Carers in rental housing most commonly leased their property from a real estate agent (40 per cent of cases), followed by social housing providers (27 per cent) and other private landlords (13 per cent). Some 44 per cent of carers who were tenants had previously been owner-occupiers, and of those to fall out of home purchase two thirds did so because of relationship breakdown. A further 17 per cent fell out of homeownership because of the cost of providing care, and an equivalent percentage were forced to return to rental housing because of the loss of employment. Interestingly, no carers who were in the rental market expected to enter homeownership in the next five years.

Fewer than 30 per cent of respondents indicated that they provide less than 40 hours of care per week. A total of 45 per cent of respondents indicated that they provided more than 100 hours of care per week, and the single biggest response to the 'How many hours of care do you provide each week?' was 168 hours, that is '24/7'.

Only 10 per cent of carers were in full-time employment, while 22 per cent were employed part time. In addition, 28 per cent reported that they had retired from the formal labour market, while 21 per cent nominated 'home duties' as their current work.

## Public policy and the housing transitions of persons with a disability

Health and disability issues have emerged as an important driver of housing careers in the 21st century in developed economies. Fully 22 per cent of households included in the Housing 21 Survey, and 19 per cent of those where the respondent was aged under 65, had one or more household members affected by a disability or long-term health condition. Some 36 per cent of respondents to the same survey reported that health or disability concerns had shaped their lifetime housing decisions. These issues are not a matter of concern in Australia alone; instead they reflect a set of global concerns and calls for action by governments. The US National Council on Disabilities estimates that 35 million households in America contain one or more persons affected by a disability (NCD, 2010). Moreover, the NCD estimates that 41 per cent of all households with one or more persons with a disability cannot afford their accommodation and that persons with a disability constitute almost 40 per cent of 'worst case' housing nationally. The NCD identifies the major policy priorities as housing affordability, physical accessibility of the housing stock, homelessness, environmental sensitivities, and limited access to public and private sector housing. Key issues across nations include the need to better integrate housing with support services, enhance the accessibility of the housing stock and ensure the provision of appropriate volumes of affordable housing.

### Integration of housing with support services

One of the challenges for governments and policy makers into the 21st century is to better integrate accommodation requirements for persons with a disability and other forms of assistance, including care or assistance packages. The housing policy environment for disability has moved beyond a stage where the processes of de-institutionalisation have unfolded (Quibell, 2004). The challenge over the coming decade is to develop and implement programmes that meet the needs of a disability-affected population living within the broader community.

Bridge et al (2003) noted in Australia that effective linkages between housing and other services for people with a disability have not been established, while the Allen Consulting Group (ACG, 2007, p 10) observed that:

> This lack of co-ordination is partly a function of the involvement of different levels of government. Commonwealth programs provide some services, while others are funded and provided at the state level. This can lead to a fragmented service offering where either people with a disability or their families must acquaint themselves intimately with the details of both State and Commonwealth Government policy arrangements. This fragmentation can, as Bridge et al (2003, p 3) observes, 'hinder efficient and fair service delivery'.

This comment highlights the multiple policy challenges to be overcome in order to produce better housing for persons with a disability. For many individuals affected by disability, it is not simply a matter of maximising support from one tier of government or the other, or even of extracting housing programmes relative to support services; instead the capacity to secure appropriate housing lies at the intersection of all these elements. In Australia and other nations, this complexity becomes more acute when we recognise the need also to integrate policies on ageing. The impacts of structural ageing within the population have to be seen to be part of the broader policy mix, as persons with a disability age and many persons acquire a disability later in life.

Ultimately, the failure to link support and housing effectively limits the scope of people with a disability to live on their own. Regardless of the direction of public policy towards encouraging independent living, if support does not allow people to take up the opportunity to live independently, policy will not succeed. This insight has been reinforced by research from the US and the UK. In the US, the NCD (2010, p 15) observed that:

> One of the most promising trends has been the increasing cross-coordination of housing with community living and support systems, funding, and service delivery. Referred to as Single Access Points, One Stop Shop, No Wrong Door, and Comprehensive Entry Point, these systems enable consumers to enter through many different 'doors' in order to receive coordinated housing and community living supports and services. Many of these initiatives, which often require new policies to enable coordinated service delivery, are based on a Money Follows the Person (MFP) framework to offer cross system, consumer-directed choice.

In the UK, Canada, New Zealand and Australia, this philosophy of assistance and service provision is referred to as 'individualised' funding and the rate of take-up and application varies considerably across and within nations (Bleasdale, 2001; Lord and Hutchinson, 2003).

## Appropriate housing supply for persons affected by disability

Research undertaken by Tually (2007) showed that state governments across Australia viewed public rental housing as the most appropriate vehicle for responding to the housing needs of those affected by disability. However, as the ACG recently noted (2007), the stock of public housing in Australia has fallen, with the AIHW (2007, p 103) observing that the number of public housing dwellings in Australia declined from 359,000 in 2001 to 341,500 in 2006. New investment in social housing by the Australian government announced in 2008 and 2009 may well see a reversal of this trend, but even then significant shortfalls are likely. Moreover, the impacts of a tightening supply of public rental housing are exacerbated by other factors, including the difficulties people with a disability have in finding accessible and appropriate public housing and 'the fact that their rents are not adjusted to reflect the higher costs of tailoring their homes to their particular needs' (ACG, 2007, p 12). Comparable declines in access to housing assistance are evident in the UK and other nations.

In Australia, current policy frameworks view social rental housing as the most appropriate mechanism for directly assisting persons affected by disability (Tually, 2007). This has contributed to a concentration of persons with a disability in the public housing stock, with fully 40 per cent of new entrants to public housing disabled (AIHW, 2003). Much of the publicly owned housing stock is seen to be physically inappropriate for persons with a disability because of the design of the dwelling, distance from public transport, and poor quality maintenance, for example. It is also appropriate to question whether the systems of public housing management are sufficiently focused on the needs of persons with a disability, given the current and growing demand from this group.

International experience can suggest ways in which social housing can become better focused on the housing needs of a population with disabilities. UK experience suggests that housing will need to change with respect to allocation processes, and the quality and design of the stock. In their work on Medical Priority Rehousing in England, Smith et al (1997) emphasised the positive impact of housing on the well-being of persons relocated for medical or disability-related reasons, including psychiatric disability. It is important to acknowledge that this housing stock is of a high quality; it has been designed for persons with a disability, and it is often clustered into groups and includes contact with a warden who can assist with a range of needs. Such a model appears to better recognise the circumstances of persons with a chronic health condition or disability who need assistance.

Over the last five years, and increasing in pace since 2007, state governments across Australia have established either new institutions for social housing provision or created the conditions for their expansion. In many instances these new entities are focused on the needs of persons affected by disability. For example, the Disability Housing Trust (DHT) was established by the Victorian government 'to promote and develop new housing options and encourage new investment in housing for people with disabilities' (ACG, 2007, p v). This initiative has subsequently grown and emerged as Housing Choices Australia but has maintained its mandate to build and let social housing units for persons with a disability, while encouraging the development of new vehicles for private investment – including family members – in disability housing. Other policy options include the use of government home-lending agencies to support access to homeownership for people with a disability. Both Keystart in Western Australia and HomeStart in South Australia have specialist packages for persons with a disability.

In the US the housing options available to persons with a disability are limited by the small size of the public rental sector, the uneven geographical spread of those public rental units that exist, the fact that much of that stock is inaccessible to persons with a disability and the failure to formally designate much of the federally subsidised private and not-for-profit housing for persons with a disability (NCD, 2010). Though Housing Choice vouchers are available to households affected by a disability, the rate of uptake varies by state (NCD, 2010).

### Universal design and the appropriateness of housing

Whether it is the NCD in the US, or a disability organisation in Europe, the physical appropriateness of the housing stock remains an issue of society-wide concern. Universal design principles in housing simply allow a greater percentage of the population to live comfortably within the housing stock. In many instances the application of universal design principles involves relatively minor modifications to built forms, for example the inclusion of grab rails (or planning for their later installation), the widening of corridors, and the removal of steps in the design of the home. In the US, Australia and the UK government sector housing providers and regulators have set targets for either the percentage of housing designed as accessible, or the proportion of new builds designed according to universal design principles. To date, however, the implementation of such standards in private construction has been limited, although there have been notable exceptions. Importantly, innovation in this area has the potential to transform substantially the housing transitions of persons with a disability over the coming decades, as more housing stock becomes accessible and the range of choice opens out for those with specific housing needs.

## Housing and disability in the 21st century: innovation or reaction?

How people with a disability move through the housing market has been one of the unexplored issues in research into housing markets in developed economies. As this chapter has shown, the housing transitions of those with a disability are not a niche issue, with almost one in five households affected. Moreover, it is not a problem limited to one nation or one point in time. It is a challenge that impinges upon all developed economies and it generates issues that will become more acute over time as the population ages, and as institutional forms of accommodation for persons with a disability become a distant memory.

The available evidence suggests that in the 21st century the housing careers of households affected by disability are flatter, more focused on the social rental sector or government-subsidised housing, and more challenged by health and disability concerns than for the general population. It is essential to acknowledge that in many important respects the housing transitions of persons with a disability are significantly different from those evident in the second half of the 20th century, when support for independent living was largely unknown and institutional forms of accommodation were common (Quibell, 2004). It could be argued that there has been policy innovation in bringing the population of persons with a disability into the mainstream of society but that transition has not translated into opportunities to participate fully in the housing market.

There are significant variations in the housing careers of persons affected by different disabilities. The housing careers of persons affected by sensory disability, mobility impairment, psychiatric disability and cognitive impairment all vary, and the source of disability can also exert a determinant influence on housing outcomes. Persons disabled through an accident or event for which they can be compensated (for example employment-related injury or road accident) may have more housing options available to them than those available to persons disabled at birth or through ill-health. In addition, housing careers of many persons with a disability are significantly constrained by their limited participation in the labour market.

## Notes

[1] It is important to discount the argument that those paying 60 per cent or more of their income on housing were living in an institutional or community care setting where living costs and housing are provided as a bundle. In common with other computer-aided telephone interview (CATI) surveys, such living arrangements were under-represented in the Housing 21 Survey.

# EIGHT

# Housing transitions, economic restructuring and the marginalised

*Andrew Beer, Debbie Faulkner and Chris Paris*

In his path-breaking book *Social Justice and the City* the eminent geographer David Harvey (1973) observed that 'the rich command space; the poor are trapped by it'. A similar observation applies to contemporary housing markets: those able to command resources have unprecedented levels of choice and opportunities for consumption, while the poor and marginalised within society are confronted by an increasingly regressive system of housing provision. The retreat from direct government intervention in housing supply is evident in many nations (already discussed in Chapter Three), and the move to 'workfare' models of welfare has coincided with a crisis of housing affordability in many nations that has squeezed the most vulnerable within society. The consequences for individuals and households have been devastating, with large-scale mortgage default and foreclosure in the US, a growing incidence of eviction in Australia, the persistence of inadequate and unhealthy housing in New Zealand, and ongoing social exclusion on large social housing estates in the UK.

For many at the bottom of the housing market or system of social housing supply there are no good choices available and they are confronted by an ongoing churn through the housing market as they shift from one precarious housing arrangement to the next. Whole groups within society are affected by these processes, and this chapter examines the housing transitions of the marginalised within contemporary developed economies. In particular, it considers those trapped within precarious housing before moving on to consider the housing fate of workers made redundant from the automotive sector. Finally, the chapter examines the housing transitions of immigrants in the UK, Ireland and Australia in order to shed light on the intersecting impacts of social policies, cultural factors, social mobility and the structure of housing markets.

## Precarious housing and movement through the market

Precarious housing has received relatively little direct attention from housing researchers, although the individual components of precariousness have been examined in detail. In part, the issue of precariousness has been examined as a matter of security of tenure, and prior research on this topic has considered the legal entitlements and obligations associated with differing tenures across jurisdictions.

Precariousness, however, is much larger than the simple presence or absence of a set of legal protections. Instead it reflects a history of movement through the housing market that is marked by frequent, involuntary relocation, often into housing that is insecure, of poor quality and/or unaffordable. Precariousness is a matter of housing transitions that are involuntary rather than voluntary, of living arrangements that do not necessarily improve and of repeated exposure to complex risks. Research in Australia by Hulse and Saugeres (2008, p 20) argued that it is possible to identify six dimensions of housing insecurity:

> mobility, housing instability, lack of privacy (within the dwelling and between the dwelling and the outside), feeling unsafe (inside and outside the dwelling), lack of belonging and lack of physical comfort ... a common thread in all of these is a lack of control over one's housing ... these dimensions are not discrete, and several interact in complex ways to contribute to, and reinforce, housing insecurity.

Persons who are precariously housed are at the threshold of entry into homelessness and, as Saegert and Evans (2003) noted, their circumstances reflect prolonged exposure to cumulative risks. Risks, for this group 'come in big bundles' and many individuals are affected by a 'cascade of troubles' rather than needing to deal with one challenge – such as unemployment – alone. Persons at risk of losing their home may be simultaneously providing care for a sick relative, working in an insecure, low-paid job, and dealing with the consequence of sole parenthood. Hulse and Saugeres (2008) reinforced the multi-dimensional nature of precariousness, noting that it had consequences for individuals that found expression in family insecurity, insecurity of the self, health insecurities, financial insecurity and employment insecurity. They noted that:

> It is this complex of interrelated insecurities that constitutes precarious living. Precarious living entails surviving from day to day. Trying to make a home in the present against the odds takes time and effort which can make it more difficult to make decisions about the longer term, such as improving educational qualifications or getting a job. The complex of insecurities means that it is difficult to single out one action which will 'untangle the web'. However, the respondents did see improving their housing security as a key to moving away from precarious living for themselves and their children. (Hulse and Saugeres, 2008, p 37)

The extent of precariousness within the housing market should not be underestimated. The Housing 21 Survey collected data on the reasons why people moved over the period 1996 to 2006. While lifestyle/aspiration factors – such as moving to a larger home or building a new home – dominated, 7 per cent of the 2,700 relocations documented were evictions or forced moves from rental housing. A further 3.5 per cent of moves were shifts to less expensive housing, and a further 2.5 per cent were as a consequence of the impact of a disability or ageing. Overall, therefore, involuntary transitions in the housing market comprised 10–12 per cent of all movement, with many moving to housing that was little, if any, better than the accommodation they had left. Over the decade to 2006, 74 per cent of all households moved three times or less and just 2.5 per cent moved more than eight times. By contrast, 60 per cent of tenants moved three times or less and 11.6 per cent moved more than eight times over that period. Clearly, there is a strong tenure dimension to frequent movement within the housing market and those households whose income or assets are insufficient to enter owner-occupation are most at risk. Age is also a critical issue, with persons aged 25–34 the most mobile, but individuals with high levels of movement come from all age groups (Beer and Faulkner, 2009, p 106).

The incidence and impact of precarious housing in contemporary society should not be underestimated. Slatter and Beer (2003a, 2003b) noted that bailiff-assisted eviction was relatively common in Australia, with approximately 1,000 such evictions per year in a jurisdiction with 80,000 private rental properties. What makes this figure more remarkable is that many people are effectively forced out of their rental homes much earlier in the legal process, such that the true rate of eviction may be 10 times that figure. Rates of eviction will clearly vary on a jurisdiction by jurisdiction basis, with some nations more, or less, punctilious in enforcing the rights of landlords. Many states in the US, for example, are supportive of landlord rights, while parts of Europe stridently protect the position of tenants. Overall, however, tenants are vulnerable, with many cycling through a range of unattractive housing options. This was the conclusion drawn by Seelig et al (2005) on the housing consumption patterns of income support recipients in Australia. They found considerable mobility within the housing market, but this activity was marked by ongoing directionless 'churn' rather than an identifiable progression to housing that was more secure, of better quality or better located.

Beer et al (2006b) examined the impact of eviction on both individuals and the system of housing provision. In many respects the findings of this study are surprising, because while 55 per cent of those interviewed were evicted from private rental housing, the remainder were not, and had in fact been ejected from either social housing or specialist homelessness services. Psychiatric disability, antisocial behaviour and substance abuse would almost certainly have contributed to this suite of terminations. Across the board, the first move of most evictees was to informal arrangements, staying with friends or relatives ('couch surfing'), with subsequent progression into either specialist homelessness accommodation or into the social housing sector. While not all evictees subsequently occupied 'welfare' housing, many did, and some 8 per cent moved immediately to more certain forms of institutional accommodation, including prisons and hospitals. This trajectory is a marker of the marginal position within society of those groups at risk of eviction.

## Economic restructuring and housing

The processes of macroeconomic restructuring can intrude rudely on the lives and housing prospects of households from across the social spectrum. Low-income and/or marginalised households are, of course, more vulnerable to these changes because they have fewer resources to sustain them in the short term, more limited opportunities for further employment, fewer skills and often more susceptible household structures. Redundancy, moreover, is an established feature of the labour markets in developed economies and this reflects both the varying fortunes of individual enterprises, cycles of prosperity and loss in some sectors and the more fundamental shifts in the well-being of some industries. For example, manufacturing industries across the developed world have witnessed wholesale employment loss as businesses have either relocated or outsourced manufacturing to the developing world, where wages are lower. In consequence there have been a series of plant closures that have pushed many out of the workforce entirely, into unemployment or into a marginal position within the labour force. For many, the housing impacts of such employment loss have been profound. The relationship between economic restructuring and subsequent housing transitions is explored here with reference to two plant closures with a high profile locally: the closure of Mitsubishi's plant at Lonsdale, South Australia in 2004 and the collapse of MG Rover in Birmingham, UK, in 2005.

### Employment loss at Lonsdale, South Australia

In April 2004 Australia's then Prime Minister John Howard announced that the Lonsdale plant of Mitsubishi Motors Australia Limited (MMAL) would be closed with a loss of 700 jobs, with a further 400 voluntary redundancies from MMAL's Tonsley Park assembly plant. The loss of just over 1,100 direct jobs in the southern part of metropolitan Adelaide was recognised as a major shock to the regional economy. Other losses were expected as businesses in the automotive supply chain felt the impact of declining demand for their products. The Australian government responded by announcing a A$45 million assistance package for the region – called the Structural Adjustment Fund (SAF) – as well as enhanced employment assistance for retrenched workers. This assistance was to be delivered via the Jobs Network, Australia's network of federally funded labour market providers. Importantly, the job losses announced in 2004 foreshadowed the complete closure in 2008 of Mitsubishi's manufacturing history in Australia. The final closure resulted in 800 redundancies, but it is important to note that the firm had been steadily shedding labour over the previous decade. All 7,000 jobs associated with this employer in the year 2000 had disappeared by 2009, and there is speculation that the head office sales functions could relocate out of South Australia in the near future.

In addition, the South Australian government committed A$10 million of assistance to displaced workers, mainly in the form of enhanced access to services.

The loss of jobs from MMAL in 2004 should be seen as part of the longer-term restructuring of the automobile industry, and manufacturing more generally, in Australia. In the mid 1970s manufacturing accounted for 25 per cent of the workforce but by 2001 it had declined to 12 per cent, even though the value of production had increased. Where once car-making plants could be found in all state capitals except Perth, by the year 2000 motor vehicle production had consolidated into a limited number of sites, with Toyota and Ford assembling vehicles in Melbourne, Mitsubishi and General Motors Holden (GMH) building cars in Adelaide and GMH also constructing engines in Melbourne.

The redundancies announced in 2004 saw workers made redundant involuntarily at the Lonsdale plant, while voluntary redundancy packages were made available at the Tonsley Park facility. The nature of the redundancy process was significant, as those in receipt of an involuntary redundancy package received five weeks of pay for every year of service up to 20 years and then one week of pay for every additional year. Workers who took a voluntary package received three weeks pay for every year of service up to 20 years and then one week of pay for every additional year of employment. Critically, redundant employees had worked an average of 19 years with the manufacturer (Beer et al, 2006c), so that many employees left with two years of salary. This payout was generous by Australian standards. The overwhelming majority of those made redundant were mature men aged from their mid 40s to late 50s who lived locally, with the majority either homeowners or home purchasers.

Interviews undertaken within six months of the redundancy (Beer et al, 2006c) with 374 of the displaced workers revealed that while 40 per cent were outright homeowners, 43.5 per cent were mortgagors, 10 per cent were renting privately and just 2 per cent were renting from the public sector. Some 141 workers, or 54 per cent of those who held a mortgage, indicated that they would use their payout to discharge all or part of their mortgage. As one ex-employee who paid off his mortgage said:

> It's the working man's dream.

While another noted:

> I had a mortgage and I thought any money that they give me I [will] pay the mortgage off. That's the best financial thing that I can do with the money, because that's a debt that's costing me, so the best thing I could do is pay that. And not that it paid it off, but it took a big chunk out of it.

A second round of interviews was completed one year after the initial interviews and during that period a further 70 displaced workers used their redundancy to pay off all or part of their mortgage. In total, therefore, some 210 of the 374 retrenched workers interviewed invested their redundancy in acquitting some or their entire mortgage.

In the first set of interviews post redundancy only 37 retrenched workers indicated that they had moved home since leaving the automotive sector, and just 69 respondents (20 per cent of the total) expected that they would need to move home as a result of their changed employment circumstances. At the second wave of interviews just 29 respondents had moved home in the previous 12 months and fully 81 per cent of workers interviewed believed that they would not need to move home or change their housing circumstances over the next 12 months. Overall the interviews showed that retrenched workers were both committed to homeownership and embedded within their region. Many had lived all their lives in southern Adelaide and one third had lived in their current neighbourhood for more than 15 years.

The Oswald (1996, 1997) thesis suggests that owner-occupation raises unemployment rates by reducing the willingness to relocate to find employment. This observation appears to hold true in the case of workers made redundant in Lonsdale, although there is a voluminous literature to show that this is not always the case. In percentage terms private tenants were more likely to be in paid employment one year post redundancy, with 51 per cent employed full time, compared with 27 per cent of outright homeowners and 32 per cent of mortgagors. Private tenants also had higher rates of employment in casual work than outright homeowners and a comparable rate with mortgage holders. The percentage of private tenants unemployed was appreciably lower than for the two owner-occupation categories, with 7.3 per cent of tenants unemployed, compared with 16 per cent of outright homeowners and 13 per cent of homebuyers.

The percentage that left the formal labour force varied appreciably by tenure: some 22 per cent of outright homeowners had left the labour force, 11.5 per cent of mortgagors had done so, but only 7.3 per cent of tenants had left the world of paid work. The age of persons in each tenure explains a proportion of the difference, but the gap between the tenures is so profound that we must conclude that there is an appreciable tenure effect. The same argument can be made with respect to those remaining in the labour market: there were real differences in employment outcomes by tenure, with private tenants more likely to find full-time employment and as likely as mortgagors to find casual employment.

The quality of employment on offer following redundancy is a critical factor in understanding why the increased incidence of owner-occupation may raise unemployment rates and discourage active participation in the labour market. Many workers, especially those with fewer formal qualifications, reported difficulties in finding work and poorer working conditions once they found work. Whereas MMAL engaged full-time permanent staff, only 107 of the 316 surveyed 18 months post redundancy were employed on a full-time basis, while 61 were employed casually and 10 were employed part time. The remainder had either left the labour force, were unemployed or were self-employed. Fully 225 of the 316 respondents (72 per cent) in the second round of interviews reported they now earned less when compared with their income prior to redundancy; only 11 per cent had incomes that matched their wages prior to redundancy and

15 per cent earned more. In many instances those who received higher wages post redundancy were the more skilled workers, such as electricians. One automotive engineer reported that his income fell from A$150,000 to A$71,000.

Finally, it is worth considering the location of employment available to retrenched workers from the automotive sector and how that has influenced labour market outcomes. MMAL was based in southern metropolitan Adelaide, a region that offers an attractive living environment distinguished by proximity to high-quality beaches, low-density suburbs with well-developed public and private gardens, and access to the Southern Vales wine region. It does not have any major large-scale industry, and the redundancies from the automotive sector announced in April 2004 significantly reduced the total stock of manufacturing employment in the region. Those seeking further work in the industry, through choice or skills, must inevitably consider employment in northern Adelaide, where blue-collar employment is both growing and available on a larger scale. Travel to the region from southern Adelaide takes a minimum of an hour or more in peak traffic periods.

## Employment loss at Longbridge, Birmingham

Roughly one year after the closure of the MMAL's Lonsdale plant, MG Rover collapsed in Birmingham, UK. The demise of MG Rover has been thoroughly documented by Bailey et al (2008). Unlike the carefully planned closure of MMAL's Lonsdale plant, MG Rover collapsed overnight and approximately 5,500 workers were made redundant with no notice. Importantly, the company's demise was part of the longer-term structural decline of automotive manufacture in the West Midlands and had followed a period of foreign purchase and then management buyout, sub-optimal production volumes and an extended period in which the currency was strong, thereby eroding the company's competitiveness.

In contrast to events at Lonsdale, workers forced to leave MG Rover did not receive substantial redundancy payments but instead were forced to rely upon government-provided assistance. As Armstrong et al (2008, p 349) observed, the UK government responded in an immediate and comprehensive fashion:

> Much of the immediate policy response to the closure of MGR was that of 'crisis management', focusing on jobs and short term financial assistance ... An aid package worth £176 million was made available, including £50 million for retraining ... up to £40 million for redundancy payments, a £24 million loan fund to help otherwise viable businesses, and £41.6 million to support ex-MGR suppliers to remain viable.

Importantly, when compared with Australia, the public sector took a much more active role in the adjustment of workers, with a more effective role in labour market training and employment assistance. Redundancy payments were a much less important part of the mix of adjustment measures.

The MG Rover plant was located at Longbridge, in Birmingham's south west, and as Bailey et al (2008) observed, its workforce – and consequently those subsequently made redundant – was highly concentrated in and around the plant. Many workers continued to live in extensive council housing estates and as a group they displayed a demography that resembled MMAL's Lonsdale plant: they were predominantly male, middle aged, blue-collar workers living in family households and with relatively low skill levels. Moreover, the average number of years worked was 19 (an exact match with Lonsdale) and roughly 40 per cent of all households were outright homeowners.

Workers made redundant by MG Rover had, on average, better outcomes than those made redundant in South Australia. As Bailey et al (2008) showed, by 2008 some 90 per cent of former MG Rover workers were employed, with 74 per cent employed full time. This brings into sharp relief the outcomes in southern Adelaide three years after MMAL's closure, where one third of workers were now under-employed (casual or part-time work) and one third had left the labour market. Moreover, outright homeowners in Birmingham were more likely than the other tenures to be employed immediately after redundancy, eight months after closure and three years post redundancy. Of course not all outcomes were positive: workers from Birmingham tended to report lower incomes and less job satisfaction in their new employment, but critically they remained employed.

### Economic restructuring and marginalisation: what role housing?

Despite their obvious similarities, the redundancy experiences of workers from Lonsdale and Longbridge tell very different stories: one was a planned withdrawal by a continuing company while the other took place without notice and as a result of the collapse of a firm. Government investment in the recovery from redundancy was greater in the UK, while the company-funded redundancies in Australia were substantial. Perhaps most importantly, very different labour market impacts were evident in the UK and Australia: workers in Birmingham were more likely to be in employment after three years, and twice as likely to be in full time employment. Homeownership appeared to be an impediment to re-employment in Australia but this was not the case in Birmingham; if anything, the opposite was true.

The contrasting outcomes in Longbridge and Lonsdale bring into focus the complex interplay between ranges of factors in determining the outcomes of large-scale redundancies. In both instances workers reported relatively low levels of residential mobility following their redundancy, but in Birmingham this was an advantage for re-employment because sustained government intervention by both the regional development agency (Advantage West Midlands) and central government had contributed to urban renaissance and the emergence of new industries (Barber and Hall, 2008). In South Australia there was less government intervention in the economy as a whole; public sector investment was focused elsewhere and, in consequence, re-employment opportunities simply did not emerge (Beer and Thomas, 2007). Whereas homeownership in Birmingham ensured that redundant workers kept their place in a revitalising labour market, in southern Adelaide workers were shackled by the bricks and mortar of their homes to a declining labour market with limited opportunities for growth. Redundancy payments simply exacerbated the problem, as many sank their payouts into their mortgages and increased their stake in a region with lifestyle benefits, but few others. Importantly, this is as much an issue of the locational dimensions of housing as the psychosocial benefits of housing: the sense of 'home'.

Clapham (2005a) noted that households can progress along a housing 'pathway' while remaining residentially inert. A comparable argument extends to the housing transitions of those made redundant: their loss of employment represents a significant shift for many in their position within the housing market. For some it will precipitate relocation. Whether housing serves as a 'buffer' during redundancy, an impediment to re-employment or as a gateway to new opportunities will not be determined by housing circumstances alone, but instead reflect the intersection of a range of personal factors and social processes. We can, however, conclude that housing will be important and that governments need to consider both regional and individual impacts.

## The housing transitions of immigrants

### Housing transitions and immigrants in the UK

Most ethnic diversity in the UK and Ireland derives from the net effects of migration, including emigration of British- and Irish-born citizens, return migration of previous emigrants, and immigration by others, as well as subsequent out-migration of some previous immigrants. Such flows have varied enormously over time both in their composition and volumes. Most immigrants to the UK between 1850 and 1950 came from Ireland, although that was part of the UK until 1921. The main other 19th-century immigrant group was Jews escaping persecution in Europe. Both Irish and Jews have been largely assimilated into the UK, despite some discrimination and prejudice, and were included within the 'white' ethnic group in the 1991 and 2001 Censuses. From the late 1950s, however, successive waves of immigrants came to the UK, initially from the Caribbean and Indian sub-continent, and more recently from almost every corner of the globe. The non-European ethnic minority population was under 100,000 in 1951 but was recorded in the 1991 Census, the first to include questions about ethnicity, at around 3 million or about 5 per cent of the total population (Peach, 1998).

Changing patterns of migration as well as the growth of minority ethnic communities occurred within changing socioeconomic, demographic and housing contexts (see Chapter Three). Thus the pattern of housing opportunities and constraints facing immigrants in the 1960s was different from those facing newcomers in the 1990s. In the meantime the children of those who arrived in the 1960s grew up through a period of profound changes, one of which was growing ethnic diversity within the UK and the emergence of 'ethnic minorities', including non-white British-born citizens, often identified collectively as 'minority ethnic groups'. The foreign-born population of the UK more than doubled between 1951 and 2001, to a total of 5 million (Rendall and Salt, 2005). Changes in employment structures and labour markets have had important implications for the work and housing market situations of immigrants and British-born ethnic minorities. More recently, the outcomes of long-term economic restructuring have combined with the recession of 2007–09 to raise further uncertainties about the future housing opportunities and transitions of an increasingly diverse mix of ethnic minority groups (Perry, 2008), with rapid growth in numbers and proportions from recent EU accession countries and from Africa and Asia.

Migration before 1945 had very little impact in terms of early 21st-century 'ethnic' categories as most in-migration was from Ireland or 'Old Commonwealth' countries including Australia, New Zealand and Canada. Despite growing immigration, there was a net *outflow* of migrants between 1945 and the early 1980s. There were similar sized inflows and outflows between 1983 and 1993 but strong net inward migration after 1994 (Horsfield, 2005). The first main wave of post-war new Commonwealth immigrants came from the Caribbean islands and the Indian sub-continent. They included large numbers of single men seeking employment in factories or public services such as the London Underground. But many families also came to work and settle in areas of labour demand, especially London and industrial cities in the Midlands and North. These newcomers entered the housing system during a period of transition, usually renting within the declining private rental sector, in 'twilight zones' around inner cities, often occupying dwellings that were then thought likely to comprise the next phase of slum clearance. They had little access to council housing, then a much more highly prized form of tenure, due to restrictive eligibility criteria and allocation procedures. Many purchased their own homes, especially immigrants from India or Pakistan, initially often older run-down inner city terraced housing. Some became landlords of sub-divided multi-occupied larger old dwellings that had been abandoned by the English middle classes on their move to leafier suburbs (Rex and Moore, 1967; Lambert et al, 1978; Henderson and Karn, 1984; Peach, 1998).

The stream of immigrants from the Caribbean, India and Pakistan reduced during the 1970s, partly due to tighter restrictions on access and partly due to the worsening economic situation. There was a noted increase in access to council housing tenancies among these groups, partly through changing eligibility criteria and allocation practices, through increased length of residence enabling them move up waiting lists, and due to growing unpopularity of council housing within the UK-born population. Homeownership grew among the Indian and Pakistani ethnic groups, but much less so among those from the Caribbean and Bangladesh. By the 1990s, therefore, there were significant differences between the housing circumstances of different ethnic groups, as well as diversity of outcomes for members of each group due to differences in socioeconomic status and income (Peach, 1998). There was no single 'minority ethnic' housing experience or sequence: rather, members of minority ethnic groups shared many of the circumstances of the majority population, differentiated by class, status, wealth and income. The diversity of opportunity and achieved housing status within the majority population ranged from a growing proportion of affluent homeowners at one extreme, to a residual underclass, often in second- or third-generation workless households, with high levels of sole parenthood. Some immigrant groups, it appeared, were more likely to be among the former category, whereas others were more likely to be included in the latter, especially following economic restructuring after 1975, with unemployment rates in the 1990s 'devastatingly high for young minority men' (Peach, 1998, p 1659).

Patterns of migration into and out of the UK changed from the mid 1980s, with population gain through net international migration increasing rapidly from 1993, adding over 100,000 people a year after 2000 to a peak of 250,000 in 2005 (Matheson, 2009). Most net additional population came from New Commonwealth countries (especially India, Pakistan and Bangladesh), recent EU accession states (especially Poland), and diverse countries in Africa and Asia, including a surge of asylum seekers and refugees (Horsfield, 2005). There was little growth in the Caribbean population: 60 per cent of the Caribbean population in 2001 had been born in Britain (Connolly, and White, 2006). During the same period, moreover, there was growing net migration *loss* of British-born citizens, from 50,000 in 1998 to over 100,000 a year after 2003 (Office of National Statistics, 2008). The overall impact has been to create an ethnic mix within the UK that has been characterised as 'super diversity', with immigrants from a vast number of countries, including destitute refugees and members of super-rich global elites (Vertovec, 2005). Unlike earlier migrant streams into the UK, most recent migrants have come from places with no colonial associations with Britain (Vertovec, 2005).

The combination of a changing housing system and an increasingly complex and diverse ethnic mix cannot be described fully here, but Tables 8.1 and 8.2 identify two key dimensions: overall change in the housing system and the

**Table 8.1: UK households, by tenure**

| | Owner-occupied | Privately rented[1] | Social renters[2] | |
|---|---|---|---|---|
| | Expressed as percentage of all dwellings | | | Total (000) |
| 1953 | 32.0 | 52.0 | 18.0 | 12,840 |
| 1971 | 50.0 | 20.0 | 29.0 | 15,940 |
| 1991 | 67.6 | 9.4 | 23.0 | 19,309 |
| 2001 | 70.4 | 10.1 | 19.5 | 20,403 |
| 2007 | 69.6 | 12.7 | 17.7 | 21,178 |

*Source:* Department for Communities and Local Government (2009)

*Notes:* [1] includes dwellings with job or business; [2] rented from councils, other public bodies and other social landlords.

dissimilar housing circumstances of different ethnic groups. Table 8.1 provides a broad picture of the changes in the tenure of households in the UK between 1953 and 2007: the rise and fall of social renting, the fall and rise again of private renting and relative stability of the proportion of home owners since 1991. The first waves of immigrants entered a changing housing system during the 1950s and 1960s and raised their children as the system *continued* to change. More recent entrants, especially since the early 1990s, came into a situation where homeownership was the norm, social renting was heavily residualised and private renting had been transformed.

Between 1991 and 2001 the British immigrant population increased by over 50 per cent to around 4.6 million, or 8 per cent of the total population of 59 million. Table 8.2 shows that in 2007–08 there were nearly 2 million immigrant households in England, representing some 9 per cent of all households, with strong tenure contrasts between ethnic groups. Indians had the highest level of homeownership (74 per cent), slightly above white British (72 per cent) and Pakistanis (68 per cent). In contrast, Africans were strongly concentrated in social and private rental housing. Caribbean and Bangladeshi households also had high levels of social rental housing and low levels of home ownership. Such variations reflect preferences as

**Table 8.2: Tenure by ethnicity of household reference person (HRP), England 2007–08**

| Ethnic group of HRP[1] | Owner-occupiers | | | Social tenants | Private tenants | Total (000) | Percentage ethnic group HRP |
| | Own outright | Buying with mortgage | All | | | | |
| | Percentage households by tenure | | | | | | |
|---|---|---|---|---|---|---|---|
| British | 34 | 38 | 72 | 17 | 11 | 17,936 | 86 |
| Other European | 22 | 27 | 49 | 14 | 37 | 1,125 | 5 |
| *All European* | *33* | *37* | *70* | *17* | *11* | *19,062* | *91* |
| Caribbean | 14 | 35 | 49 | 41 | 11 | 269 | 1 |
| African | 4 | 24 | 28 | 44 | 28 | 246 | 1 |
| Indian | 28 | 45 | 74 | 7 | 20 | 387 | 2 |
| Pakistani | 29 | 40 | 68 | 16 | 16 | 221 | 1 |
| Bangladeshi[2] | 9 | 29 | 38 | 47 | 15 | 92 | <0.5 |
| Chinese[2] | 15 | 37 | 52 | 13 | 35 | 100 | <0.5 |
| Mixed | 11 | 29 | 39 | 33 | 28 | 121 | 1 |
| Other | 9 | 28 | 37 | 28 | 35 | 466 | 2 |
| *All ethnic minority* | *16* | *34* | *50* | *26* | *24* | *1,902* | *9* |
| **All** | **31** | **37** | **68** | **18** | **14** | **20,964** | **100** |

*Source:* Department for Communities and Local Government (2009, Table 1.13)

*Notes:* [1] excludes cases for which ethnic group is unknown; [2] high sampling error due to small size and population clustering well as relative positions within class and labour market structures, with Caribbean and Bangladeshi household members more likely to be unemployed or in low-wage manual employment than Indians, who were well represented in business and professional occupations (Clark and Drinkwater, 2007). Bangladeshis arrived in the UK significantly later than Pakistanis and Indians, mainly during the 1980s, 'when it may have been easier for those on low incomes to access social housing and (paradoxically) more difficult to get onto the homeownership ladder' (Housing Corporation and CIH, 2008, p 4). Many recent arrivals have few opportunities except in low-paid jobs or, in some cases, the informal economy.

Household structures also affected tenure circumstances, most notably the extremely high proportion of Caribbean sole parents. The surge in immigration from the mid 1990s resulted in a number of non-European groups moving into privately rented accommodation. At the same time, the high proportion of non-European residents in social housing reflects its relatively undesirable status among the mainstream population, which has a higher level of homeownership, especially outright ownership. The Housing Corporation and CIH (2008) expected that the high proportion of non-European households in social housing would increase over the next decade due to inter-related factors: continuing immigration and international marriages; economic disadvantage among some non-European groups leaving them dependent on social housing; limited or no opportunity for new non-European households to use parental equity to enter home ownership; greater likelihood of living in areas of more plentiful social housing; and being in housing need, especially through overcrowding.

The emergence of super-diversity in ethnic terms has made it harder than ever to generalise about 'ethnic' housing circumstances and transitions in the UK (Robinson et al, 2007; Perry, 2008). Whereas refugees, asylum seekers and especially illegal migrants will continue to experience the most stressful housing circumstances, other non-European group members are members of the global super-rich with one or two of their many homes in England. In October 2007, for example, almost half of the country homes in south-east England valued at £5 million and over were purchased by foreigners as 'Russian oligarchs and tycoons from Asia and the Middle East emulate the lifestyle of Britain's landed gentry' (Gadher and Davies, 2007).

## Housing transitions and immigrants in Ireland

At the start of the 1990s Ireland was among the most ethnically homogeneous countries in the world, with a demographic history over 150 years characterised by emigration of native-born citizens and virtually no inward migration. Housing provision was dominated by homeownership within a largely agricultural economy that had never undergone significant industrialisation. That changed dramatically from the early 1990s with the economic boom and a switch from net out-migration to booming in-migration, including many overseas-born persons with Irish citizenship by virtue of their parents or grandparents who had emigrated from Ireland during previous generations (Paris, 2005).

There was no significant ethnic minority immigration into Ireland until the 'Celtic Tiger' economic boom of the 1990s. Surging growth in jobs and incomes attracted a flood of immigrants, including returning Irish-born citizens as well as economic migrants from across the globe, refugees and asylum seekers. The boom included rapid growth in housing construction and prices and strong demand for private rental housing and home purchase. The ethnic composition of the population changed rapidly during this turbulent period, though to a lesser extent overall than in the UK. Around 4 per cent of the population was recorded as black and minority ethnic in 2006, the first time that the Irish Census included a question on ethnicity.

The recent migrant stream into Ireland was very similar to the post-industrial and post-colonial movement into the UK from the early 1990s – highly diverse, from many origins, including especially recent EU accession countries, with large numbers of asylum seekers and refugees and uncertain numbers of illegal immigrants. The migration surge occurred within a booming housing market and strong growth in private renting.

The rapid growth of the overseas-born population in Ireland has been too recent for large spatially defined ethnic communities to have emerged by the latest Census in 2006. The population remained predominantly white across the country as a whole (94 per cent), with around 3.5 per cent in immigrant groups and 0.5 per cent Irish Travellers concentration. There was no spatial equivalent to the UK concentrations of immigrants during the 1950s and 1960s into former industrial areas, because there *were* no equivalent areas, but there was a high concentration of work in the Dublin metropolitan region and other major cities, especially Cork, Galway and Limerick. Recent migrants tended to concentrate in private rental housing. Many refugees and asylum seekers were accommodated in council-owned dwellings, especially in unpopular estates, and some migrants gained access to homeownership.

Ireland has been massively affected by the global financial crisis, with extensive job losses, deteriorating public finances and massive falls in new housing and other construction. Thousands of new homes remain unsold, negative equity is widespread among homebuyers who purchased after 2003, and house prices are expected to fall by 40–50 per cent from their peak of 2007 (O'Halloran, 2010). Many recent immigrants have left, especially those from recent EU accession countries, and there has been a resumption of net out-migration since 2007. The Irish government has taken draconian measures, cutting public sector pay, imposing job caps, raising new taxes and creating a new institution to take over much of the debt of banks and property developers. Future housing transitions remain uncertain especially for non-European groups, many having little choice but to remain in Ireland, dependent on public resources while hoping for an upturn in the economy. Longer-established citizens and residents retain high levels of homeownership, and for those in work there is no longer a significant affordability issue regarding homeownership, though loan finance remains severely restricted. This extremely turbulent environment is unlikely to change significantly for possibly many years to come.

### Housing transitions and immigrants in Australia

Immigration has been integral to Australia's growth and development resulting in Australia being one of the most culturally diverse countries in the world. Numerous waves of immigration have occurred since 1945. In the immediate post-war period the major influx of immigrants was from Europe in particular the countries of Italy, Greece, Germany and the Netherlands followed soon by immigrants from the UK and Ireland (Figure 8.1). In the 1970s and 1980s these groups declined as new groups of immigrants arrived, particularly from South East Asia and New Zealand. In the 1990s and the first years of this century countries in the Middle East, such as Iraq, Asian countries such as China, India and Indonesia and African countries such as Sudan and South Africa have all contributed significant numbers to Australia's population growth (ABS, 2007f).

The timing of these different waves of immigration influence household type (Figure 8.2). As revealed in the Housing 21 Survey, a greater proportion of respondents of European origin are in single-person households or couple-only households (21 and 39 per cent respectively), while more recent immigrants

**Figure 8.1: Decade of arrival in Australia of persons born overseas**

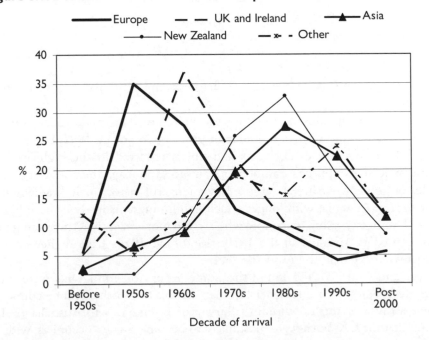

*Source:* Housing 21 Survey

**Figure 8.2: Household type, by selected birthplace groups**

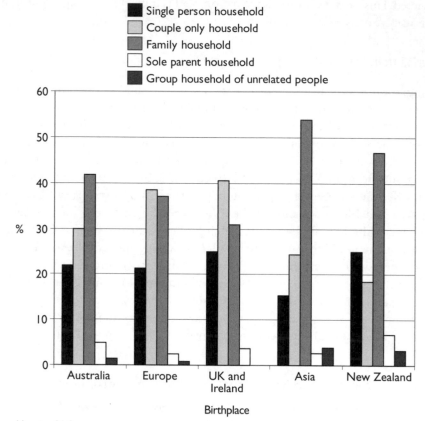

Source: Housing 21 Survey

(originating from Asia or New Zealand, for example) are likely to form family households.

There is a clear consensus within the literature that owner-occupation is the preferred tenure of many immigrant groups (Coughlan, 1991; Hassell with Hugo, 1996; Burnley et al, 1997), and this is reflected in the high levels of homeownership or purchase among migrants to Australia in the post-war period. Rates of homeownership are affected by a range of factors including length of residence in Australia, with longer established immigrants likely to have higher rates of homeownership than more who arrived more recently. Many immigrants who settled in Australia in the 1950s, 1960s and 1970s have higher rates of homeownership than the Australian-born.

Beer and Cutler (1999) found that some groups of immigrants were more likely to progress to homeownership than arrivals from other source countries. Their analysis of the Longitudinal Survey of Immigrants to Australia (LSIA) found that the UK-born were most likely to become owner-occupiers, with 38 per cent entering this tenure within 18 months of arrival in Australia. They were followed by the North and Western Europe-born (34 per cent), the North and Central America-born (31 per cent) the Eastern Europe-born (24.6 per cent) and the South-East Asia-born (22 per cent). At the other end of the spectrum, just 10.1 per cent of South Asia-born arrivals, 10.6 per cent of Middle East- and North Africa-born settlers and 10.9 per cent of South America-born immigrants were owner-occupiers within 18 months of arrival. However, it is important to recognise that this tenure distribution does not reflect preferences but is heavily filtered by the ability to enter home purchase, and this in turn is a function of visa category, resources, support networks and other factors.

Similar trends are evident from the Housing 21 Survey, with homeownership rates higher among longer-established immigrants (Figures 8.3 and 8.4). Migrants who settled in Australia prior to the 1960s had very high rates of outright ownership. For those from mainly English-speaking countries, 76 per cent were outright owners and another 8 per cent were paying a mortgage. Slightly fewer immigrants from non-English-speaking countries were outright owners at the time of the survey (73 per cent), but many more (19 per cent) were mortgage holders. These data suggest that 92 per cent of immigrants from non-English-speaking backgrounds would become outright owners compared with 84 per cent of persons from mainly English-speaking backgrounds. A small proportion of immigrants appear to have remained in rental accommodation.

The change in this pattern over the last 15 or so years is striking. In the 1990s and since the year 2000 it has become increasingly difficult for people from non-English-speaking backgrounds to enter the homeownership market. At the time

**Figure 8.3: Decade of arrival in Australia of immigrants from mainly English-speaking countries, by tenure**

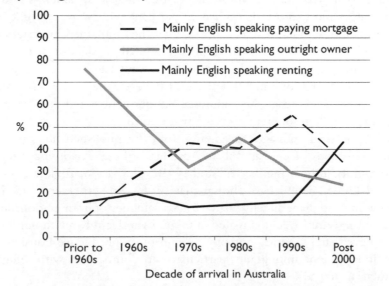

*Source:* Housing 21 Survey

**Figure 8.4: Decade of arrival in Australia of immigrants from mainly non-English-speaking countries, by tenure**

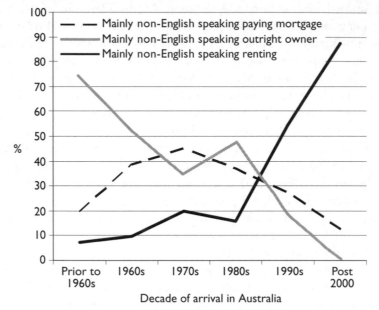

*Source:* Housing 21 Survey

of the Housing 21 Survey only 27.3 per cent of persons who arrived in Australia in the 1990s from a non-English-speaking background were paying a mortgage and only 18 per cent were outright owners. This compares with 54.8 per cent of persons who arrived in the 1990s from a mainly English-speaking country who were paying a mortgage and another 29 per cent who were outright owners. Immigrants in the rental market reported that they remained in rental housing because of cost barriers: either the difficulty of saving a deposit or the inability to afford mortgage payments. In fact, 45.6 per cent had not been able to save a deposit, while an additional 21.1 per cent believed they could not afford the repayments on a mortgage. An additional 8.9 per cent stated they were recent immigrants and therefore renting was a first option.

One of the clear messages to emerge from the published literature on the housing transitions of new arrivals to Australia is the effect of visa category of arrival. Significantly, a number of studies (Burnley, 1976; Tonkin et al, 1993; Beer and Cutler, 1999) have shown that success in settlement and housing outcomes in Australia is directly related to visa category of immigration: business-nominated and employer-nominated immigrants and family reunion immigrants tend to have better housing outcomes – and more productive housing careers – than independent immigrants, particularly in comparison with refugee and humanitarian arrivals.

Over time, changes in government policy and structural conditions have influenced the ability of refugee and humanitarian arrivals to become established in the housing market. While achieving success in the housing market has always been difficult for refugees and humanitarian migrants, in the past the government has provided 'on arrival' subsidised accommodation and even interest-free home loans (Cox, 1996). While relatively few get access to public and community housing, since the late 1990s refugee and humanitarian migrants have been exposed to the vagaries of the private rental market. According to the Refugee Council of Australia (2009, p 51) '...complete reliance on the private rental market to meet the housing needs of new refugees has created a number of serious and complex challenges'. At all stages of the process of finding and maintaining accommodation refugee and humanitarian settlers face challenges: knowledge of available properties, inspecting properties, applying for properties, competing in an auction-type market, a lack of rental history, unemployment, discrimination by real estate agents, discrimination and exploitation by landlords, a lack of understanding of the responsibilities of landlords and the rights of tenants, rents in excess of 50 per cent of weekly income, and overcrowding and poor-quality housing. In addition, access to the Integrated Humanitarian Settlement Strategy, the government's assistance programme for new arrivals, is limited to the first six months post arrival (Refugee Council of Australia, 2010), a period of time often shorter than the first lease on a property. Many immigrants face housing stress and increased vulnerability to homelessness, and in the current crisis in housing affordability affecting all Australians their ability to enter homeownership or secure good-quality rental housing is restricted.

## Marginalised groups and housing: mobility, immobility and adverse outcomes

Housing is a primary determinant of well-being in developed economies, and while its influence may not be as profound as that of position in the labour market or health, it is pervasive, cumulative and ongoing. The ability to make successful transitions through the housing market is critical as the failure to do so can reinforce dependence on welfare payments, expose the individual to discrimination, make it more difficult to find employment and rule out avenues for wealth accumulation or even reduced living costs. Market-based economies tend to punish the disadvantaged, and those who 'fail' within the housing market are no exception. In Australia, for example, in several states the use of formal and informal databases by landlords to check on the rental history of low-income home seekers effectively excludes some households from tenancies. The discussion in this chapter has shown that a percentage of households in developed nations are precariously housed and their housing market transitions are marked by frequent moves, the risk of eviction and unaffordable housing. In key respects the concept of a housing transition speaks most clearly to the circumstances of this group, as there is no sense of a housing 'career' or progression.

Economic restructuring can mean that groups that previously occupied a stable position within the housing market suddenly find themselves vulnerable. The analysis of labour market outcomes from Longbridge and Lonsdale shows that these events completely reframe a household's position within the market and could well generate the need to relocate. Critically, however, the impact housing plays in mediating redundancy largely reflects its location. Therefore its impact is either positive, ensuring access to a growing labour market, or negative, handcuffing the household to a region with limited prospects. Economic restructuring also influences the housing transitions of immigrant groups because, as this chapter has shown, economic circumstances fundamentally shape rates of immigration, economic opportunities upon arrival, the capacity to gain access to a range of tenures and the chance to enter homeownership. Importantly, there is no one sequence of housing transitions for immigrants in any of the nations considered here. Some immigrant groups fare better than others, and these outcomes are a function of the timing of arrival, the period of residence, language ability, educational attainment, position in the labour market and cultural preferences. We can, however, conclude that some immigrant communities arrive into migrant-receiving countries at risk and that their disadvantages are then compounded within the housing market.

# NINE

# Conclusion: negotiating the housing market over the next decades

Housing remains central to life in the 21st century: it is a major determinant of well-being, it provides a mechanism for wealth accumulation, it offers an avenue for self-expression, it is a carrier of social status and it carries significant costs for both individuals and society. It can also serve to reinforce inequality in society and either catapult individuals into adversity or further reinforce the marginal position of disadvantaged groups. Throughout *Housing Transitions* we have argued that the relationship between households and their housing has changed over the last four decades and that an ongoing recasting of this relationship is to be expected. This chapter re-examines the assumptions that led to the major research project that underpins this book and draws out the key lessons we have uncovered on the dynamics between housing and the life course in the 21st century. It also casts light on how housing markets and systems of housing supply are likely to evolve over the coming decades and what this will mean for populations.

## From housing careers to housing transitions

As noted in the Preface, the research that led to this monograph arose out of discussions between policy makers and an Australian research institution on the issues of housing careers and how such housing careers may change in the 21st century. Policy makers were concerned to understand how housing careers may be transformed and what that may mean for the provision of government assistance into the future. In particular, government bodies in Australia were concerned about three questions of policy relevance. First, over the coming decades what will be the impact of the ageing of the 'baby boom' cohort in terms of housing and the demand for housing assistance? Second, is the apparent decline in entry into homeownership among 25- to 34- year-olds robust, and what are the implications for the demand for housing assistance in the long term? Third, what forms of government housing assistance will be necessary and appropriate in the 21st century given changes in household structure, labour markets and philosophical shifts in attitudes to government intervention? All three were pertinent questions and were subsequently answered through the research programme (Beer and Faulkner, 2009).

Policy-focused analysis of this nature and extent inevitably throws up more fundamental questions of a conceptual nature. Importantly, mounting evidence of the sequence of housing occupancies now found across developed economies challenged the concept of a 'housing career' that had served as a foundation stone of housing research in the developed world for at least 40 years. At the same time, the continuation of empirical relationships between labour market position, stage in the life cycle, region and policies undermines the value of a 'housing pathways' approach founded on the subjective position of individuals. If what we think about housing is the only reality worth knowing, why do so many groups exhibit common consumption patterns? Clearly, there are objective policy processes and housing market drivers leading to observable commonalities and these need to be recognised, accepted, understood and built into our future understanding of the role of housing within society and its dialectical relationship with the economy, demography, cultural values, public sector policies and health.

Other researchers have previously used the term transitions to reflect upon and highlight stages in the life course and their relationship with one or more dimensions of the housing system. McNaughton (2008) examined the empirical and theoretical dimensions of the transitions into homelessness and, in common with this book, explicitly linked changes in housing outcomes to the emergence of a 'risk' society. Importantly, she recognised that both structure and agency remain pivotal in understanding housing and homelessness outcomes in contemporary society:

> Whilst it may be argued that there has always been a *degree* of complexity to the transitions people made over their life course (Goodwin and O'Connor 2005), it is now also recognised that there are more options, choices, and unpredictability (Furlong and Evans 1997). So to what degree has individualisation really taken hold or changed the ontological experience of social life in late modernity? There may be more 'choice', fluidity, or options, however there are also still clear 'plots' or 'scripts' that are collectively recognised in different societies and cultures.... Ezzy (2001) argues that transitions over the life course should take an 'integrative' course – for example, someone moving from the parental home to their own, moving into a larger home to have children, or move somewhere for new employment, are all transitional stages that maintain an individual's integration to society over their life course' (McNaughton, 2008, p 30).

Ezzy's (2001) observation on the integrative role of transitions over the life course speaks directly both to Clark et al's (2003) observation that a limited number of housing sequences accounted for 75 per cent of lifetime housing in the US. It also reflects our findings on trends in Australia's housing market. Structural factors clearly shape the decisions of individuals. These factors result in convergence for large sections of the population, but the same processes increasingly generate a greater diversity of outcomes for at least some groups in society. In *Housing Transitions*, the experiences of persons with a disability and those living precarious lives illustrate the widening gaps between some population groups.

McNaughton (2008) also situated her analysis of homelessness within critical realism and noted that the objective of a realist ontology is to generate causal explanations and theories on how particular outcomes arose. Causation, from this perspective, however

> ... is not viewed positivistically – as something that occurs in a linear relationship: that A causes B. Rather it is recognised that events occur due to a complex relationship of causation embedded in an entire interconnected social system.... Uncovering causation from a critical realist perspective is about uncovering the different mechanisms that can explain certain outcomes, without asserting that these same factors will necessarily *always* lead to that outcome, for *all* people (Fitzpatrick 2005). (McNaughton, 2008, pp 40–41)

McNaughton's (2008) research was based on 28 in-depth interviews with homeless persons and therefore diverges fundamentally from the research reported in *Housing Transitions,* where the major body of evidence is quantitative in nature. We would argue, however, that both perspectives are consistent with critical realism as each provides a foundation that permits theory building that sheds light on the multiple and hidden structural forces shaping society. Within this philosophy of knowledge *Housing Transitions* illuminates the structural processes – demographic, economic, governmental, social, historical and aspirational – that have fundamentally recast the relationship between housing and the life course in Australia and many other developed economies. On the other hand, we would acknowledge that further work is needed in this area to strengthen the account of agency in 21st-century housing transitions and the ways in which individuals and households, negotiate, broker and attach meaning to their movements through the housing stock. Such analysis is necessary, but unfortunately it was beyond the scope of our already substantial research programme. That said, we remain firm in our belief that the term housing transitions and its conceptualisation is of considerable value to contemporary scholarship on housing because of the way it unshackles researchers from a focus on linear progression, while acknowledging both convergence across society and divergence between groups.

The concept of housing transitions represents the multiple, and often conflicting, processes in the 21st century shaping movement through the housing market over the life course. Key determinants of an individual's decision at all life stages include their demography (that is, their stage in the life course), their labour market position, their consumption aspirations, their health or disability status, and their previous housing history. Importantly, the relative impacts of each of these factors will vary both over time and over the life course and this variation will find expression at both the individual and societal levels. For example, in many developed economies the global financial turmoil from 2007 onwards emphasised position in the labour market in determining housing outcomes. But over coming years, as financial markets return to a measure of stability, demographic factors such as the ageing of the baby boomer generation may, once again, overshadow other drivers in the housing system. At an individual level, consumption aspirations are present at all stages in the life course, but may only play a determining role in mid life when wealth and income peak.

In recognising the movement away from 20th-century housing careers to 21st-century housing transitions it is important to acknowledge the capacity of individuals to express choice within the housing market. We recognise, of course, that 'choice' is a problematic concept because not everyone is able to exert choice over their housing circumstances, and choice is itself socially constructed. While acknowledging these difficulties we argue that the concept of choice – as problematic or messy as it is – remains fundamental to understanding housing outcomes and their relationship to the life course in the 21st century. At a conceptual level it is important for a number of reasons. First, in virtually all developed economies the overwhelming majority of housing is allocated according to market processes, either through the purchase of housing or through rental markets. This trend has in fact strengthened over the last two to three decades, with the winding back in many nations of social housing supply and direct government intervention in the market. Put simply, for most people, for most of their lives, it is the market that determines where they live, in what type of housing and in which type of household structure. There are, of course, exceptions but they are limited, and in some nations even social housing systems now use 'choice based letting'. Second, by focusing on the decisions households make we must inevitably acknowledge that 'choice' is constrained, which in turn focuses attention on the processes limiting the range of possibilities available to various groups within society. Third, the issue of choice speaks to the ethnography of individual accounts of individual housing experiences. Clapham (2005a) contended that ethnographic approaches were necessary to put into practice his 'housing pathways' framework. Significantly, such qualitative research inevitably canvases the choices, or restrictions on choice, confronting individuals and their households.

The housing transitions perspective represents both a departure from previous theoretical constructs and the evolution of established scholarship in this area. Inevitably there remains a tension between the idea of individuals 'progressing' up a ladder of housing opportunities and situations on the one hand and, on the other, a perhaps less optimistic focus on changing position within the housing market per se. We would suggest that this tension can be overcome by focusing on the sequence of housing that individuals and households occupy over the life course. From this perspective, it is possible to recognise that some households exhibit housing careers marked by upward mobility, increasing consumption and opportunities for wealth accumulation, but these represent a subset of a much wider set of housing sequences evident within society.

Alternative housing sequences observed and now understood within the 21st century include pathways into and out of homelessness, the 'churning' of marginalised individuals and groups through precarious housing, the movement of the older population to purpose-built aged accommodation and the potential succession of accommodation they will occupy at the end of life, and the transcontinental housing arrangements of those working in global enterprises and industries. Each of these sets of housing transitions is important and in many ways reflects different class or labour market positions. We should acknowledge that earlier work, such as that of Clark et al (2003), recognised considerable fragmentation in the way in which households moved through the market but chose to set aside the 'outliers' within the data and instead focused on describing and understanding the major transitions. We would argue that such an approach can no longer be sustained and that instead it is important to develop a better understanding of the full spectrum of housing outcomes. Whereas housing careers made sense in a society and a time of middle-class stability, a more diverse economy and polity throws such propositions into question. Importantly, the latter part of the 20th century and the first decade of the 21st century have witnessed a widening of housing outcomes, with more advantageous consequences for some and deleterious conditions for others. In turn, these housing outcomes have implications for our understanding of the lifetime relationship between housing market position and the life course. They are reviewed in the following section.

## Housing transitions in the 21st century: risk, opportunity and policy challenges

Over the past two decades there has been an evident increase in the range of housing outcomes in developed economies. In large measure this has been part of a much broader shift to a 'risk society', which has entailed the erosion of established institutions and social supports that underpinned the industrial-era society and at the same time emphasised 'individualisation', with a greater range of opportunities available for some. This transformation has resulted in greater complexity within housing markets and in the sequence of housing over the life course. Increasing income inequality has contributed to this complexity, as has the ageing of the population, widespread immigration in developed economies, economic restructuring, the incidence of disability within the population and, in many nations, a movement away from direct welfare provision to more targeted and market-based approaches.

The impact of disability on housing transitions in the 21st century highlights the ways in which housing outcomes over the life course have become more complex. As the Housing 21 Survey showed, some 22 per cent of households in Australia included at least one person with a disability, and 19 per cent of households with a respondent aged under 65 reported at least one member with a disability or long-term health condition. Broadly comparable rates of incidence are evident in other nations. Disability, therefore, is an unavoidable feature of housing in contemporary societies, but it is important to ask how this has changed over the last 20 or 30 years. The answer to this is multi-faceted and includes both shifts in public policies and in societal norms. Importantly, there has not been a substantial increase in the rates of lifetime disability within the population. The rates of disability associated with ageing have increased as more people live for longer, but the percentage of the population affected by lifetime disabilities has been relatively static. Innovation in healthcare and medical technology may have reduced the incidence of some specific disabilities, but increased the occurrence of others. There has, however, been a substantial shift away from institutional forms of care to housing within the broader community. This shift has been driven by both the demands of the population affected by disability and the priorities of government with respect to welfare outlays and the quality of services they offer. In the 21st century, therefore, a higher percentage of persons with a disability live within the broader community and therefore within the stock of housing available to the population generally. This has implications for the population affected by disability – including carers and other family members – who must compete for accommodation with households in which all adults are able to work. They must also select from among a housing stock that was essentially designed and built without any thought as to how individuals may be impaired.

Disability, of course, does not simply affect the housing of those with lifetime impairment. Virtually all individuals within society will experience impairment at some stage in life, and the overwhelming majority of the aged live with some form of disability. Complexity in housing outcomes, therefore, is apparent both across the population as a whole and in the individual's experience of housing through their life course.

Risk within the housing market can, of course, be derived from a range of social, demographic, economic, and environmental sources. In contemporary Australia, for example, climate change appears to have increased the risk associated with bushfires, with some households in locations previously assessed as being in marginal risk now confronted by a much greater threat to both property and life. More commonly, however, households are confronted by socially constructed risks, of which the recent turmoil in global financial markets is a telling example. Many of the households that have fallen out of homeownership in the US, the UK, New Zealand and Australia since 2007 will never re-enter owner-occupation. The financial crisis of the past three years will have a permanent impact on their housing market circumstances and completely recast their housing transitions for the remainder of their lives.

The changing profile of risk in housing markets in the 21st century calls into question the nature of government intervention in housing and the philosophies of assistance they pursue. In broad terms, the last two decades have witnessed a movement away from direct government engagement with housing markets and at the same time more limited welfare support for disadvantaged individuals and groups. In the past, housing policy in nations such as Canada, the UK, Australia and New Zealand was based on the provision of social housing for households in need, with support often provided indefinitely. In some jurisdictions this policy framework has changed, with New South Wales, South Australia and Queensland, for example, introducing limited tenure within social housing. At the same time governments have pursued housing policies that are broadly consistent with 'third way' philosophies of government, and these interventions place greater emphasis on providing 'point in time' assistance. That is, governments seek to offer help that is seen to allow households to 'get back on their feet'.

Our analysis suggests that both philosophies of housing assistance are misplaced and out-of-step with 21st-century realities. On the one hand, many households do not have a 'housing career' to resume, and a reliance on short-term policy levers results in some households in indefinite receipt of 'short term' housing assistance. On the other hand, the conventional policy framework, based on indefinite residence in social housing, appears blind to the demographic realities of the 21st century. For example, only 10 per cent of respondents to the Housing 21 Survey (250 households) had ever applied for public housing and some 160 households had been offered social housing at some stage. Only 22 households (less than 1 per cent) were currently on the waiting list and approximately 5 per cent of respondents lived in social housing at the time of the interview. Critically, social housing is a small tenure and the stock of households assisted is minute relative to the level of need within the community. Moreover, households do not necessarily remain in social housing for extended periods as they relocate to other living and tenure arrangements (Seelig et al, 2005). More broadly, in the 21st century government interventions need to be better attuned and more sensitive to the processes of household dissolution. There is a need, therefore, for a more fine-grained approach to housing assistance, with policies that can accommodate a range of outcomes that match the breadth of circumstances affecting persons of low income in housing need.

The broad-scale social, economic and demographic processes that have been documented in *Housing Transitions* provide grounds for specific policy changes that in many respects fundamentally refocus housing programmes. It is inevitable that over the coming years there will be a growing demand for housing policies and programmes that better meet the needs of persons with a disability. We have argued through the course of this book that one of the most fundamental differences between housing transitions in the 21st century and housing careers in the 20th century is the large scale and acknowledged presence of disabled persons in the home. Whereas in the 20th century home was a place for the provision of care to children, demographic and policy change has meant that in the 21st century home will be a place for the provision – and receipt – of care for the adult population. Ageing is part of this equation, as is the trend to accommodate persons with a lifetime disability in the community. Some of the responses that governments will need to investigate include the development of a cohort of specialist housing providers, and their subsequent strengthening; the mandated application of universal housing design principles in new housing construction; and a repositioning of priorities for housing assistance. In the medium to longer term governments will need to investigate and implement programmes that assist persons with a disability, and family members with care responsibilities, into home ownership.

The ageing of the population will constitute a second key driver of housing policy reform in most developed nations over the coming decades. In most developed economies the percentage of the population aged over 65 will double over the next three decades and this will have enormous impacts on both government budgets and the housing stock. For some, older age will present few housing challenges, but others will be confronted by significant difficulties, especially if they enter older age while resident in an insecure tenure such as private rental housing. The research presented in *Housing Transitions* has shown that already 11 per cent of persons aged over 65 in Australia live in the private rental market where they are confronted by insecure leases, high housing costs and often poor-quality housing. Both the number and percentage of older persons in this circumstance will rise in the near future as the first waves of the baby boom generation passes the age of 65. Inevitably there will be an increased demand for housing assistance, as well as other forms of support. The coming generations of older persons, for example, are much more likely to be affected by social isolation because of their more fluid household structures and greater levels of residential mobility. In the future housing policies will need to be better integrated with other government services in order to create communities that better meet the needs of a population that has a greater percentage of members at home rather than at work.

Demographic change has been an important determinant of social change in many advanced economies over the previous two decades and it is likely that many of the evident trends will either be sustained or gather pace. One of the key challenges for government policy will be the ways in which existing programmes are adapted to take account of these changes. Household dissolution offers a case in point: in many ways the processes and outcomes associated with the breakup and dispersion of households are as important for the housing market as household formation. Household dissolution generates additional demand for housing, affects the disposable incomes and resources of the affected individuals and may trigger a departure from homeownership. Governments will need to consider this suite of processes and develop policy solutions that better meet the demands of a 21st-century population.

In Australia and many other nations one way of resolving the looming demographic challenges will be to strengthen programmes that maintain existing home purchasers in that tenure. Governments currently subsidise owner-occupation in a number of ways, ranging from mortgage deductibility in the US, to home purchase assistance grants in Australia and specialised loans in the UK. However, relatively little attention is paid to maintaining households in that tenure once they have gained a foothold. This focus on entry into the tenure rather than its maintenance is myopic in the extreme, as it ignores the substantial personal and financial costs associated with falling out of homeownership. The nations that have served as the focus of analysis in this book – Australia, the US and the UK – have all promoted home purchase over an extended period and it is now time to recognise that in some instances further investment is both justified and necessary. Baker et al (2010) noted in their study of low- and modest-income recipients of housing assistance in Australia that many home purchasers reported that they were worried because they could not afford to maintain their home and felt that they were at risk of dispossession. The costs to society and government of these households leaving homeownership are substantial and amply justify additional assistance to maintain them in their tenure.

## Global housing transitions: linkages, convergence and divergence

In the 21st century it is self evident that we live within a global economy. The near instantaneous flow of information and financial transactions has contributed to greater levels of economic integration between economies, as has the reduction of tariff and other trade barriers. Economic integration has contributed to a growing convergence in some dimensions of the housing market and housing market experiences, while significant differences remain because of regulatory frameworks, historical legacies and the nature of the local environment.

### Financial markets – turmoil, recovery and status quo

The turmoil within financial markets that has been evident across developed economies since 2007 has reinforced once again the ways in which housing markets are linked globally. The sub-prime mortgage crisis in the US precipitated much of the instability in the finance sector as lending institutions and investors discovered that many assets were now without value and house prices had been inflated by questionable lending practices. In many developed economies the financial crisis precipitated at that time – and the consequent crisis associated with the collapse of Lehman Brothers – resulted in a dip in housing markets. In the US, the UK, New Zealand and parts of Europe (including, notably, Spain) house prices fell, while in Australia house prices first stalled and then remained quiescent. Significant house price declines were not recorded in Australia because of the continuing shortfalls in supply, the economic stimulus measures introduced by the Australian government and the ongoing strength of the economy. Critically then, while there was convergence in some parts of the globe, there was also divergence, with local conditions and opportunities exerting a determinant influence.

The financial crisis first evident from 2007 will eventually come to a conclusion and the affected economies should return to economic growth. What then are the implications for the housing transitions in the affected economies? We would argue that the financial crisis will have a profound and lasting impact on some groups within the economy, especially those who have lost their homes or are otherwise disadvantaged. One of the outcomes of housing and finance sector turmoil has been a tightening of the regulatory environment and more limited access to housing finance – especially for the less well off in society. This trend is likely to continue, though weaken over time, as demands for both economic growth and better access to housing finance begin to overwhelm more cautionary approaches. However, for the majority of housing consumers the recent perturbations in financial markets are likely to be a mere hiccup in their lifetime consumption patterns. These economies remain fundamentally affluent and many households continue to hold significant wealth in housing and other assets. We foresee that their engagement with the housing market will resume a comparable trajectory to that evident in the recent past.

## Housing consumption across the globe

Housing markets and housing systems have also experienced greater levels of integration at a global scale. For some this integration has taken place directly and at a very personal level, with Paris (2008a, 2008b) and others documenting the growing incidence of individuals owning a second home in other nations. Entire urban developments in the Middle East, South East Asia, and the warmer parts of Europe have been established for the international market. The implications for local economies are profound, as are the flow-on effects for the housing experiences of the purchasing individuals or households. At one level it represents a simple case of 'hyper consumption' and the capacity of individuals to express housing choice at a global scale, but at the same time it reflects a set of historically and culturally specific circumstances and conditions. It implies, for example, an ongoing capacity to meet the cost of more than one home; continuing access to low-cost travel, especially airfares; a sense of dislocation from the local community, both within the host and origin countries; and household arrangements that are sufficiently flexible to allow cyclical relocation. Households where one or more persons provide primary care for someone in another household would not be able to engage in the requisite ongoing travel.

The growth of the international second-home market has contributed to convergence in housing markets across the globe both by strengthening financial ties and creating personal experiences of housing and/or homeownership that span international borders. Whether this market persists, however, is open to question as the weakening since 2007 of many European currencies, including the euro and the pound sterling, as well as economic downturn, will have reduced the spending capacity of many actual and aspirational second-home owners. As will be discussed below, environmental concerns may also impinge upon this market in coming years.

There are other ways in which individual housing transitions find expression on a global scale: for a growing proportion of both upwardly mobile young people and those in middle age at the peak of their career. In the past, migration to another country to find work was a long-term prospect, but increasingly those who work in the financial services sector, biotechnology, computing science, health or other key components of the knowledge economy cycle through international labour markets as they build their work portfolio. Some 6 per cent of moves through the housing market recorded in the Housing 21 Survey were associated with immigration and/or a return from a period spent overseas. The latter was more significant numerically than the former, with large numbers of both young adults and mid-age adults from Australia spending periods in Europe, North America and other parts of the world. This is a new driver within contemporary housing markets and one that may have unexpected spillover effects. It was notable that the economic downturn in the UK from 2007 resulted in the involuntary return to Australia of many who had previously worked in London's financial markets. In most cases they returned to Sydney, Melbourne or one of the other metropolitan centres, where they resumed the housing they owned and consequently evicted the tenants who had lived in their homes while they had worked in the UK. Comparable experiences would potentially have been evident in other parts of the global economy, as individual businesses closed branch offices and repatriated staff to headquarters, while in other cases staff were shed from the labour force and returned home. Unlike the global market for second homes, it is difficult to believe that this trend will not recur once global economic prosperity is restored, or at least re-emerges on the horizon. This conclusion is based on recognition that there is a global demand for skilled labour and that in many labour markets there is under-supply. There are also strong personal reasons why individuals would seek out these opportunities. The implication is that global housing transitions will continue and so an increasing proportion of the non-immigrant population will include significant international experience in the sequence of housing they occupy through their lifetime.

## Prospects: housing transitions over the coming decades

In their fundamental dynamics housing markets and the various components that constitute them are remarkably stable. Change is a constant feature of housing markets but it tends to be gradual, incremental and cumulative. In part this stability is a consequence of the importance of housing to the economy, to society and individuals. It is simply too important to be subject to radical change, and a society where housing is primarily provided through the market has too many decision makers to bring about wholesale change in a short period. Regulatory reform can have a profound impact but the consequences often take some time to emerge. For example, as discussed in Chapter Three, the sub-prime crisis in the US was the consequence of decades of regulatory reform. Even then, the housing market collapse triggered by the sub-prime crisis resulted in a return to previous conditions – with many low income households in the US forced back into low-rent accommodation – rather than precipitating the emergence of fundamentally new housing forms. Systems that are heavily reliant on direct government provision are more susceptible to substantial change in direction, but even the effects of the sale of council housing in the UK took decades to become fully evident. This stability in housing markets suggests that future change in the housing transitions of the residents of developed nations are likely to take place over an extended period. This in turn implies that it is more difficult to identify the key drivers of future housing experiences because their full impact is only evident after a prolonged period. Despite this caveat, we will conclude with a discussion of two factors that we consider will exert a critical influence on individuals and their housing through their life course.

## Housing and environmentally sustainable development

Across the globe, and especially in developed economies, there is a growing awareness of the need to move towards environmentally sustainable development. In part this reflects the growing debate on climate change and carbon pollution, but it should be acknowledged that there are other environmental debates relevant to housing, including the consumption of agricultural land, the impact of storm water run–off, and locally the generation of air pollution, water contamination and the proliferation of solid waste.

Housing is important both in terms of the consumption of resources and in the generation of waste. It exerts an impact in its construction and in its ongoing occupation. Housing also contributes indirectly to transport-related energy consumption; in particular the desire for low-density housing has contributed to urban sprawl in the US, Canada, Australia, New Zealand and parts of Europe. Many of the key shifts in housing consumption evident over the last two decades documented in this book result in greater levels of resource consumption for an increasing percentage of the population. The environmental consequences are clear: a faster rate of resource depletion, additional pollution and a built form increasingly out of step with community expectations on sustainability.

The concern for environmental sustainability will exert a number of impacts on the lifetime experience of housing in the coming decades. Most importantly, it is likely to contribute to increasing housing costs as the supply of land for urban development is restricted and as new housing construction is required to meet increasingly stringent standards. The same price pressures will also discourage the building of larger dwellings or the large-scale extension of housing. At the same time, the increasing cost of energy will result in higher house prices in more accessible locations, potentially reducing affordability in neighbourhoods currently occupied by low-income households. These are fundamental shifts that in large measure challenge our current understanding both of housing markets and the operation of cities. Over recent decades the trend in many nations, such as the US, Ireland and Australia, has been to larger homes, and we suggest that this will be reversed. In the US, many inner-city areas have been abandoned by the middle classes, but increasing fuel costs and the ongoing need to gain access to employment will create an inexorable push for centralisation. Such pressures are inevitable even in nations that do not take measures to address climate change because the days of relatively inexpensive energy, especially liquid fuels, are limited.

The restructuring of cities and housing markets over the coming years as a consequence of environmental concerns will have a profound impact on the relationship future generations will have with their housing. In all likelihood they will find entry into the home purchase market more difficult, they will be more likely to live both in smaller housing and in higher-density housing than currently, they will probably not engage in additional housing consumption at mid life, and they will be most unlikely to own a second home for their own use. It is inconceivable that, except for the wealthiest, they would own a home in a second country. Their housing preferences will be shaped by these expectations, with a greater focus on access to local services and increased preferences for well-designed housing and neighbourhoods.

## The ageing of the population

The populations of all developed economies are ageing rapidly, and the structural ageing of populations will have a profound impact on housing markets and the lifetime experiences of housing over coming decades. Demographic processes are an example, par excellence, of long-term structural change that is in many ways immutable. The reality is that for most developed nations their short- to medium-term demographic futures have already been determined because the scale of population processes is so great while the rate of change in these dynamics is relatively slow. Of course, not all nations will be affected equally, with the US, for example, having a younger age profile than the majority of the developed world. However, the ageing of the population will affect most nations. Large-scale immigration will not offer a solution to structural ageing in the longer term because over coming decades there will be increasing competition for immigrants, especially as global population moves towards a peak mid 21st century.

The ageing of the population is not simply a matter of the progressive ageing of the baby boom population. In many developed economies Generation X, which followed the baby boom generation, is as large, if not larger, and therefore nations will be confronted by at least 50 years with older populations. The implications for housing markets are profound. Key questions include:

- Will there be a demand for the larger housing that older residents seek to vacate in later life?
- What forms of housing assistance will governments be able to afford given increasing demands for healthcare and income support for aged residents?
- Will new housing forms be developed to meet the needs of the aged population?
- Will there be a need for innovation in tenure arrangements or in the financing of housing in older age?

The ageing of the population and their consequent demand for housing will have a significant impact on the lived experience of housing, on the housing industry and on governments. The impact of population ageing on the lived experience of housing will be profound: girls born in the year 2008 in Australia had a life expectancy at birth of just less than 84 years while boys born in the same year had a life expectancy at birth of 79 years. By the time both sexes reach the age of 20 their life expectancies will have risen by another five years or so. Similar life expectancies are recorded in other nations, and especially outside their disadvantaged groups. If achieved age continues to rise, albeit at a declining rate, by 2060 or 2070 a large percentage of the population will have spent the major part of their lives as older people, potentially living in purpose-built aged housing. This has implications for the built form of the housing stock, the way housing is funded and the need to offer services in addition to accommodation. One of the consequences will be the need to build 'lifetime housing', that is, dwellings that are able to accommodate persons in every housing transition, including those when they may be affected by a disability. The challenge for governments will be to fund and provide services and housing that support all sections of the aged population. While many will be able to meet their needs from their own resources, others will not, and for many disadvantaged older people direct government provision of housing may be the only workable solution. Potentially we may see a situation emerge whereby governments across the developed world re-engage with the direct provision of housing, but unlike the 1950s and 1960s, when they were concerned to provide housing for families, on this occasion housing will be targeted to the aged.

## The role and scope of further research

It is not possible to forecast all the processes and outcomes that will reshape the relationship between persons and their housing over their lifetimes. However, we can be sure that it will remain an important and dynamic relationship and one which reflects a full range of social, economic and environmental pressures. Housing transitions in the first decade of the 21st century differ from those acknowledged and understood a generation previously. There will be a continuing need to examine this issue to better inform public policy, assist communities with their housing needs and, perhaps most importantly, continue to contribute to the understanding of society. Over time the need for cross-national research and scholarship in this area will grow as the differing policy positions nations adopt on climate change adaptation and amelioration, income support, economic development and the taxation of housing will exert a subtle but powerful influence on housing outcomes. Both large-scale quantitative analysis and more detailed qualitative investigations will be needed to realign our understanding of the relationship between housing outcomes and the life course, as well as capture new patterns within the housing market. Researchers have long been fascinated by the intersection between the life course and housing processes and the durability of this research tradition suggests a further wealth of insights over the coming years.

# References

Abramson, M. (2008) 'Housing careers in a changing welfare state – a Swedish cohort study', *Housing, Theory and Society*, vol 25, no 4, pp 231-54.

ABS (Australian Bureau of Statistics) (2004a) *Household and family projections Australia 2001-2026,* Cat No 3236.0, Canberra: ABS.

ABS (Australian Bureau of Statistics) (2004b) *Disability, ageing and carers: summary of findings Australia*, Cat No 4430.0, Canberra: ABS.

ABS (Australian Bureau of Statistics) (2005) *Job search experience Australia,* Cat No 6222.0, Canberra: ABS.

ABS (Australian Bureau of Statistics) (2007a) 'Lifetime marriage and divorce trends', *Australian Social Trends,* Cat No 4102.0, Canberra: ABS.

ABS (Australian Bureau of Statistics) (2007b) *Job search experience Australia*, Cat No 6222.0, Canberra: ABS.

ABS (Australian Bureau of Statistics) (2007c) *Housing occupancy and costs 2005-06,* Cat No 4103.0.55.001, Canberra: ABS.

ABS (Australian Bureau of Statistics) (2007d) *Household wealth and wealth distribution Australia*, Cat No 6554.0, Canberra: ABS.

ABS (Australian Bureau of Statistics) (2007e) *Basic community profile Australia*, Canberra: ABS.

ABS (Australian Bureau of Statistics) (2007f) *Migration 2005-06,* Cat No 3141.0, Canberra: ABS.

ABS (Australian Bureau of Statistics) (2008a) *Yearbook Australia*, Cat No 1301.0, Canberra: ABS.

ABS (Australian Bureau of Statistics) (2008b) *Population projections Australia 2006-2101*, Cat No 3222.0, Canberra: ABS.

ABS (Australian Bureau of Statistics) (2009a) 'Home and away; the living arrangements of young people', *Australian social trends,* Cat No 4102.0, Canberra: ABS.

ABS (Australian Bureau of Statistics) (2009b) *Job search experience Australia,* Cat No 6222.0, Canberra: ABS.

ABS (Australian Bureau of Statistics) (2009c) *Housing mobility and conditions Australia,* Cat No 4130.0.55.002, Canberra: ABS.

ABS (Australian Bureau of Statistics) (2010) *Australian labour market statistics,* Cat No 6105.0, Canberra: ABS.

ACG (Allen Consulting Group) (2007) 'Development of a model for families and individuals to invest in housing provided by the disability Housing Trust', Sydney, unpublished.

AHURI (Australian Housing and Urban Research Institute) (1998) 'Who's moving from home ownership into rental', *Quarterly Housing Monitor,* vol 3, p 3.

AIHW (Australian Institute of Health and Welfare) (2003) *Disability prevalence and trends, disability series,* AIHW Cat No DIS 34, Canberra: AIHW.

AIHW (Australian Institute of Health and Welfare) (2007) *Current and future demand for specialist disability services*, Canberra: AIHW.

AIHW (Australian Institute of Health and Welfare) (2009) *Australia's welfare 2009*, No 9, Cat No AUS 117, Canberra: AIHW.

Allon, F. (2008) *Renovation nation: our obsession with home,* Kensington: UNSW Press.

Allwood, D. and Rogers, N. (2001) *Moving yarns: aboriginal youth homelessness in Metropolitan Adelaide*, Adelaide: Department of Human Services.

Anderson, M. Bechhofer, F. and Kendrick, S. (1994) 'Individual and households strategies', in M. Anderson, F. Bechhofer and J. Gershundy (eds) *The social and political economy of the household*, Oxford: Oxford University Press.

Andrew M (2010) 'The changing route to owner occupation: the impact of student debt', *Housing Studies*, vol 25, no 1, pp 39-62.

Armstrong, K., Bailey, D., de Ruyter, A., Mahdon, M. and Thomas, H. (2008) 'Auto plant closures, policy responses and labour market outcomes: a comparison of MG Rover in the UK and Mitsubishi in Australia', *Policy Studies*, vol 29, no 3, pp 343-55.

Ashcraft, A. and Schuermann, T. (2008) 'Understanding the securitization of subprime mortgage credit', Federal Reserve Bank of New York, Staff Report no. 318 (available at www.newyorkfed.org/research/staff_reports/sr318.pdf).

Atkinson, R. and Flint, J. (2004) 'Fortress UK? Gated communities, the spatial revolt of the elites and time-space trajectories of segregation', *Housing Studies*, vol 19, no 6, pp 875-92.

Atkinson, R. And Jacobs, K. (2008) *Public housing in Australia: stigma, home and opportunity*, Housing and Community Research Unit, Paper No 1, University of Tasmania, Hobart: Housing and Community Research Unit.

Atterhog, M. (2005) *Importance of government policies for home ownership rates, an international survey and analysis,* Working Paper No 54, Royal Institute of Technology, Stockholm: School of Architecture and the Environment.

Australian Financial System Inquiry (1981) *Final report* (Campbell Committee), Canberra: Australian Government Publishing Service.

Australian Financial System Inquiry (1984) *Final report* (Martin Committee), Canberra: Australian Government Publishing Service.

Badcock, B.A. and Beer, A. (2000) *Home truths: property ownership and housing wealth in Australia*, Melbourne: Melbourne University Press.

Bailey, D., Chapain, C., Mahdon, M. and Fauth, R. (2008) *Life after Longbridge: three years on. pathways to re-employment in a restructuring economy*, Birmingham: The Work Foundation.

Baker, A. (2007) 'Generational reform: the health implications of housing change'. Paper presented to the ENHR 2007 International Conference, 'Sustainable Urban Areas', Rotterdam, unpublished.

Baker, E. Beer, A. Wood, G. and Raftery, P. (2010) 'Gatekeepers and pathways: the impact of administrative processes in shaping access to housing assistance', paper presented to the Australasian Housing Researchers Conference, November, Auckland.

Banks, J., Emmerson, C. and Oldfield, Z. (2004) 'Not so brief lives: longevity and wellbeing in retirement', in I. Stewart and R. Vaitilingam (eds) *Seven ages of man and women*, Swindon: ESRC, pp 28-31.

Barber, A. and Hall, S. (2008) 'Birmingham: whose urban renaissance? Regeneration as a response to economic restructuring', *Policy Studies,* vol 29, no 3, pp 281-93.

Barker, K. (2004) *Review of housing supply, delivering stability: securing our future housing needs, final report*. London: HM Treasury.

Baum, S. and Wulff, M. (2003) *Housing aspirations of Australian households*, Final Report, Melbourne: Australian Housing and Urban Research Institute.

Baxter, J. and McDonald, P. (2004) *Trends in home ownership rates in Australia: the relative importance of affordability trends and changes in population composition*, Final Report, Melbourne: Australian Housing and Urban Research Institute.

Baxter, J. and McDonald, P. (2005) *Why is the rate of home ownership falling in Australia?* Research and Policy Bulletin 52, Melbourne: Australian Housing and Urban Research Institute.

Beck, U. (1992) *Risk society: towards a new modernity*, London: Sage.

Beck, U. (2000) *The brave new world of work*, Cambridge: Polity Press.

Beer, A. (1992) 'A dream won, a crisis born? Home ownership and the housing market', in C. Paris (ed) *Housing Australia*, Melbourne: Macmillan, pp 147-72.

Beer, A. and Cutler, C. (1999) 'Housing needs and preferences of immigrants', Canberra: Department of Immigration and Ethnic Affairs, unpublished.

Beer, A. and Faulkner, D. (2009) *21st century housing careers and Australia's housing future*, Final Report, Melbourne: Australian Housing and Urban Research Institute.

Beer, A. and Paris, C. (2005) 'Sustainable housing paradigms? The impact of reforms on the social housing sector in South Australia and Northern Ireland', *South Australian Geographical Journal*, vol 104, pp 38-50.

Beer, A. and Thomas, H. (2007) 'The politics and policy of economic restructuring in Australia: understanding government responses to the closure of an automotive plant', *Space and Polity*, vol 11, no 3, pp 243-62.

Beer, A., Faulkner, D. and Gabriel, M. (2006a) *21st century housing careers and Australia's housing future*, Positioning Paper, Melbourne: Australian Housing and Urban Research Institute.

Beer, A., Slatter, M., Baulderstone, J. and Habibis, D. (2006b) *Evictions and housing management*, Final Report, Melbourne: Australian Housing and Urban Research Institute.

Beer, A., Baum, F., Thomas, H., Lowry, D., Cutler, C., Ziersch, A., Verity, F., Jolley, G., McDougall, C. (2006c) *An evaluation of the impact of retrenchment at Mitsubishi focussing on affected workers, their families and communities: implications for human services policies and practices*, Adelaide: Department of Health.

Beer, A., Kearins, B. and Pieters, H. (2007) 'Housing affordability and planning in Australia', *Housing Studies*, vol 22, no 1, pp 11-24.

Beer, A., Faulkner, D., Baker, E., Tually, S., Raftery, P. and Cutler, C. (2009) *Our homes, our communities, the aspirations and expectations of older people in South Australia*, Adelaide: ECH.

Berry, M., Dalton, T. and Nelson, A. (2009) *Mortgage default in Australia: nature, causes and social and economic impacts*, Positioning Paper, Melbourne: Australian Housing and Urban Research Institute.

Berry, M., Dalton, T. and Nelson, A. (2010) *Mortgage default in Australia: nature, causes and social and economic impacts*, Final Report No 145, Melbourne: RMIT Research Centre, Australian Housing and Urban Research Institute.

Billari, F.C. and Liefbroer, A.C. (2007) 'Should I stay or should I go? The impact of age norms on leaving home', *Demography*, vol 44, no 1, pp 181-98.

Billari, F.C., Philipov, D. and Baizan, P. (2001) 'Leaving home in Europe: the experience of cohorts born around 1960', *International Journal of Population Geography*, vol 7, pp 339-56.

Birdsall-Jones, C.L. and Christensen, W.J. (2007) *Aboriginal housing careers in Western Australian towns and cities*, Positioning Paper, Melbourne: Australian Housing and Urban Research Institute.

Blakely, E. and Snyder, G. (1999) *Fortress America: gated communities in the US*, Chicago: The Brookings Institute.

Blatter, J. (2004) '"From places of place" to "spaces of flows"? Territorial and functional governance in cross-border regions in Europe and North America', *International Journal of Urban and Regional Research*, no 28, vol 3, pp 530-48.

Bleasdale, M. (2001) 'Empowerment through individualised funding', paper presented to the 'Sharing the Road' Conference, Brisbane: Griffith University.

Blyth, M. (2008) 'The politics of compounding bubbles: the global housing bubble in comparative perspective', *Comparative European Politics*, vol 6, no 3, pp 387-406.

Bochel, C., Bochel, H. and Page, D. (1999) 'Housing: the foundation of community care', *Health and Social Care in the Community*, vol 7, no 6, pp 492-501.

Bonvalet, C. and Ogg, J. (2008) 'The housing situation and residential strategies of older people in France', *Ageing and Society,* vol 28, part 6, pp 753-78.

Bracher, M., Santow, G., Morgan, S.P. and Trussell, J. (1993) 'Marriage dissolution in Australia: models and explanations', *Population Studies*, vol 47, no 3, pp 403-25.

Bridge, C., Cockburn-Campbell, J., Flatau, P., Whelan, S., Wood, G. and Yates, J. (2003) *Housing assistance and non shelter outcomes*, Melbourne: Australian Housing and Urban Research Institute.

Bridge, C., Mathews M., Phibbs P., and Adams T. (2009) *Reverse mortgages and older people: growth factors and implications for retirement decisions*, Positioning Paper No 123, UNSW-UWS Research Centre, Melbourne: Australian Housing and Urban Research Institute.

Brink, S. (1990) 'International policy trends in housing the elderly in developed countries', *Ageing International*, vol 17, no 2, pp 13-20.

Brink, S. (1998) *Housing older people: an international perspective*, New Brunswick, New Jersey: Transaction Publishers.

Brink, S. (2002) The ageing population challenge for policy makers. Submission to the Australian Parliamentary Inquiry into Ageing (available at www.aph.gov.au/house/committee/ageing/strategies/subs/sub49.pdf).

Burnley, I. (1976) 'Greek settlement in Sydney 1947-71', *Australian Geographer*, vol 13, no 3, pp 200-14.

Burnley, I., Murphy, P. and Fagan, R. (1997) *Immigration and Australian cities*, New South Wales: The Federation Press.

Carliner, M. (1998). 'Development of federal homeownership policy', *Housing Policy Debate,* vol 9, no 2 (available at www.mi.vt.edu/data/files/hpd 9(2)/hpd 9(2)carliner.pdf).

Carmichael, G.A., Webster, A. and McDonald, P. (1996) *Divorce Australian style: a demographic analysis*, Canberra: Research School of Social Sciences, Australian National University.

Cassells, R. and Harding, A. (2007) *Generation WhY?,* AMP. NATSEM Income and Wealth Report issue 17, Canberra: National Centre for Social and Economic Modelling.

Castles, I. (1998) 'The really big trade off: home ownership and the welfare state in the new world and old', *Acta Politica*, vol 33, no 1, pp 5-9.

Chamberlain, C. and MacKenzie, D. (2008) Australian Census Analytic Program, *Counting the Homeless, Australia, 2006*, Cat No. 2050.0, Canberra: Australian Bureau of Statistics.

Chiuri, M.C. and Jappelli, T. (2003) 'Financial market imperfections and home ownership: a comparative study', *European Economic Review*, vol 47, pp 857-75.

Clapham, D. (2002) 'Housing pathways: a post modern analytical framework', *Housing, Theory and Society*, vol 19, no 2, pp 57-68.

Clapham, D. (2004) 'Housing pathways – a social constructionist research framework', in K. Jacobs, J. Kemeny and D. Manzi. (eds) *Social constructionism in housing research*, Basingstoke: Ashgate, pp 93-116.

Clapham, D. (2005a) *The meaning of housing: a pathways approach*, Bristol: Policy Press.

Clapham, D. (2005b) 'The "really big tradeoff" between home ownership and welfare: Castle's evaluation of the 1980 thesis and a reformulation 25 years on', *Housing Theory and Society*, vol 22, no 2, pp 59-75.

Clark, K. and Drinkwater, S. (2007) *Ethnic minorities in the labour market: dynamics and diversity*, York: Joseph Rowntree Foundation.

Clark, W.A.V. and Huang, Y. (2003) 'The life course and residential mobility in British housing markets', *Environment and Planning A*, vol 35, pp 323-39.

Clark, W., Deurloo, M. and Dielemann, F. (2000) 'Housing consumption and residential crowding in US housing markets', *Journal of Urban Affairs*, vol 22, no 1, pp 49-63.

Clark, W., Deurloo, M. and Dielemann, F. (2003) 'Housing careers in the United States: modelling the sequencing of housing states', *Urban Studies*, vol 40, pp 143-60.

Cobb-Clark D.A. (2008) 'Leaving home: what economics has to say about the living arrangements of young Australians', *The Australian Economic Review*, vol 41, no 2, pp 160-76.

Commonwealth of Australia (2002) *Intergenerational Report 2002-03*, Budget Paper No 5, Canberra: Treasury.

Commonwealth of Australia (2007) *Intergenerational Report 2007*, Canberra: Treasury.

Commonwealth of Australia (2008a) 'The road home: the homelessness white paper', Canberra: Department of Families, Housing, Community Services and Indigenous Affairs.

Commonwealth of Australia (2008b) *A decent quality of life: inquiry into the cost of living pressures on older Australians,* Canberra: The Senate Standing Committee on Community Affairs.

Commonwealth of Australia (2010) *Australia to 2050: future challenges*, Canberra: Treasury.

Connolly, H. and White, A. (2006) 'The different experiences of the United Kingdom's ethnic and religious populations', *Social Trends 36th edition*, Office of National Statistics, Basingstoke: Palgrove Macmillan, pp 1–8, accessed on 25 January at http://www.statistics.gov.uk/downloads/theme_social/Social_Trends36/Social_Trends_36.pdf

Côté, J. and Bynner, J.M. (2008) 'Changes in the transition to adulthood in the UK and Canada: the role of structure and agency in emerging adulthood', *Journal of Youth Studies*, vol 11, no 3, pp 251-68.

Coughlan, J. (1991) *Housing characteristics of Australia's three Indo Chinese communities, 1976-86*, Brisbane: Griffith University.

Cox, D. (1996) *Understanding Australian settlement services*, Canberra: Bureau of Immigration, Multicultural and Population Research, Department of Immigration and Multicultural Affairs.

Crossley, T.F. and Ostrovsky, Y. (2003) 'A synthetic cohort analysis of Canadian housing careers, social and economic dimensions of an ageing population', (SEDAP) Research Paper No. 107, Ontario, Canada: McMaster University.

Daglish, T. (2009) 'What motivates a subprime borrower to default?' *Journal of Banking and Finance*, vol 33, pp 681-93.

Daly, M. (1982) *Sydney boom, Sydney bust, the city and its property market, 1850-1981*, Sydney: George Allen and Unwin.

Dargavel, R. and Kendig, H. (1986) 'Political rhetoric and program drift: House and Senate debates on the Aged and Disabled Persons' Homes Act', *Australian Journal on Ageing*, vol 5, pp 23-31.

Davison B., Kendig, H., Stephens, L. and Merrill, V. (1993) *My place: older people talk about their homes*, Canberra: Australian Government Publishing Service.

*Demographia*, (2006) Second annual Demographia international housing affordability survey (available at www.demographia.com).

Department for Communities and Local Government (2007) *Homes for the future: more affordable, more sustainable*, London: Department for Communities and Local Government.

Department for Communities and Local Government (2009) Live tables (available at www.communities.gov.uk/corporate/researchandstatistics/publicdatasources/housing/livetables/).

Department of Families, Housing, Community Services and Indigenous Affairs (2009) *Housing Assistance Act 1996 annual report 2006-07*, Canberra: Department of Families, Housing, Community Services and Indigenous Affairs.

Department of Health and Ageing (2008) *Home and community care program minimum data set 2007-08 annual bulletin,* Canberra: Australian Government Department of Health and Ageing.

Department of Health, Housing, Local Government and Community Services (DHHLGCS) (1993) *Aged care reform strategy mid term review,* stage two report, Canberra: Australian Government Publishing Service.

Deurloo, M.C., Clark, W.A.V. and Dieleman, F.M. 1994) 'The move to housing ownership in temporal and regional contexts', *Environment and Planning A*, vol 26, pp 1659-70.

Diamond, I. (2004) 'Foreword', in I. Stewart and R. Vaitilingam (eds) *Seven ages of man and women*, Swindon: ESRC, p 5.

Dieleman, F. (1994) 'Social rented housing: valuable asset or unsustainable burden?', *Urban Studies*, vol 31, no 3, pp 447-63.

Dijst, M., Lanzendorf, M., Barrendregt, A. and Smit, L. (2005) 'Second homes in Germany and the Netherlands, ownership and travel impact explained', *Tijdshrift voor Economishe en Sociale Geografie*, vol 96, no 2, pp 139-52.

DiMartino, D., Duca, J. and Rosenblum, H. (2007) 'From complacency to crisis: financial risk taking in the early 21st century', Federal Reserve Bank of Dallas, Economic Letter, vol 2, no 12.

Dodson, J. (2007) *Government discourse and housing*, Basingstoke: Ashgate.

Dolan, A., McLean, P. and Roland, D. (2005) 'Home equity, retirement incomes and family relationships', paper prepared for the 9th Australian Institute of Family Studies Conference, 9-11 February, Melbourne.

Doling, J. and Ronald, R. (2010) 'Home ownership and asset based welfare', *Journal of Housing and the Built Environment*, vol 25, pp 165-73.

Dorling, D., Rigby, J., Wheeler, B., Ballas, D., Thomas, B., Fahmy, E., Gordon, D. and Lupton, R. (2007) *Poverty, wealth and place in Britain, 1968 to 2005*, York: Joseph Rowntree Foundation.

Dorn, N. (2009) 'Ponzi finance, regulatory capture and the credit crunch', SSRN (available at http://ssrn.com/abstract=1365250)

Dunn, J. (2000) 'Housing and health inequalities: review and prospects for research', *Housing Studies*, vol 15, no 3, pp 341-66.

Dupuis A. and Thorns D. (1996) 'Meaning of home for older home owners', *Housing Studies*, vol 11, pp 485-501.

Econsult (1989) *Rural centres housing study*, Canberra: Australian Government Publishing Service.

ECOTEC Research and Consulting Ltd and the Joseph Rowntree Foundation (2009) *Young people's housing transitions*, York: Joseph Rowntree Foundation (also available at www.jrf.org.uk).

Edwards, B., Higgins, D. and Zmijewski, N. (2007) 'The families caring for a person with a disability study and the social lives of carers', *Family Matters*, vol 76, pp 8–17.

Ellis, L., Lawson, J. and Roberts-Thomson, L. (2003) 'Housing leverage in Australia', Research Discussion Paper, Sydney: Reserve Bank of Australia.

Encel, S. (1993) 'Work and opportunity in a changing society', in K. Sanders (ed) *Ageing: law, policy and ethics, directions for the 21st century*, Proceedings of a Symposia held at the University of Melbourne, 1992, pp 122–8. Epsing-Anderson, G. (1990) *Three worlds of welfare capitalism*, Cambridge: Cambridge University Press.

Ezzy, D. (2001) *Narrating unemployment*, Aldershot: Ashgate.

Farmer, M. and Barrell, R. (1981) 'Entrepreneurship and government policy: the case of the housing market', *Journal of Public Policy*, vol 1, no 3, pp 307–32.

Faulkner, D. (2001) *Linkages among housing assistance, residential (re)location, and use of community health and social care by old-old adults*, Positioning Paper, Melbourne: Australian Housing and Urban Research Institute.

Faulkner, D. and Bennett, K. (2002) *Linkages among housing assistance, residential (re) location, and use of community health and social care by old-old adults*, Final Report, Melbourne: Australian Housing and Urban Research Institute.

Faulkner D., Tually S., Baker E., and Beer, A. (2007) 'Report on the outcomes of focus groups for the South Australian Ageing Atlas: ageing and its implications for social and planning policy', Report prepared for Planning SA, unpublished.

Feijten, P. (2005) 'Union dissolution, unemployment and moving out of home ownership', *European Sociological Review*, vol 21, no 1, pp 59–71.

Feijten, P. and Mulder, C.H. (2002) 'The timing of household events and housing events in the Netherlands: a longitudinal perspective', *Housing Studies*, vol 17, pp 773–92.

Feijten, P. and Mulder, C.H. (2005) 'Life-course experience and housing quality', *Housing Studies*, vol 20, no 4, pp 571–87.

Feijten, P. and van Ham, M. (2007) 'Residential mobility and migration of the divorced and separated', *Demographic Research*, vol 17, Article 21, pp 623–54.

Ferri, (2004) 'Thirty-something: time to settle down?', in I. Stewart and R. Vaitilingam (eds) *Seven ages of man and women*, Swindon: ESRC, pp 20–3.

Fine, M. (2007) 'Uncertain prospects: aged care policy for a long-lived society', in A. Borowski, S. Encel and E. Ozanne (eds) *Longevity and social change in Australia*, Sydney: University of New South Wales Press, pp 265–95.

Fitzpatrick, S. (2005) 'Explaining homelessness, a critical realist perspective', *Housing, Theory and Society,* vol 22, no 5, pp 1–17.

Flatau, P., Hendershott P., Watson, R. and Wood, G. (2003) *What drives housing outcomes in Australia? Understanding the role of aspirations, household formation, economic incentives and labour market interactions,* Positioning Paper, Melbourne: Australian Housing and Urban Research Institute.

Flatau, P., Hendershott, P., Watson, R. and Wood, G. (2004) *What drives Australian housing careers? An examination of the role of labour market, social and economic determinants,* Final Report, Melbourne: Australian Housing and Urban Research Institute.

Flood, J. and Baker, E. (2010) *Housing implications of economic, social and spatial change,* Final Report, Melbourne: Australian Housing and Urban Research Institute.

Florida, R. (2002) *The rise of the creative class: and how it's transforming work, leisure and everyday life,* New York: Basic Books.

Fopp, R. (2008) 'Social constructionism and housing studies: a critical reflection', *Urban Policy and Research*, vol 26, no 2, pp. 159-76.

Ford, J., Rugg, J. and Burrows, R. (2002) 'Conceptualising the contemporary role of housing in the transition to adult life in England', *Urban Studies*, vol 39, no 13, pp 2455-67.

Forrest, R. (1987) 'Spatial mobility, tenure mobility and emerging social divisions in the UK housing market', *Environment and Planning A*, vol 19, pp 1611-30.

Forrest, R. and Kemeny, J. (1983) 'Middle class housing careers: the relationship between furnished renting and owner occupation', *Sociological Review*, vol 30, pp 208-22.

Franklin, B. (2002) 'On the elusiveness of grand theory', *Housing, Theory and Society,* vol. 19, no 3, pp 140-2.

Fukuda, S. (2009) 'Leaving the parental home in post-war Japan: demographic changes, stem-family norms and the transition to adulthood', *Demographic Research*, vol 20, article 30, pp 731-816.

Fukuyama, F. (1992) *The end of history and the last man,* New York: The Free Press.

Furlong, A. and Cartmel, F. (2007) *Young people and social change: new perspectives* (2nd edn), Buckingham: Open University Press.

Furlong, A. and Evans, K. (1997) 'Metaphors of youth transitions: niches, pathways, trajectories or navigations', in J. Bynnner, L. Chisholm and A. Furlong (eds) *Youth, Citizenship and Social Change in a European Context,* Aldershot: Avebury (Ashgate).

Gadher, D. and Davies, H. (2007) 'Shires fall to foreign land rush', *The Sunday Times*, 28 October.

Gallent, N., Mace, A. and Tewdr-Jones, M. (2005) *Second homes: European perspectives and UK policies,* Aldershot: Ashgate.

Galster, G., Tatian, P. and Smith, R. (1999) 'The impact of newcomers who use Section 8 certificates on property values', *Housing Policy Debate*, vol 10, no 4, pp 879-912.

Gardner, N. (2010) 'First-home buyers struggle as interest rates rise', *The Sunday Mail* (Qld), 31 January.

Giddens, A. (1984) *The constitution of society*, Cambridge: Polity Press.

Giddens, A. (1990) *The consequences of modernity*, Cambridge: Polity Press.

Giddens, A. (1991) *Modernity and self-identity: self and society in the late modern age*, Stanford: Stanford University Press.

Giddens, A. (1998) *The third way: the renewal of social democracy*, Cambridge: Polity Press.

Giddens, A. (1999) 'Risk and responsibility', *Modern Law Review*, vol 62, no 1, pp 1-10.

Giddens, A. (2000) *The third way and its critics*, Cambridge: Polity Press.

Glaeser, E. and Gyourko, J. (2005) 'Urban decline and durable housing', *Journal of Political Economy*, vol 113, no 2, pp 345-75.

Globe and Mail (2009) 'Subprime lending market', *The Globe and Mail* (available at www.canadamortgagehub.com/Mortgage_News/)

Goodwin, J. and O'Connor, H. (2005) Exploring complex transitions: looking back at the 'golden age' of 'from school to work', *Sociology*, 39:2, pp 201-220.

Gottliebsen, R. (2002) 'Living on a leveraged edge', *The Weekend Australian*, 18-19 May.

Gram-Hanssen, K. and Bech-Danielsen, C. (2008) 'Home dissolution: what happens after separation?', *Housing Studies*, vol 23, no 3, pp 507-22.

Green-Pedersen, C., Van Kersbergen, Km and Hemerijck, A. (2001) 'Neo-liberalism, the 'third way' or what? Recent social democratic welfare policies in Denmark and the Netherlands', *Journal of European Public Policy*, vol 8, no 2, pp 307-25.

Guerrero, T.J. (2001) *Youth in transition: housing, employment, social policies and families in France and Spain*, Aldershot: Ashgate.

Gwyther, G. (2007) 'Women's housing transitions after significant relationship breakdown: A qualitative approach', Sydney: University of Sydney, unpublished.

Hall, P., Thomas, R., Gracey, H. And Drewett, R. (1973) *The containment of urban England*, 2 vols, London: Allen and Unwin.

Hanson J. (2001) 'From "special needs" to "lifestyle choices": articulating the demand for "third age" housing', in S. Peace and C. Holland (eds) *Inclusive housing in an ageing society, innovative approaches*, Bristol: The Policy Press, pp 29-53.

Harmer, J. (2009) *Pension review report*, Canberra: Department of Families, Housing, Community Services and Indigenous Affairs.

Harts, J. and Hingstman, L. (1986) *Verhuizin-gen op eenrij: een analyse van individual everhuis geschiedenissen*, Utrecht: University of Utrecht, Department of Geography.

Harvey, D. (1973) *Social justice and the city*, London: Edward Arnold.

Hassell, in association with Hugo, G. (1996) *Immigrants and public housing*, Department of Immigration and Multicultural Affairs, Canberra: Australian Government Publishing Service.

Havet, N. and Penot, A. (2010) *Does homeownership harm labour market performance: a survey*, Working Paper 1012, St-Etienne, Lyon: Groupe d'analyse et de theorie economique.

Headey, B., Warren, D. and Wooden, M. (2008) *The structure and distribution of household wealth in Australia: cohort differences and retirement issues*, Social Policy Research Paper No 33, Melbourne: Melbourne Institute of Applied Economic and Social Research, University of Melbourne.

Helleiner, J. (2000) *Racism and the politics of culture*, Toronto: University of Toronto Press.

Henderson, J. and Karn, V. (1984) 'Race, class and the allocation of state housing in Britain', *Urban Studies*, vol 21, pp 115-28.

Hewett, J. (2007) 'Under mortgage pressure', *The Australian,* 20 October (available at www.theaustralian.com.au/business/property/under-mortgage-pressure/story-e6frg9gx-1111114684241).

Hewitt, B., Baxter, J. and Weston, M. (2005) 'Marriage breakdown in Australia: the social correlates of separation and divorce', *Journal of Sociology*, vol 41, no 2, pp 163-83.

Heywood, F., Oldman, C. and Means, R. (2002) *Housing and home in later life*, Buckingham: Open University Press.

Hill, M. (1959) *Housing finance in Australia, 1945-56*, Melbourne: Melbourne University Press.

Hill, M. (1974) 'Housing finance', in R. Hirst and R. Wallace (eds) *The Australian capital market*, Melbourne: Cheshire.

Hillman, K.J. and Marks, G.N. (2002) 'Becoming an adult: leaving home, relationships and home ownership among Australian youth, longitudinal surveys of Australian youth', Research Report No 28, Victoria: Australian Council for Educational Research and Commonwealth Department of Education, Science and Training.

Hogan, W. (2003) *Historical perspectives: the evolution of the Australian government's involvement in supporting the needs of older people. Review of pricing arrangements in residential aged care* (Background Paper no. 4), Canberra: Department of Health and Ageing.

Holdsworth, C. and Morgan, D. (2005) *Transitions in context: leaving home, independence and adulthood*, Buckingham: Open University Press.

Horsfield, G. (2005) 'International migration', in Chappell, R. (ed) *Focus on people and migration*, Basingstoke: Office of National Statistics (Palgrave Macmillan), pp 115-129, accessed on 25 January 2011 at http://www.statistics.gov.uk/statbase/product.asp?vlnk=12899

Hou, F. (2010) 'Homeownership over the life course of Canadians: evidence from Canadian censuses of population', Research Paper in the Analytical Studies Branch Research Paper Series, Cat No 11FOO19M-No 325, Ontario: Statistics Canada.

House of Representatives Standing Committee on Expenditure, (1982) *In a home or at home: accommodation and home care for the aged,* Report from the House of Representatives Standing Committee on Expenditure, October, Canberra: Australian Government Publishing Service.

Housing Corporation and CIH (Chartered Institute of Housing) (2008) *Housing needs and aspirations of minority ethnic communities*, Coventry: CIH (available at www.housingcorp.gov.uk/upload/pdf/Housing_ethnic_minorities.pdf).

HIA (Housing Industry Association) (1990) *Housing towards 2000*, Canberra: HIA.

Howe, A. (2003) 'Housing an older Australia: More of the same or something different?' Housing Futures in an Ageing Australia Conference, Melbourne: Australian and Housing and Urban Research Institute and The Myer Foundation.

HUD (US Department of Housing and Urban Development) (2009) HUD historical background (available at www.hud.gov/adm/about/admguide/history.cfm)

HUD (US Department of Housing and Urban Development) (2010) *Report to Congress on the root causes of the foreclosure crisis*, Office of Policy Development and Research (available at www.huduser.org/portal/publications/hsgfin/foreclosure_09.html)

Hughes, J. (2007) 'Caring for carers: the financial strain of caring', *Family Matters,* vol 76, pp. 32-3.

Hugo, G. (1986) 'Population aging in Australia: implications for social and economic policy', Papers of the East-West Population Institute, No 98, Honolulu: East-West Center.

Hugo, G. (2003) 'Australia's ageing population', *Australian Planner*, vol 40, no 2, pp 109-18.

Hugo, G. (2007) 'New questions in the 2006 population census: some initial findings', *People and Place,* vol 15, no 3, pp 53-6.

Hulse, K. and Saugeres, L. (2008) *Housing insecurity and precarious living: an Australian exploration*, Final Report, Melbourne: Australian Housing and Urban Research Institute.

Iacovou, M. (2002) 'Regional differences in the transition to adulthood', *The Annals of the American Academy of Political and Social Sciences*, vol 580, pp 40-69.

Iacovou, M. (2004) 'Patterns of family living', in R. Berthoud and M. Iacovou (eds) *Social Europe,* Cheltenham and Northampton: Edward Elgar, pp 21-45.

Jackson, N. (2002) 'The Higher Education Contribution Scheme – a HECS on the family?' Joint Special Issue, *Journal of Population Research and NZ Population Review*, pp 105-19.

Jackson, R. and Bridge, H. (1988) 'Housing', in W. Vamplew (ed) *Australian historical statistics*, Sydney: Fairfax Syme.

Jacobs, K. (2002) 'Useful in some approaches but not others', *Housing, Theory and Society*, vol 19, no 2, pp 74-6.

Jacobs, K. (2008) 'Contractual welfare ideology and housing management practice: the deployment of tenant incentive schemes in Australia', *Urban Policy and Research*, vol 26, no 4, pp 467-81.

Jacobs, K. and Atkinson, R. (2008) 'Theoretical concerns in Australian housing and urban research', *Housing Theory and Society*, vol 25, no 3, pp 157-63.

Jacobs, K., Kemeny, J. and Manzi, T. (2004) *Social constructionism in housing research*, Aldershot: Ashgate.

James, A. (2009) 'Growing old in non metropolitan regions: intentions and realities', Melbourne: Flinders University, School of Geography, Population and Environmental Management, unpublished PhD thesis.

Jenkins, A., Rowland, F., Angus, P. and Hales, C. (2003) *The future supply of informal care, 2003 to 2013*, Canberra: Australian Institute of Health and Welfare.

Jessop, B. (1990) *State theory: putting the capitalist state in its place*, Cambridge: Polity Press.

Jessop, B. (1997) 'The entrepreneurial city: re-imaging localities, redesigning economic governance, or restructuring capital?', in N. Jewson and S. MacGregor (eds) *Transforming cities: contested governance and new spatial divisions*, London: Routledge, pp 28-41.

Jessop, B. (2002) 'Liberalism, neoliberalism and urban governance: a state theoretical perspective', *Antipode*, vol 34, no 2, pp 452-72.

Jones, A. Howe, A. Tilse, C., Bartlett, H. and Stimson, B. (2010) *Service integrated housing for Australians in later life,* Final Report, Melbourne: Australian Housing and Urban Research Institute.

Jones, A., Bell, M., Tilse, C. and Earl, G. (2007) *Rental housing provision for lower income older Australians*, Positioning Paper, Melbourne: Australian Housing and Urban Research Institute.

Jones, G. (2004) 'A risky business: experiences of leaving home among young rural women', *Journal of Youth Studies,* vol 7, no 2, pp 209-20.

Jones, M. (1972) *Housing and poverty in Australia*, Melbourne: Melbourne University Press.

Jordan, A., Wurzel, R. and Zito, A. (2005) 'The rise of 'new' policy instruments in comparative perspective: has governance eclipsed government?', *Political Studies*, vol 53, pp 477-96.

Kearns, A. and Turok, I. (2000) Power, responsibility and governance in Britain's new urban policy, *Journal of Urban Affairs*, vol 22, no 2, pp 175-91.

Kelly, S. (2003) 'Self provision in retirement? Forecasting future household wealth', Canberra: University of Canberra, National Centre for Social and Economic Modelling (NATSEM).

Kelly, S. (2009) *Don't stop thinking about tomorrow*, Canberra: AMP. NATSEM.

Kelly, S. and Harding, A. (2005*) Love can hurt, divorce can cost, financial impact of divorce in Australia,* AMP. NATSEM Income and Wealth Report No. 10, Canberra: AMP. NATSEM.

Kelly, S. and Harding, A. (2007) *Baby boomers – doing it for themselves*, AMP. NATSEM Income and Wealth Report, no 6, Canberra: AMP. NATSEM.

Kelly S., Harding A. and Percival R. (2002) 'Live long and prosper? Projecting the likely superannuation of the baby boomers in 2020', Paper presented at the 2002 Australian Conference of Economists Business Symposium, 4th October, Canberra: NATSEM.

Kemeny, J. (1983) *The great Australian nightmare*, Melbourne: Georgian House.

Kemeny, J. (1992) *Housing and social theory*, London: Routledge.

Kemp, P. (2009) 'The transformation of private renting', in P. Malpass and R. Rowlands (eds) *Housing, markets and policy*, London: Routledge.

Kendig, H. (1979) *New life for old suburbs*, Sydney: George Allen and Unwin.

Kendig, H. (1981) *Buying and renting: household moves in Adelaide*, Canberra: Australian Institute of Urban Studies.

Kendig, H. (1984) 'Housing careers, life cycle and residential mobility, implications for the housing market', *Urban Studies*, vol 21, no 3, pp 271-83.

Kendig, H. (1990a) 'A life course perspective on housing attainment', in D. Myers (ed) *Housing demography: linking demographic structures and housing markets*, Madison: University of Wisconsin Press, pp 133-56.

Kendig, H. (1990b) 'Ageing, policies and politics', in H. Kendig and J. McCallum (eds) *Grey policy, Australian policies for an ageing society*, Sydney: Allen &Unwin.

Kendig, H., Paris, C. and Anderton, N. (1987) *Towards fair shares in Australian housing*, Canberra: Highland Press.

Khasawneh, R. (2008). 'Ratings, regulation and risk', *Risk*, vol 21, no 7, p 69, Retrieved 7 February, 2010, from ABI/INFORM Global (Document ID:1528216011).

Kim, H. and McCann, P. (2008) 'Supply chains and locational adjustment in the global automotive industry', *Policy Studies*, vol 29, no 3, pp 255-67.

King, P. (1996) *The limits of housing policy: a philosophical investigation*, London: Middlesex University Press.

King, P. (2002) 'Who needs postmodernism?', *Housing, Theory and Society*, vol 19, no 2, pp 76-8.

Kroehn, M. Hutson, K. Faulkner, D. and Beer, A. (2007) *The housing careers of persons with a disability and family members with care responsibilities for persons with a disability*, Melbourne: Australian Housing and Urban Research Institute.

Kupke, V. (2007) 'Factors important in the decision to buy a first home', paper presented at the 14th Pacific Rim Real Estate Society Conference, Kuala Lumpur.

Kupke, V. and Marano, W. (2002) *The implications of changes in the labour market for the owner aspirations, housing opportunities and characteristics of first home buyers,* Final Report, Melbourne: Australian Housing and Urban Research Institute.

Lambert, J, Blackaby, B. and Paris, C. (1978) *Housing policy and the state: allocation, access and control*, London: Macmillan.

Larner, W. (2005) 'Neoliberalism in (regional) theory and practice: the stronger communities action fund in New Zealand', *Geographical Research*, vol 43, no 1, pp 9-18.

Leo, C. and Anderson, K. (2006) 'Being realistic about urban growth', *Journal of Urban Affairs*, vol 28, no 2, pp 169-89.

Leo, C. and Brown, W. (2000) 'Slow growth and urban development policy', *Journal of Urban Affairs*, vol 22, no 2, pp 193-213.

Lewis, J. (2006) 'Repartnering and the management of risk', *International Journal of Law, Policy and the Family*, vol 20, no 2, pp 151-68.

Lord, J. and Hutchinson, P. (2003) 'Individualised support and funding: building blocks for capacity building and social inclusion', *Disability and Society*, vol 18, no 1, pp 71–86

Lowe, P. (2010) 'Some challenges for the future', address to the UDIA National Congress 2010 by Assistant Governor', Sydney, 10 March.

Lund, B. (2006) *Understanding housing policy*, Bristol: Policy Press.

MacGee, J. (2009) 'Why didn't Canada's housing market go bust? Economic commentary', Federal Reserve Bank of Cleveland (available at www.clevelandfed. org/research/commentary/2009/0909.cfm)

Macklin, J. (2009) 'Improved indexation for Australia's pensioners', media release, Minister for Families, Housing, Community Services and Indigenous Affairs, Commonwealth of Australia, 24 August.

Mallett, S., Bentley, R., Baker, E., Mason, K., Keys, D., Kolar, V. and Krnjacki, L. (2011) *Precarious housing and health inequalities*, Melbourne: VicHealth.

Malpass, P. and Rowlands, R. (eds) (2009) *Housing, markets and policy*, London: Routledge.

Mandic, S. (2008) 'Home-leaving and its structural determinants in Western and Eastern Europe: an exploratory study', *Housing Studies*, vol 23, no 4, pp 615–37.

Mathers, C.D. (2007) 'The health of older Australians', in A. Borowski, S. Encel, and E. Ozanne (eds) *Longevity and social change in Australia*, Sydney: University of New South Wales Press.

Matheson, J. (2009) 'National statistician's annual article on the population: a demographic review', *Population Trends*, 138, pp 7–21 (available at www.statistics. gov.uk/downloads/theme_population/Pop-trends-winter09.pdf).

May, J. (1999) 'Housing histories and homeless careers: a biographical approach', *Housing Studies*, vol 14, no 4, pp 613–38.

Mayer, C., Pence, K. and Sherlund, S. (2009) 'The rise in mortgage defaults', *Journal of Economic Perspectives*, vol 23, no 1 (accessed through Proquest ABI/Inform).

McCrone, D. (2004) 'Getting by and making out in Kirklady', in M. Anderson, F. Bechhofer and J. Gershundy (eds) *The social and political economy of the household*, Oxford: Oxford University Press.

McDonald, P. and Baxter, J.(2005) 'Home ownership among young people in Australia: in decline or just delayed?', *Australian Journal of Social Issues*, vol 40, no 4, pp 471–87.

McDonald, P. and Brownlee, H. (1992) 'Living day to day: families in the recession', *Family Matters*, no 31, pp 8–13.

McDowell, L. (1997) 'The new service class: housing, consumption and life style among London bankers in the 1990s', *Environment and Planning A*, pp 2061–78.

McIsaac, S.J. (1997) 'Identity in the institutional setting: a status passage analysis', paper presented at the 16th Congress of the International Association of Gerontology, 19–23 August, Adelaide, Australia.

McNaughton, C. (2008) *Transitions through homelessness: lives on the edge*, Basingstoke: Palgrave Macmillan.

McNelis, S. (2007a) *Older persons in public housing: present and future profile*, Research Paper, Melbourne: Australian Housing and Urban Research Institute.

McNelis, S. (2007b) 'Independent living units: managing and renewing an ageing stock', *Australasian Journal on Ageing*, vol 26, pp 109–114.

McNelis, S. and Herbert, T. (2003) *Independent living units: clarifying their current role as an affordable housing option for older people with low assets and low incomes*, Final Report, Melbourne: Australian Housing and Urban Research Institute and Swinburne Monash Research Centre.

Merette, M. (2002) 'The bright side: a positive view on the economics of aging', *Choices*, vol 8, no 1, Montreal, Quebec: Institute for Research on Public Policy.

Merlo, R. and McDonald, P. (2002) *Outcomes of home-ownership aspirations and their determinants,* Final Report, Melbourne: Australian Housing and Urban Research Institute.

Ministry of Social Development (2009) *The social report,* Wellington: Ministry of Social Development.

Minnery, J. and Zacharov, R. (2006) *The quality of housing careers*, Melbourne: Australian Housing and Urban Research Institute.

Molgat, M. (2002) 'Leaving home in Quebec: theoretical and social implications of (im)mobility among youth', *Journal of Youth Studies*, vol 5, no 2 pp 135–52.

Morris, A. (2007). 'On the edge: the financial situation of older renters in the private rental market in Sydney', *Australian Journal of Social Work*, vol 42, no 3, pp 337–50.

Mulder, C. (2000) 'Leaving home in the Netherlands: when and in which housing', paper for Leaving Home : a European Focus workshop, September, Rostock, Germany.

Mulder, C. (2003) 'The housing consequences of living arrangement choices in young adulthood', *Housing Studies*, vol 18, no 5, pp 703–20.

Mulder, C.H. (2006a) 'Home-ownership and family formation', *Journal of Housing and the Built Environment*, vol 21, no 3, pp 281–98.

Mulder, C. (2006b) 'Population and housing: a two-sided relationship', *Demographic Research*, vol 15, no 13, pp 401–12.

Mulder, C.H. and Hooimeijer, P. (2002) 'Leaving home in the Netherlands: timing and first housing', *Journal of Housing and the Built Environment,* vol 17, pp 237–68.

Mulder, C.H. and Wagner, M. (1998) 'First-time home-ownership in the family life course: a West German–Dutch comparison', *Urban Studies*, vol 35, no 4, pp 687–713.

Mulder, C.H. and Wagner, M. (2001) 'The connections between family formation and first-time home ownership in the context of West Germany and the Netherlands', *European Journal of Population*, vol 17, pp 137–64.

Mullins, D. and Murie, A. (2006) *Housing policy in the UK*, Bristol: Policy Press.

Mullins, D. and Pawson, H. (2009) 'The evolution of stock transfer in the UK: privatisation or re-nationalisation?', in P. Malpass and R. Rowlands (eds) *Housing, markets and policy*, London: Routledge.

Muntaner, C., Lynch, J. and Smith, G. (2000) 'Social capital and the third way in public health', *Critical Public Health*, vol 10, no 2, pp 107-24.

Myers, D. (1999) 'Cohort longitudinal estimation of housing careers', *Housing Studies*, vol 14, no 4, pp 473-90.

Nadauld, T. and Sherlund, S. (2009) 'The role of securitization process in the expansion of subprime credit', Finance and Economic Discussion Series, Divisions of Research and Statistics and Monetary Affairs, Federal Reserve Board (available at www.federalreserve.gov/Pubs/Feds/2009/200928/200928pap.pdf).

(NCD) (National Council on Disability) (2010) 'The state of housing in America', Washington DC: NCD.

Neutze, M. (1978) *Australian urban policy*. Sydney: George Allen & Unwin.

Neutze, M. and Kendig, H. (1991) 'Achievement of home ownership amongst postwar Australian cohorts', *Housing Studies*, vol 6, no 1, pp 3-14.

Northern Ireland Housing Executive (2009) *Housing research bulletin,* issue 8, Spring, Belfast: NIHE.

OECD (2009) *Society at a glance: OECD social indicators*, Paris: OECD (available at www.oecd.org/els/social/indicators/SAG).

Office of National Statistics (2008) *Social Trends 38th edition*, the Office of National Statistics, Basingstoke, Palgrave Macmillan (available at www.statistics.gov.uk/downloads/theme_social/Social_Trends38/Social_Trends38.pdf).

Office of National Statistics (2009) *Social trends 39th edition,* Office for National Statistics, Basingstoke: Palgrave Macmillan (available at www.statistics.gov.uk/socialtrends39/)

O'Halloran, B. (2010) 'Property prices continue to fall', *The Irish Times* (available at www.irishtimes.com/newspaper/finance/2010/0705/1224274034754.html)

Olsberg, D. and Winters, M. (2005) *Ageing in place: intergenerational and intrafamilial housing in transfers and shifts in later life*, Final Report, Melbourne: Australian Housing and Urban Research Institute.

O'Neill, P. (2008) 'The role of theory in housing research: partial reflections on the work of Jim Kemeny', *Housing, Theory and Society*, vol 25, no 3, pp 164-76.

O'Neil, P. and Argent, N. (2007) 'Neoliberalism in Antipodean spaces and times', *Geographical Research*, vol 43, no 1, pp 2-8.

Oswald, A. (1996) 'A conjecture on the explanation for high unemployment in the industrialised nations: Part 1', Working Paper 475, Warwick Economic Research Papers, Warwick: Warwick University.

Oswald, A. (1997) 'A theory of homes and jobs', Warwick Economic Research Papers, Warwick: Warwick University.

Paris, C. (1992) *Housing Australia*, South Melbourne: Macmillan.

Paris, C. (2005) 'Housing and the migration turnaround in Ireland', *Urban Policy and Research*, vol 23, no 3, pp 287–304.

Paris, C. (2008a) *Second homes in Northern Ireland*, Final Report, Belfast: Northern Ireland Housing Executive.

Paris, C. (2008b) 'Re-positioning second homes within housing studies: household investment, gentrification, multiple residence, mobility and hyper-consumption', *Housing, Theory and Society*, vol 22, no 4, pp 1-19.

Paris, C. (2010) *Affluence, mobility and second home ownership*, Abingdon: Routledge.

Parkin, A. and Hardcastle, L. (2004) *The impact of targeting housing assistance*, Adelaide: Department of Families and Communities.

Pastalan, L.A., (1997) 'An introduction to international perspectives on shelter and service issues for aging populations', in L.A. Pastalan (ed) *Shelter and service issues for aging populations: international perspectives*, Binghamton, New York: The Haworth Press, p 38.

Patiniotis, J. and Holdsworth, C. (2005) 'Seize that chance! Leaving home and transitions to higher education', *Journal of Youth Studies*, vol 8, no 1, pp 81-95.

Payne, J. and Payne, G. (1977) 'Housing pathways and stratification: a study of life chances in the housing market', *Journal of Social Policy*, vol 23, pp 125-156.

Peace, S. (2003) 'The development of residential and nursing home care in the United Kingdom', in J. Katz and S. Peace (eds) *End of life in care homes: a palliative care approach*, Maidenhead: Open University Press, pp 16-42.

Peach, C. (1998) 'South Asian and Caribbean ethnic minority housing choice in Britain', *Urban Studies*, vol 35, no 10, pp 1657-80.

Pearse, H. (2003) *The social and economic impact of student debt*, Carlton South, Victoria: Council of Australia.

Peck, J. (2001) *Workfare states*, New York: Guilford Press.

Peck, J. and Theodore, N. (2001) 'Exporting workfare/importing welfare to work: exploring the politics of Third Way policy transfer', *Political Geography*, vol 20, no 4, pp 427-60.

Peck, J. and Tickell, A. (2002) 'Neoliberalizing space', *Antipode*, vol 34, pp 380-404.

Percival, R. and Kelly, S. (2004) *Who's going to care? Informal care and an ageing population,* Canberra: National Centre for Social and Economic Modelling.

Percival, R., Payne, A., Harding, A. and Abello, A. (2007) *Honey I calculated the kids … it's $537,000 – Australian child costs in 2007*, AMP. NATSEM Income and Wealth Report No. 18, Canberra: AMP. NATSEM.

Perry, J (2008) *The housing and neighbourhood impact of Britain's changing ethnic mix*, York: Joseph Rowntree Foundation.

Phillipson, C. (2007) 'The "elected" and the "excluded": sociological perspectives on the experience of place and community in old age', *Ageing and Society*, vol 27, part 3, pp 321-42.

Pickert, K. (2008) 'A brief history of Fannie Mae and Freddie Mac', *Time,* 14 July (available at www.time.com/time/business/article/0,8599,1822766,00.html).

Pickvance, C. (1974) 'Life cycle, house and residential mobility: a path analytic approach', *Urban Studies*, vol 11, pp 171-88.

Powell, M. (2000) 'New labour and the third way in the British welfare state: a new and distinctive approach', *Critical Social Policy,* vol 20, no 1, pp 39-60.

Power, S. and Whitty, N. (1999) 'New labour's education policy: first, second or third way', *Journal of Education Policy*, vol 14, no 5, pp 535-46.

Productivity Commission (2004) *First home ownership*, Report no. 28, Melbourne: Productivity Commission Australian Government.

Productivity Commission (2006) *Report on Government Services*, Canberra: Steering Committee for the Review of Government Services Provision.

Przeworksi, A. and Teune, H. (1970) *The logic of comparative social inquiry*, New York: Wiley.

Qu, L. and Weston, R. (2008) 'Snapshots of family relationships', report for the 2008 National Families Week, Melbourne: Australian Institute of Family Studies.

Quibell, R. (2004) 'The living history project: the lived experiences of people with disability and parents of people with disability in the period 1981-2002', Victoria: Scope Vic Ltd.

Refugee Council of Australia (2009) *Australia's Refugee and Humanitarian program community views on current challenges and future directions*, Canberra: Refugee Council of Australia.

Refugee Council of Australia (2010) *Australia's Refugee and Humanitarian program 2010-11 community views on current challenges and future directions*, Canberra: Refugee Council of Australia.

Rendall, M. and Salt, J. (2005) 'The foreign-born population', in Chapell, R (ed) *Focus on people and migration*, Basingstoke: Office of National Statistics, chapter 8, pp 132-152, accessed on 25 January 2011 at http://212.58.231.23/downloads/theme_compendia/fom2005/08_FOPM_ForeignBorn.pdf 9

Reserve Bank of Australia (2005) *Survey on housing equity and injection*, Reserve Bank Bulletin, October, pp 1-12.

Rex, R. and Moore, J. (1967) *Race, community and conflict: a study of Sparkbrook*, Oxford: Oxford University Press.

Richards A. (2008) 'Some observations on the cost of housing in Australia', address to The Melbourne Institute 2008 Economic and Social Outlook Conference, Reserve Bank of Australia, Melbourne, 27 March.

Roberts, D., Hugo, G., Bradley, H., Coffee, N. and Golan, S. (2005) *The emerging housing needs of indigenous South Australians*, Adelaide: Department for Families and Communities.

Roberts, M. (1997) 'Housing with care: housing policies for an ageing Australia', *Ageing International*, vol 23, no 3-4, pp 90-106.

Robinson, D., Reeve, K. and Casey, R. (2007) *The housing pathways of new immigrants*, York: Joseph Rowntree Foundation (available at www.jrf.org.uk/publications/housing-pathways-new-immigrants).

Rochman, H. and McCampbell D.Z. (1997) *Leaving home: stories*, New York: Harper Collins.

Rose, N. (2001) 'Community, citizenship and the third way', in D. Meredyth and J. Minson (eds) *Citizenship and cultural policy*, London: Sage, pp 1-17.

Rowles, G.D. (1993) 'Evolving images of place in aging and "aging in place"', *Generations*, vol 17, no 2, pp 65-70.

Rudd, K. (2010) Building Australia's future: beginning a building decade for a stronger Australia, speech to Australia Day Reception, National Gallery of Victoria, Melbourne, 18 January (available at www.pm.gov.au/node/6416).

Rugg, J. and Ford, J. (2004) 'Housing advantage? The role of students renting in the constitution of housing biographies in the United Kingdom', in J. Rugg and J. Ford (eds) *Journal of Youth Studies*, vol. 7, no 1, pp 19-34.

Saegert, S. and Evans, G. 2003 'Poverty, housing niches and health in the United States', *Journal of Social Issues,* vol 59, no 3, pp 569-89.

Santarelli, E. and Cottone, F. (2009) 'Leaving home, family support and intergenerational ties in Italy: some regional differences', *Demographic Research*, vol 21, article 1, pp 1-22.

Saugeres, L. (2008) '21st century housing careers of people with a disability and carers: a qualitative study', Melbourne: Australian Housing and Urban Research Institute.

Saunders, P. (1978) 'Domestic property and social class', *International Journal of Urban and Regional Research*, vol 6, no 2, pp 205-22.

Saunders, P. (1979) *Urban politics*, Harmondsworth: Penguin.

Saunders, P. (1981) *Social theory and the urban question*, London: Hutchinson.

Saunders, P. (1984) 'Beyond housing classes: the sociological significance of private property rights and means of consumption', *International Journal of Urban and Regional Research*, vol 8, no 3, pp 202-27.

Saunders, P. (1990) *A nation of home owners*, London: Unwin Hyman.

Sayer, A. (1992) *Method in social science: a realist approach,* London: Routledge.

Sayer, A. (2000) *Realism and social science,* London: Sage.

Schwartz, H. (2008) 'Housing, global finance and American hegemony: building conservative politics one brick at a time', *Comparative European Politics*, vol 6, no 3, pp 262-85.

Seelig, T., Hoon Han, J., O'Flaherty, M., Short, P., Haynes, M., Baum, S., Western, M. and Jones, A. (2005) *Housing consumption patterns and earnings behaviour of income support recipients over time,* Positioning Paper, Melbourne: Australian Housing and Urban Research Institute.

Sheehan, G. and Hughes, J. (2001) 'Division of matrimonial property in Australia', Australian Institute of Family Studies Research Paper No 25, Melbourne: AIFS.

Sheen, V. (2002) 'Home equity conversion: getting the policy right and getting the product right for older Australians', paper presented to Changing Needs, Growing Markets Conference, Sydney, 18 February.

Shorten, B. (2008) 'National disability strategy', discussion paper', Canberra: Department of Families, Communities, Housing and Indigenous Affairs.

Slatter, M. and Beer, A. (2003a) 'Evictions and housing management', Adelaide: Australian Centre for Social Science Research.

Slatter, M. and Beer, A. (2003b) *Housing evictions in South Australia: a study of bailiff assisted evictions,* Adelaide: Australian Centre for Community Services Research.

Smith, S., Alexander, A. and Easterlow, D. (1997) 'Rehousing as a health intervention: miracle or mirage?', *Health and Place*, vol 3, no 4, pp 203-16.

Smyth, B. and Weston, R. (2000) 'Financial living standards after divorce: a recent snapshot', Australian Institute of Family Studies Research Paper No 23, Melbourne: AIFS.

Smyth, P., Reddel, T. and Jones, A. (2004) 'Social inclusion, new regionalism and associational governance: the Queensland experience', *International Journal of Urban and Regional Research*, vol 28, no 3, pp 601-15.

Somerville, P. (2002) 'But why social constructionism?', *Housing, Theory and Society*, vol 19, no 2, p 80.

Somerville, P. and Bengtsson, B. (2002) 'Constructionism, realism and housing', *Housing, Theory and Society,* vol 19, no 3, pp 121-36.

Spicer, I. (2007) 'Disability and family carers', *Family Matters*, vol 76, pp 30-1.

Sprigings, N (2008) 'Buy-to-let and the wider housing market', *People, Place & Policy Online*, no 2 (available at http://extra.shu.ac.uk/ppp-online).

Stewart, I. and Vaitilingam, R. (eds) (2004) *Seven ages of man and women*, Swindon: ESRC.

Stutchbury, M. (2010) 'Renovation boom masks shortage of new houses', *The Australian*, 11 March (available at www.theaustralian.com.au/business/renovation-boom-masks-shortage-of-new-houses/story-e6frg8zx-1225839329178).

Tanton, R., Nepal, B. and Harding, A. (2008) *Wherever I lay my debt, that's my home*, AMP. NATSEM Income and Wealth Report No 19, Canberra: AMP. NATSEM.

Tarr, D.G. (2009) 'The political, regulatory and market failures that caused the US financial crisis: what are the lessons?' (available at http://ssrn.com/abstract=1322297).

Taylor, J. (1997) 'The contemporary demography of Indigenous Australians', *Journal of the Australian Population Association*, vol 14, no 1, pp 77-115.

Thorns, D.C. (1981) 'The implications of differential rates of capital gain from owner occupation for the formation and development of housing classes', *International Journal of Urban and Regional Research*, vol 5, no 2, pp 205-17.

Tinker A. (1997) 'The environment of ageing', *Philosophical Transactions of the Royal Society of London, Series B Biological Science*, vol 352, Issue 1363, pp 1861-69.

Tomaney, J. and Bradley, D. (2007) 'The economic role of mobile professional and creative workers and their housing and residential preferences: Evidence from North East England', *Town Planning Review*, vol 48, no 4, pp 511-30.

Tonkin, S. and Williams, L with Ackland, R. (1993) *The relationship between visa category and the demand for housing. Results from the Longitudinal Survey of Immigrants to Australia (LSIA) Pilot*, Canberra: Australian Government Publishing Service.

Troy, P. (1991) *The benefits of owner occupation, urban research program*, Working Paper No 29, Canberra: Australian National University.

Tually, S. (2007) *A brief review of the integration of state and territory housing and disability policies in Australia,* Melbourne: Australian Housing and Urban Research Institute.

Tually, S. (2008) *Overview of findings: housing 21 qualitative survey*, Adelaide: Southern Research Centre, Australian Housing and Urban Research Institute.

Uren, D. (2010) 'Nation back on growth track', *The Australian*, 2 March, p 1.

US Bureau of the Census, Historic housing data – ownership (available at www. census.gov/hhes/www/housing/census/historic/owner.html).

US Bureau of the Census, Homeownership rates for the US and Regions: 1965 to present (available at www.census.gov/hhes/www/housing/hvs/historic/index.html).

US Department of Veterans' Affairs (2009) Legislative history of the VA home loan guaranty program (available at www.homeloans.va.gov/pdf/history.pdf).

VanderHart, P.G. (1995) 'The socioeconomic determinants of the housing decisions of elderly homeowners', *Journal of Housing for the Elderly*, vol 11, no 2, pp 5-35 and co-published in L.A. Pastalan, *Housing decisions for the elderly: to move or not to move*, Binghamton, New York: The Hawthorn Press, Chapter 2, pp 5-35.

Vertovec, (2005) *The emergence of super-diversity in Britain*, Working Paper 25, Oxford: ESRC Centre on Migration, Policy and Society.

Watson, S. (1988) *Accommodating inequality. gender and housing*, Sydney: Allen and Unwin.

Watt, P. (2005) 'Housing histories and fragmented middle class careers', *Housing Studies*, vol 20, no 3, pp 359-82.

Weston, R., Stanton, D., Qu, L., and Soriano, G.(2001) 'Australian families in transition' *Family Matters*, no 60, pp12-23.

Whitehead, M. (2003) 'In the shadow of hierarchy: meta-governance, policy reform and urban regeneration in the West Midlands', *Area*, vol 35, no 1, pp 6-14.

Whittington, L.A. and Peters, H.E. (1996) 'Economic incentives for financial and residential independence', *Demography*, vol 33, pp 82-97.

Williams, P. (1984) 'The politics of property: home ownership in Australia', in J. Halligan and C. Paris (eds) *Australian urban politics*, Melbourne: Longman Cheshire, pp 167-92.

Williams, P. (2003) 'Home ownership and changing housing and mortgage markets: the new economic realities', in R. Forrest and J. Lee (eds) *Housing and social change: east west perspectives,* London: Routledge, pp. 162-182.

Wilson Center (2009) 'Weathering the economic crisis: lessons from Canada', Centerpoint (available at www.wilsoncenter.org).

Wincup, E., Buckland, G. and Bayliss, R. (2003) *Youth homelessness and substance abuse,* London: Home Office.

Wood G., Watson R., and Flatau P. (2003) *A microsimulation model of the Australian housing market with applications to Commonwealth and State policy initiatives*, Final Report, Melbourne: Australian Housing and Urban Research Institute..

Wulff, M. and Maher, C. (1998) 'Long term renters in the Australian housing market', *Housing Studies*, vol 13, no 1, pp 83-98.

Wyn, J. and Dwyer, P. (1999) 'New directions in research on youth in transition', *Journal of Youth Studies*, vol 2, pp 5-21.

Yates, J. (1996) 'Towards a reassessment of the private rental market', *Housing Studies,* vol 11, pp 35-51.

Yates, J. (2002) *Housing implications of social, spatial and structural change*, Final Report, Melbourne: Australian Housing and Urban Research Institute.

Yates, J. (2003) *Tax concessions and subsidies for Australian homebuyers and home owners*, Research and Policy Bulletin No 27, Melbourne: Australian Housing and Urban Research Institute.

Yates, J. and Bradbury, B. (2009) 'Home ownership as a (crumbling) fourth pillar of social insurance in Australia', Luxembourg Wealth Study Working Paper Series, Working Paper No 8, Luxembourg: Luxembourg Income Study (LIS).

Yates, J. and Bradbury, B. (2010) 'Home ownership as a crumbling fourth pillar of social insurance in Australia', *Journal of Housing and the Built Environment*, vol 25, pp 193–211.

Yates, J. and Gabriel, M. (2006) *Housing affordability in Australia,* National Research Venture 3, Housing Affordability for Lower Income Australians, Research Paper 3, Melbourne: Australian Housing and Urban Research Institute.

Yates, J. and Milligan, V., with Berry, M., Burke, T., Gabriel, M., Phibbs, P., Pinnegar, S. and Randolph B. (2007) *Housing affordability: a 21st century problem,* Final Report, Melbourne: Australian Housing and Urban Research Institute.

Yates, J., Kendig, H., and Phillips, B., with Milligan V. and Tanton R. (2008) *Sustaining fair shares: the Australian housing system and intergenerational sustainability*, Research Paper No 11, Melbourne: Australian Housing and Urban Research Institute.

Young C. (1996) 'Are young people leaving home earlier or later', *Journal of Population Research,* vol 13, no 2, pp 125–152.

Young, C.M. (1987) 'Young people leaving home in Australia: the trend towards independence', Australian Family Formation Project, Monograph No 9, Department of Demography, Research School of Social Sciences, Canberra: Australian National University.

# Index

Page references for figures and tables are in *italics*